The Shores of Connemara

Séamas Mac an Iomaire

Translated and annotated by
Padraic de Bhaldraithe

This translation first published in 2000 by Tír Eolas ©, Newtownlynch, Kinvara, Co. Galway.
Original Irish language edition entitled 'Cladaí Chonamara', Government of Ireland ©.
Translated and annotated by Padraic de Bhaldraithe ©.
Reproductions from original etchings by Sabine Springer ©.
Reprinted in 2006.

Acknowledgements for illustrations:
National Museum of Ireland, Folklife Division, photographs on pages 7, 18, 37, 38, 40, 48, 118, 131, 132, 151, 159, 160.
University College Dublin, Department of Irish Folklore, photographs on pages 36, 39, 129, 130, 136, 138, 140, 141, 164.
Kevin Dwyer, aerial photograph on page 3.
National Library of Ireland, photograph on page 28.
Anne Korff, cover and photographs on pages 9, 10, 12, 15, 42.
Cillian Roden, photographs on pages 11, 13, 14, 41.
Marcus Barrett, photograph on page 32.
Drawing on page 35 courtesy of D.G. Bennet (from *The Galway Hooker* by Richard J. Scott).

ISBN 1 873821 14 X
ISBN 9 781873 821145

British Library Cataloguing in Publication Data.
A catalogue record for this book is available from the British Library.

Cover and layout: Anne Korff and Johan Hofsteenge.
Typesetting: Johan Hofsteenge.
Printed in Ireland by Betaprint.

Fuarthas cúnamh ó Údarás na Gaeltachta don athchló seo.

This book is dedicated to the
Connemara Environmental Education Centre,
Letterfrack, Co. Galway.

I thought there was nowhere on the surface of the earth which bettered it for beauty and adornment, and it was hard to beat for fun and pastime.

Map of area described in The Shores of Connemara

(English version of names from Ordnance Survey of Ireland, Discovery Series No 44 and Admiralty Charts 2096 and 2709).

MAIN MAP (RIGHT)

1. *Maidhm an Urláir* Floor Rock
2. *Cruach na Caoile* Croaghnakeela Island [Deer Island]
3. *Loch na Lannach*
4. *Cill Chiaráin* Kilkieran
5. *Cruach na Cora* St. Macdara's Island
6. *Roisín an Chalaidh* Rusheenacholla
7. *Bealach na Srathra* Straddle Pass
8. *Maínis* Mweenish Island
9. *An Trá Mhóir*
10. *Carraig na bPortán* Carricknaburptaun Rocks
11. *Fínis* Finish Island
12. *Carraig an Mhíle* Mile Rock
13. *Trá Dheiscirt*
14. *Oileán Lachan* Duck Island
15. *Carraig an Ghlainigh* Carrickalusk
16. *Inis Múscraí* Inishmuskerry
17. *An Charraig Fhada*
18. *Oileán Barra (Bior)* Birmore Island
19. *Sceirde Mór* Skerdmore
20. *Dún Ghudail* Doonguddle
21. *Dúleic* Carrickadoolagh
22. *Mullán na mBod* Bullaunabaud [Carricknamackan Little]
23. *Carraig na Meacan* Carricknamackan
24. *Carraig Iolra* Eagle Rock
25. *Carraig na hEilite* Seal Rock
26. *Leitir Mealláin* Lettermullan
27. *An Aird Mhóir* Ardmore
28. *Trá an Ghoirtín* Gorteen Beach
29. *Inis Ní* Inishnee
30. *Inis Leacain* Inishlackan
31. *An Foiriún (Thuaidh)* Feraun (North)
32. *Cloch na Rón* Roundstone
33. *Carna* Carna

INSET (BELOW)

1. *Loch na Lannach*
2. *Roisín an Chalaidh*
3. *Trá Bolg*
4. *Trá na hAille*
5. *An Meall Rua*
6. *Trá Fhada Mhainse*
7. *Trá Dheiscirt*
8. *An Aircín Thoir*
9. *An Aircín Thiar*
10. *Carraig na mBan*
11. *An Trá Mhóir*
12. *Cartúr*
13. *Feithearnach*
14. *Portach Mhainse*
15. *Bealach na Srathra*
16. *Tobar Cholm Cille*
17. *Carraig na bPortán*

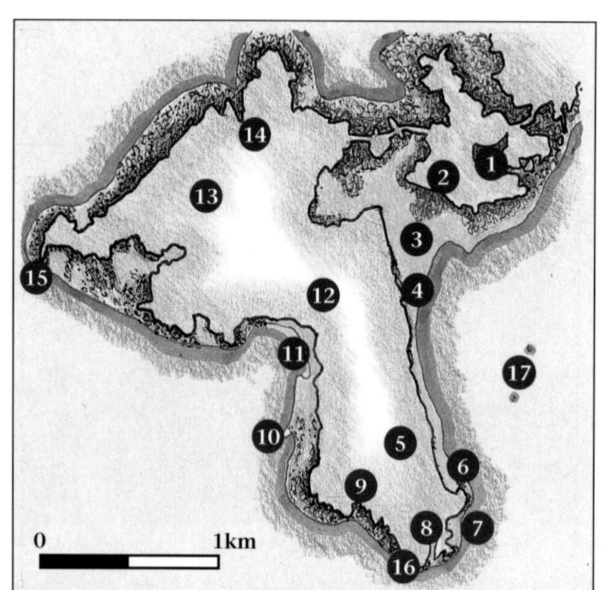

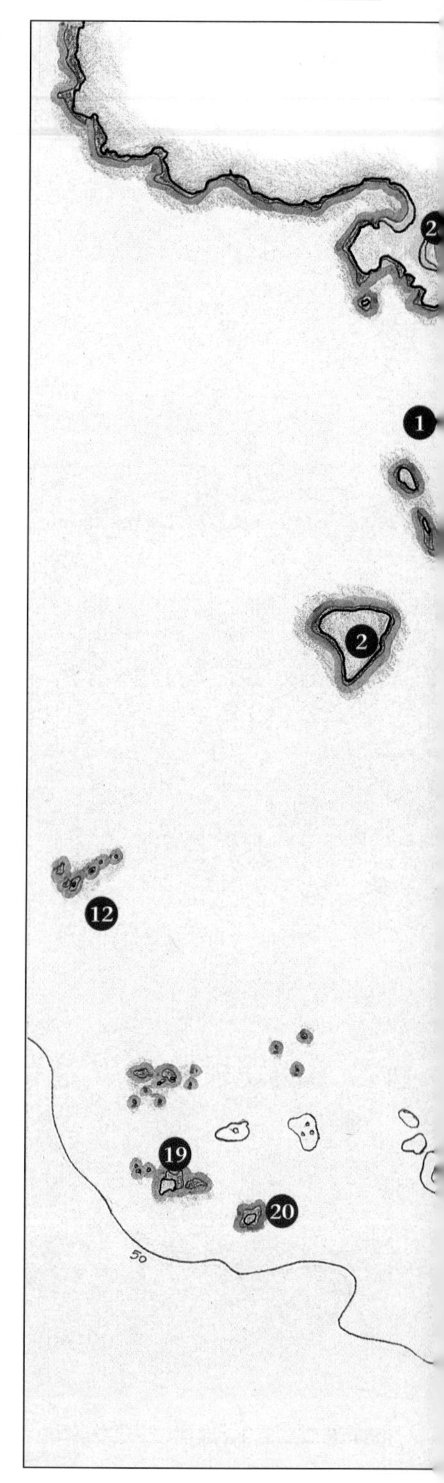

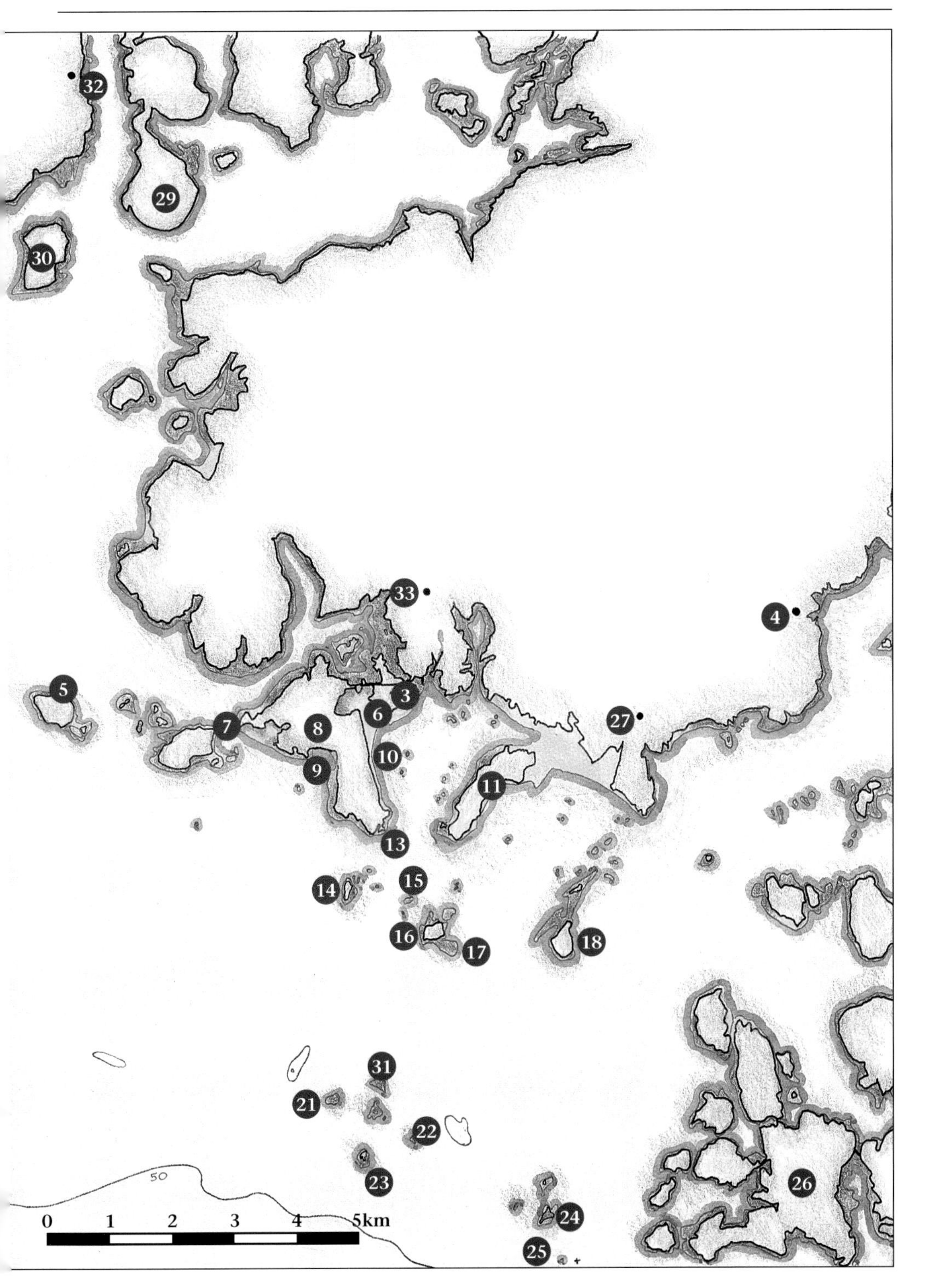
32
29
30
33
4
5
7
8
3
6
10
27
9
11
13
14
15
16
17
18
31
21
22
23
50
26
24
25
0
1
2
3
4
5km

CONTENTS

Turf transport by currach across Greatman's Bay.

FOREWORD

"The clever boat wrights of this Connemara shore took quickly to the new models presented to them by the Congested Districts Board . . . The púcáns or gleoteogs take the place filled by the donkey and cart in districts not so cut up by arms of the sea. The peat is taken to the market, the weed gathered for kelp or for manure, by these boats; in them also, the supplies of flour and meal arrive, the cattle go to the fair and the people to mass. The youngsters quickly become sailors and for excitement, smart sailing and close contest, nothing can beat a púcán race at one of the local regattas. All these craft are built on exquisitely graceful lines under water, but the tumble home above the water and the immense strength of their frames tend to give them a clumsy appearance."

W.S.Green

THE BOOK

These words were written almost a century ago by W.S. Green, Inspector of Fisheries in the then newly established Department of Agriculture in Dublin. Green's young boys learning how to sail, the way city children learn to ride bicycles, tell of a coastal people whose way of life was totally entwined with the sea. But how little has been told of such people in the English speaking cities of modern Ireland. Things could have remained so indefinitely but for a wonderful book written by a man from *Maínis* (Mweenish Island) over seventy years ago. The book, written in Irish, was the unexpected result of an illness suffered by the author Séamas Mac an Iomaire, soon after he emigrated to America.

The result was *Cladaigh Chonamara*, one of the most interesting books written on the natural history of Ireland. So many books on nature are simply culled from earlier writing and repeat endlessly the same mixture of true and false stories. Others are factually interesting, but are written in the dry detached style that is now obligatory for scientific reports. They screen out any sense of a living creature's individuality or beauty, nor are they aware of any vocabulary that allows them to express what value the animal or plant has for them.

Mac an Iomaire follows another road. He brings together the sea and the shore, the animals and plants that live there and the lives of the people who depend on them for their existence. This combining may be more than just his own skill, for in a strange way there seems to have been an unusual wholeness about the life of this coastal community. The material base of prosperity was very narrow – fishing, seaweed cutting and turf collecting, along with a little farming. Many people must have experienced harsh poverty, but this spare material existence seems to have coincided with an amazing imaginative life which certainly included the fish and seaweeds of the always visible ocean. To read Mac an Iomaire is to bury, once and for all, the myth that the people of Ireland were a race of thalassophobes incapable of observing their natural surroundings. Instead we gain an insight into a resourceful people who developed a maritime economy, strong enough to maintain their community intact through the horrors of famine and a culture rich enough to provide insights into the natural world, deeper than what is available to most city dwellers of today.

For many travellers the sea is, at best, an unvaried backdrop to the landscape they move through; that the water itself is also a territory is a less widespread idea. But it is exactly this point of view that underlies Mac an Iomaire's understanding of his home place. For him his locality was summed up in the phrase *Imeallbhord Chonamara*, which could be translated as the coastline or border of Connemara, encompassing the coast, the shallow inshore water and the offshore rocks and islands. This sense of living on a border or edge resonates with the actual geography of south Connemara.

LANDSCAPES AND SEASCAPES

Maínis is located near the very western edge of Ireland, the immensity of the Atlantic is all that lies beyond. Nearly all the inhabitants of south Connemara live along the coast or on the islands, the interior consists of low granite hills and empty bog-land, which cannot be farmed. So the community is suspended between two empty spaces – the bog-land and the sea. Traditionally the bog provided fuel and the sea, food and cash from seaweed gathering and fishing. The little good land between bog and sea provided potatoes, oats and grazing. But the boundary between land and ocean is not simple; instead it twists and coils over many miles, forming islands and peninsulas, inlets and bays. This fretwork geography is the result of the bedrock, an ancient granite which was much weathered before the glaciation, and easily eroded and destroyed by that event. The mainland north of *Maínis* is a long peninsula called *Iorras Aithneach,* or the peninsula of the storms, an apt name. It lies between the two large bays of *Cill Chiaráin* and *An Bheirtreach Bhuí,* (Kilkieran and Bertraghbuoy). At the start of the 20th century the islands, though small in area, used to be the most densely populated part of the coast. The larger islands are inshore; to the south and west, smaller uninhabited islands give way to barren rocks and submerged reefs. On the south-western horizon, about seven miles offshore, lie *Na Sceirdí* or the Skird Rocks, a cluster of reefs and islets that mark both the end of the land and the start of the open ocean. Below *Na Sceirdí* an underwater cliff of about sixty metres separates the shallow coastal ledge, that runs north to the land, from the sea floor which slopes rapidly to depths greater than a hundred metres. Many miles further to the west the sea bed finally encounters the continental slope and falls thousands of metres to the abyssal plain of the Atlantic.

It's a beautiful place in the summer when the sea is a flat board like a big silvery mirror around the islands, the smooth sandy beaches resplendent and glittering under the shimmering sun, everything in full growth, the birds of the air happily singing and warbling up in the blue sky, gulls and other sea birds fishing and swimming in the mouth of the waves, every animal, every insect and all, without worry or otherwise, happy with life, people here and there on the beaches swimming and bathing in the healthy brine.

Left: As for land, few possess it, small fields are full of stones and in some places have not even a foot of soil. The sandy ground is not much good for any crop.

Below: With the amount of swell and tossing of the sea from day to day and from year to year, there are storm beaches of big stones that are as round as eggs on top of the shore.

A lot of it grows on Carraig na Meacan. *Indeed, a lot of all kinds of* dúilfheamainn *grows on it, about half an acre of high cliffs and a storm beach of big stones that are as round as eggs on the south east side of it. There are many caves with seals on the south-west side and deep tidal pools on the north-east side where red seaweed stays. This is the easiest side to come ashore if the sea is quiet. Indeed, it's a very rough place even in summer and it's terrible altogether in winter and only on certain days can it be approached.*

This was the area, between *Na Sceirdí* (Skird rocks) and the coast, that provided *Maínis* with its livelihood. Though little visited by outsiders, it is an area of great beauty. There is no better way of stepping into Mac an Iomaire's world than to sail south and west to *An Sceirde Mór* (Skerdmore). On a calm day, when the Atlantic swell has abated and a light easterly wind blows, it is possible to land in the small cove on the south side of the rock. Once ashore you follow in the footsteps of generations of seaweed gatherers and make your way to the crest of the rock. Here about sixty feet above the sea, the inlets, reefs, channels and islands of the Connemara coast can all be seen spread out over the wide sea. To the north-west lie the low black reefs of the Mile Rocks, barely breaking on this calm day. Immediately to the north lie the confused mass of rocks, breakers and dangerous channels that run from *An Sceirde Mór* for about 3km. To the east lie *Carraig na Meacan* (Carricknamackan), the only rocks sheltered enough to support some stunted vegetation, further east close to *Ceann Gúlam* (Golam Head), lies *Carraig Iolra (*Eagle Rock). Beyond these small islets are the farmed or still inhabited islands; dome shaped *Cruach na Caoile* (Deer Island) to the north, *Oileán Mhic Dara* (MacDara's island) with its small oratory, *Maínis* low and flat, its white houses and strand bright against the dark blue of the sea. *Fínis* (Finish), its eroding sand hills gleaming brightly. The large islands of *Leitir Móir* (Lettermore), *Leitir Mealláin* (Lettermullen) and *Garmna* (Gorumna) form an archipelago along the eastern horizon. In the far distance, the Connemara hills – *Cnoc Mordáin* above Kilkieran, the *Beanna Beola* (Twelve Bens), *Iorras Beag* (Errisbeg) and far out to the north-west, the tiny volcanic hill of Doon – set the landward limits of this coast. But this is only the view to the north and east. In the south at no great distance is *An tOileán Iarthach* (Eeragh) at the extreme west end of the Aran Islands, but to the south-west there is nothing but the sea, vast and stretching out to America.

The coastline is wild and rough on the south and west sides. The swell of the sea has eaten away the place where the land is soft. Those indentations that stretch in through the land like arms of the sea are called aircíní *or creeks and great bold hard projections of big granite rocks stretch out to challenge the breakers.*

OCEANOGRAPHY AND MAC AN IOMAIRE'S WORLD

In *Cladaigh Chonamara*, the mood of the sea is expressed in terms of colour, strength and surface state, but there are other ways of noting change in the sea which are not mentioned, especially changes in the plankton and water masses. The main reason for this is that rather precise measurements are needed to distinguish such changes. Such measurements are only possible in a laboratory, such as the Shellfish Research Laboratory of University College Galway, which was established near Carna in 1973. I had the immense good fortune to study the sea and plankton between *Maínis* and the Skirds some sixty years after Mac an Iomaire left for America. A great part of that good fortune was that our small research vessel belonging to the Shellfish Research Laboratory was skippered by the late Padraig Casey, a native of *Maínis* who was totally familiar with the traditions and knowledge explored in *Cladaigh Chonamara*. Along with Marcus Hernon he introduced the sea, rocks and islands of *Imeallbhord Chonamara* to me during the many days we spent studying plankton and fishing off the Skirds.

This work showed me the oceanographic features which underlay many of Mac an Iomaire's observations and it may add to his account to summarize them here. Briefly the productivity of the area is linked to the upwelling of nutrient-rich water from the sea bed to the south of the Golam Head /Skirds line. This upwelling is strongest during big spring tides, when a large patch of slightly colder plankton-rich water reaches the surface over the underwater escarpment. Possibly due to richer feeding, this area holds the largest populations of pollack and coalfish and is the best area to see seabirds such as shearwaters (perhaps the black birds of Mac an Iomaire), gannets, petrels and auks; it is very noticeable that they are seen most often in this plankton-rich area. Indeed there are noticeable colonies of grey seals, shags and perhaps cormorants both on the Skirds and Namacken rocks. Mac an Iomaire was well aware of the good fishing here as his account of his expedition with Máirtín Mhicil Sheáin Phádraig from *Bóithrín na Trá* and Labhcás Pháidín Ó Nia from *Garraí na nGéabha* shows. Indeed the very place where he tells of catching nine pollack in a few minutes . . . *"The Duck Island big shingle beach over Duleic and the white house at the edge of Leitir Calaidh over the peak of Na Foiriúin rocks"*, was only a few yards from where in 1986 we found the greatest population of coalfish and pollack and linked this abundance to the upwelling of cold plankton-rich water.
Mac an Iomaire specifically notes that the presence of sea birds is an indicator of good fishing, a link that holds to this day and can now be extended to include plankton and nutrient-rich seawater. While the people of *Maínis* did not study plankton, they may well have been aware that spring tides promoted upwelling and hence productivity and concentrations of fish and birds, for one of the great spring tides was known as *'The big spring tide of the birds in May'*, which coincided with the greatest upwelling and plankton bloom of the year, so great that in its aftermath I remember seeing the inlet off the Skirds clogged with floating copepods and other small animals.

It was a lovely sight to watch, some of them sailing close to the wind below, some of them in irons beside each other and some of them luffing each other. They ploughed the seas with great strength, a bright surge of a wave in front of their stem that was spraying up on their bows.

A look now and again from Seán under the clew of the mainsail, when he was going east through Bealach na Srathra, *and telling Micil to stand on the forward platform holding on with his hand to the luff of the staysail for support. To keep a sharp look out, that there was a submerged rock somewhere ahead.*

While spring tides may have promoted growth, neap tides in summer allow great masses of offshore water to flood onto the coastal shelf. Very often this water is saltier and warmer than the usual coastal water and strange animals are carried in with it. Mac an Iomaire's account of the flying fish off the Skirds strikes me as entirely accurate. Close to the mainland shore the sea is shallower and no deep water upwells, consequently fewer fish are found here. Seaweed, however, grows abundantly in the well-lit shallows and oysters used grow in some quantity.

In winter as Mac an Iomaire relates, the sea is in turmoil, huge storms sweep in from the west and it is a frequent sight to see waves break over the sixty feet high peaks of the Skirds. In this season the short dark days prevent the growth of plankton but many brown seaweeds grow best at this time, a fact which explains the harvesting cycle of the kelp burners. Unexpectedly, winter seawater beyond the Skirds can be relatively warm and harbours plankton species normally found far to the south. I still recall my own amusement in using a guide to the algae of Florida to help me identify organisms collected in mid winter. Mac an Iomaire's tale of the barrel-fish, a native of warmer waters, illustrates this unusual characteristic of the Atlantic coast. However it is not certain that this warm water comes from the Gulf Stream, recent research and satellite images suggest that warm water also travels north along the edge of the continental shelf.

A CLASH OF TRADITION

Cladaigh Chonamara may serve to correct Irish people's assumptions about their forefathers' relation with the sea but there are deeper reasons for studying the book. Mac an Iomaire teaches us two vital points about how we should relate to nature, firstly that we should learn to watch the world that surrounds us, and secondly that we should learn to express the world of emotions inside us that always and immediately responds to what we see. Not only was Mac an Iomaire aware of the maritime world; he also rather liked what he knew and was born into a culture that had varied and wonderful opinions about many of its animal neighbours. These Mac an Iomaire reports in great detail, creating an impression of a people who relied on the sea and its creatures but who also had a strong emotional tie to these creatures.

This emotional tie is what is now so weak in our own culture. Science in its relentless search for "objectivity" has desiccated our emotional response to nature and all the facts in the world won't substitute for a rooted sense of the value of nature which encompasses us. By now many ecologists view, with great foreboding, the impact on nature of a society bereft of emotional awareness. But read Mac an Iomaire whenever you need to re-establish this sense of the wonderful, read for example about the *tonachán*.

The *tonachán* is a denizen of *Maínis*, also known as a *dreancaid mhara*. English speakers will recognize it as the sand-hopper and will have come across it along the shoreline of every sandy beach, where it leaps and hops amongst the drift seaweed and flotsam of the tide mark. Apparently, it appreciates a sociable life.

"The tonachán trá is like the míol críonna or the dreancaid mhara. He is always working at ebbing tide, making small holes under the sand. He is no bigger than two inches in length, but very lively. He raises his hard pointy little head from time to time to look around and see how the labour is going. I haven't a clue why he works so hard. He doesn't live in his holes. Usually there are a huge crowd of them together, helping each other loyally and stoutly."

I thought there was nowhere on the surface of the earth which bettered it for beauty and adornment, and it was hard to beat for fun and pastime.

I suppose, in a scientific sense, this is total rubbish. The facts are more or less correct, although two inches sounds very large. The error is in the interpretation, any attempt to attribute human concerns to *tonacháns* is heresy and would drive the editor of a scientific journal into frenzy.

C.M. Yonge, in his classic natural history book, *The Sea Shore* says of the sand-hopper *". . . [it] may occur in immense numbers: "not millions but cartloads" was the comment of one observer. It burrows in sand under weed and other debris along the strand line"*. He then quotes an extract from the English Archdeacon W. Paley who in the early 19th century wrote a once influential book *Natural Theology*; *"Walking by the sea side, in a calm evening, on a sandy shore, with an ebbing tide, I have frequently remarked the appearance of . . . young Shrimps, in the act of bounding into the air from the shallow margin of the water or from the wet sand. If any motion of a mute animal could express delight, it was this; if they had meant to make signs of their happiness they could not have done it more intelligibly. "* It so happens that one of the great foundation myths of science is the overthrow by Darwin of this earlier emotional and religious interpretation of nature championed by many others besides Paley. Yonge, like other great 20th century naturalists, is firmly in the scientific camp. *"We may quote with approval, the description if not the explanation encountered"* is his dry comment on the above report.

By co-incidence, another naturalist was charting sea shore life along the west coast of another continent, at the same time as Mac an Iomaire was writing *Cladaigh Chonamara*. Ed Ricketts, the model of John Steinbeck's Doc, the hero of *Cannery Row* and *Sweet Thursday*, published his description of Pacific intertidal life, *Between Pacific Tides* in 1938. His approach was more detailed and stuck closer to the usual form of a natural history, he makes no excursions into fishing or weed gatherings and his taxonomy is carefully worked out. Nevertheless he clearly saw nature from an angle not too distant from that of Mac an Iomaire. We return to hoppers:

"Observers with a trace of sympathy for bohemian life should walk with a flash light along a familiar surfy beach at half tide on a quiet evening. The huge hoppers will be holding high carnival – leaping about with vast enthusiasm and pausing to wiggle their antennae over likely looking bits of flotsam seaweed." So now we have anarchy, Paley thinks they are leaping for joy, Mac an Iomaire thinks they are working in a *meitheal*[1], and now one of the founders of marine studies in California imagines they are holding a carnival. Yonge prefers the more basic drive of hunger.

Ricketts may not be typical of American scientists, but his industry and knowledge of his subject was such that his book has now gone into five editions, even though he died in 1948. Unfortunately, academic science has not warmed to Rickettsian interpretations any more than to Paley's view. Like all dominant ideologies, it hasn't hesitated to protect its turf. In the preface to the fifth (1985) edition is this ominous editorial note *". . . and I confess to having deleted or toning down a few Rickettsian statements that, although of long standing, seemed by now too anthropomorphic, teleological or metaphysical."*

A similarity in opinions between a 19th century Church of England clergyman, a Californian biologist and an Irish fisherman suggests a world view of fairly universal appeal. But it is this world view that science has felt impelled to conquer. The only way

[1] meitheal = co-operative work group

of resolving the matter however, is to get the *tonachán* himself to tell us what he is at . . . and there alas, our inquiry ends. Only with great difficulty, can we fully comprehend the humour of those people who have lived with us for years on end, and such an understanding is a rare and valuable experience. Nothing we know at present, can even help us decide if the *tonachán* has any sort of humour (how many neurons do you need, to feel like jumping in the air for the hell of it?). Neither Mac an Iomaire, nor Paley, nor Ricketts, nor Yonge, have the slightest inkling of what real feelings, if any, occupy the brain of a sand-hopper. All their opinions are reflections, not on the essentially unknowable nature of the leaping *dreancaid mhara*, but on the feelings that the animal inspires in them.

In the last analysis, Mac an Iomaire is not telling us about sand-hoppers, he is telling us about himself. His world is full of observation, warmth, passion and attachment because these are the values that occupy his own mind, these are the values that governed the relationship between the people of *Maínis* and the sea that surrounded them. If we feel at home when reading *The Shores of Connemara* it is not because we are surrounded by a benevolent if quick tempered nature, but because we are surrounded by benevolent (and quick tempered?) people. When we turn to our modern literature about the sea – our journals of marine science – we realise that we are surrounded by people, about whom we know little beyond their names, who seem to be devoid of any value or feeling, except that there are no values they care to communicate. How we interpret or react to the endless facts and hypotheses which this colourless multitude has laid before us, we must decide for ourselves. Science has nothing further to say. The model on offer is the model of the feelingless universe. As models go, this one is not always the least useful. But if one late August night you find yourself three miles south of *An Sceirde Mór* recovering a plankton net, and as it breaks surface, it flashes and glows in the dark, when the myriad animals protest their capture, don't bother seeking reports of similar wonders in the science library. Instead read Mac an Iomaire, and match your experience with that of others who have also lain off *Na Sceirdí* late at night, and marvelled at the sea.

Cilian Roden
September 2000

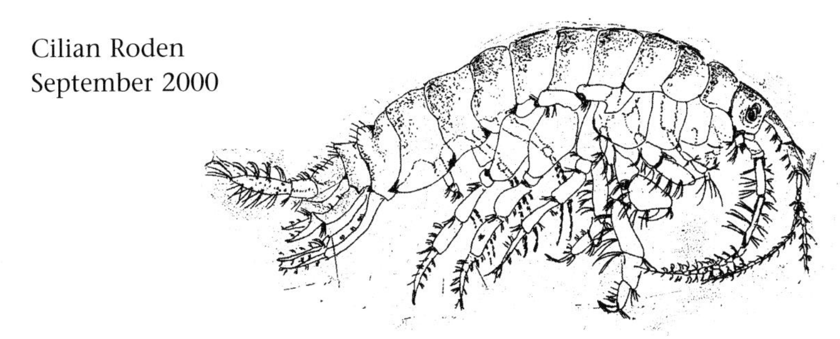

References

Ricketts, E.F. Calvin, J. and Hedgpeth, J.W. (1985) Between Pacific Tides, 5th edition revised by D.W. Philips. Stanford University Press, California.

Roden, C.M. and Raine, R. (1994) Phytoplankton blooms and a coastal thermocline boundary along the west coast of Ireland. Estuarine, Coastal and Shelf Science, 39, 511-526.

Yonge, C.M. (1949) The Sea Shore, Collins, London.

INTRODUCTION

Séamas Mac an Iomaire was born on the 13th January 1891 on *Maínis*, an island off the coast of Connemara that was joined shortly afterwards to the mainland by a causeway leading to the village of Carna. According to the Census of 1901, his father Coleman (Cóilín) was married to Barbara (Bairbre) and they had three sons – James (Séamas), Kerrins (Ciarán), John (Seán) and one daughter Mary (Máire). His father spoke both Irish and English whereas his mother spoke Irish only. His people owned a shop in a part of *Maínis* called *An Meall Rua*. His father, Cóilín, like many shopkeepers in Connemara, owned a sailing vessel to carry goods and cargo from Galway. For a period of about twelve years, from some time in 1915 or 1916 until the year of his death in 1927, he carried on this trading route from Galway to *Cill Chiaráin* and other points west. His boat was one of the more famous of the Galway Hookers and was known as *An Áirc* or *Bád Chloch an Phionna*.[1] Séamas, or Jimín as he was known by his neigbours, attended the local national school on the island. The schoolteacher had no Irish and the medium of instruction, as was the norm at the time, was the English language, of which the children had little or none. The life of the island community was interwoven with the seashore and the inshore waters of the coastal area and Séamas learned the skills associated with this way of life – fishing, cutting seaweed and other such activities. He was also living in a community that was rich in songs, storytelling and other expressions of folklore and he acquired this heritage in the usual way. He began writing and a piece he had submitted to *Ireland's Own* on a drowning tragedy off Carna during the pattern of MacDara in 1907 earned him a prize and probably spurned him on to continue writing.[2] He became interested in the national movement for independence and joined the Irish Volunteers. His family was also involved and Séamas and his father and one of his brothers were each arrested and imprisoned for their activities. His home was raided in 1919 by the military and the police who removed a quantity of his collection of folklore. This did not deter him and he continued to write and in the interest of security he placed his writings in tin boxes and buried them in the sand dunes of *Maínis*. His essays and stories along with songs he collected were published in the monthly *An Stoc* between 1919 and 1926. He was asked by Colm Ó Gaora, writer, leader of the Irish Volunteers in the Rosmuc area and member of the national executive council of *Conradh na Gaeilge* (The Gaelic League), to become involved in the teaching of Irish through the scheme of *múinteoirí taistil* (travelling teachers) initiated by the League.

[1] This vessel, which was built in the yard of the renowned Casey boatwrights in Maínis, was in commission until she was abandoned in heavy weather in the Bay of Biscay in the summer of 1988. It is rumoured that she was salvaged and taken to a port in the north of Spain.

[2] The author referred to this tragedy in his book *Conamara Man* and gave the date, incorrectly, as 1904.

A loaded hooker approaching the swing bridge at Béal an Daingin at the upper end of Greatman's Bay. This passage was often used by boats sailing to Cill Chiaráin as it saved boats from a long beat against the wind around Golam Head.

237

sgéiṫeann sí de féir nádúir
nuair a ṫagas an t-am.
Imṫigeann siad amaċ ar an
ḃoṫairín san n-geiṁreaḋ ~~de~~
do féir a n-dúṫċas, mar ḃéarfas
go leor eile aċ iad.

---

dóig 12b

Luaċóg, Luaċóga

Ḃaineann na Luaċóga le treiḃ na n-eascon, aċt fáġtear cineál aca i loċáin fíor-uisge nó i sruṫáin nó i n-áit a m-bíonn roinnt uisge aċt an cineál eile i loċáin sáile sa gealaċ. Ní'l aon ḃaċ ainṁin a ḃíos orṫa; an ċuid a ḃíos i n-aice an ġainiṁ bíonn siad níos ḃáine ná na cinn a ḃíos le fáġail i láib. Timċeall le seaċt nó oċt de orḋlaiġ ar faḋ a ḃíos cuid aca. Is baoite mait í cé an craiceann a ḟeannaḋ di, go h-áiriḋ an luaċóg ġeal-ḃuiḋe a ḟáġtear i n-aice an ġainiṁ: meallann sí an breac ḋí ċlipe é.
Ní'l caoi ar ḃiṫ is fusa iad a fáġail ná, má

Snáṫaḋ Mara, Snáṫaḋa Mara

Ḃuaileann siad seo isteaċ 'ugainn ón ḃomain, i ḃtús an tsaṁraiḋ. Is minic a ḃíos siad le fágail ṫríḋ an sgoiṫċ nuair a caiṫtear i ḋtír í le oibriú na farraige. Go deiṁin, is aisteaċ an ḃreaċ é: ceaṫair nó cúig de ordlaiġ ar fad, caol ar ḋéanaṁ na snáṫaide móire, craiceann cruaiḋ air agus é cineál sliogánaċ, go mór-mór amaċ 'na tosaiġ.

Ar maiṫ an baoite mangaċ é, agus le linn iad a ḃeiṫ le fágail tagann a lán cluiċí eile aniar ón ḃfarraige. Leanann siad féin a ċéile agus ní le gean dá ċéile, mar ḃíonn sé ~~i n-a~~ ṫroiḋ agus ~~i n-a~~ ṁarḃú ar feaḋ an tsarais, iad féin a' marḃaċtáil ar a ċéile. An dream beag a ḃíos tíar leis. Ní ḃíonn aon ṫruaiġe ag an láidir don lag.

Pages of the original manuscript of Cladaigh Chonamara.

He trained initially in *Tuar Mhic Éadaigh* in Mayo and taught in the area around Boyle in Roscommon and in Wicklow. He subsequently went to *Coláiste na Rinne* in *An Rinn*, Co. Waterford and after gaining a teaching certificate there he got a job teaching in Enniscorthy. He applied for a permanent teaching position in Sligo but was not offered it on account of his refusal to take the oath of allegiance that was required of all public servants of the new Free State.

He emigrated to the USA in 1926, gaining entry via Canada, after failing to get a visa from the United States consulate in Dublin because of his perceived poor command of the English language. In a letter that he wrote to Professor Tomás Ó Máille of University College Galway from New York in 1937 he expressed his aggrievement at not being offered a permanent position in Wicklow and in Wexford and suggested that younger teachers who had influence with the masters had been the cause of this. When Séamas reached New York he renewed his aquaintance with an Irish-American called Seosamh Daibhéid who was to become a close friend and mentor of his. Seosamh was born in Brooklyn of Irish parents. He left school at an early age and got to know Connemara people in New York, learning Irish from them and teaching it in the New York Gaelic Society. Séamas began teaching classes in the Gaelic Society but eventually decided on a more permanent position with a railway company, working mostly underground, spending months on end without seeing the light of day. He contracted TB and was hospitalised. Seosamh Daibhéid encouraged him to continue writing while he was recuperating and so the embryo of *Cladaigh Chonamara* developed.

Séamas wrote (in Irish) "I was in bed when I wrote most of the pieces as I was not allowed to get up. The doctor told me there was no harm in writing three or four pages a day, that is, after having already spent six months on the flat of my back not being allowed stir. I often wrote eight pages a day, although the doctor doesn't know that yet, but it's said "*nuair a thugtar banlámh don bhodach go dtabharfaidh sé féin slat leis*" (give him an inch and he'll take an ell). I would get so immersed in such desirable memories that I would forget altogether that I was in a foreign country lying on the flat of my back with TB. As well as that I would often be talking in my sleep . . . I'd be back in Connemara hauling pots or long-lines or nets, or maybe even cursing the dogfish or the starfish . . . I would awaken suddenly out of these memories when I'd look out through the window at the cars and the electric traffic lights turning green and red from time to time, the noise and bustle of the city reminding me where I was."

It was suggested to Seosamh Daibhéid by Professor Tomás Ó Máille that he help Mac an Iomaire by way of advice and by editing of the draft pieces he was writing. Daibhéid engaged himself in this work and also wrote to *An Gúm*, the publishing section of the Department of Education, at the end of 1927 outlining the work in hand and asking for it to be published. He received a reply in early 1928 and there followed protracted correspondence between Daibhéid and *An Gúm*. The draft of *Cladaigh Chonamara* was in *An Gúm* for a year before a decision was taken to publish it. In December 1932 Seosamh received word from *An Gúm* that the work was to be completely re-edited. He was not very happy about this and decided to give up his editorial work but continued to advise Mac an Iomaire on the text. He stated (in Irish) "If the editor of *An Gúm* is going to re-edit my work then I would rather leave all the work to him and not have my name as editor on the book at all. I won't be responsible for someone else's work, whether it's good or bad. When Tomás Ó Máille suggested that I edit these drafts, he said he was willing to read the proofs . . ." The book finally appeared in 1938 and the preface, written by Professor Ó Máille, made no mention of the part played by Seosamh Daibhéid.

Séamas continued working with the railroad company until his retirement in 1960. He visited his native home from time to time and supported the foundation of the Marine Biology Station set up by University College, Galway at *Crumpán*, between *Maínis* and *Carna*. He died on the 15th of November in 1967.

Cladaigh Chonamara, when first published, consisted of 247 pages and a number of coloured plates that were taken from the book *The Sea-Shore* by Janet-Harvey Kelman and the Rev.Theodore Wood, published by Thomas Nelson & Sons, Ltd. *Cladaí Chonamara* was later republished in 1985 by *An Gúm*, with a number of drawings and photographs. This latter edition made the book more accessible to today's reader of Irish, mainly by standardisation of spelling and by printing it in roman script, without losing the flavour of the language of the region in which it was set. The aim of this present edition is to bring *Cladaí Chonamara* to a wider audience by providing an English translation and to make annotations.

Cladaigh Chonamara did not set out to identify the flora and fauna in a scientific context and thus no Latin or scientific names were presented (with the notable exception of the wrasse *Crenilabrus rupestris*). Mac an Iomaire used three main groupings of organisms in his book – *An Fheamainn* ("seaweed"), *Iascán Trá* ("small shore fish" – this included mostly invertebrates and did not include finfish), *Iasc na Farraige* ("fish of the sea"). It was probably not the intention of the author to arrange the grouping and the sequence of the descriptions of the organisms in a way that would reflect the accepted taxonomy of the time. For example, the cuttlefish (a mollusc) appeared amongst "fish of the sea" (finfish), and cartilaginous fish appeared in various places among the teleosts or bony fish. Similarly, the hermit crab (a crustacean) appeared next to the winkles (molluscs) and the acorn barnacle (a crustacean) appeared with the molluscs (between the limpets and the bivalves). The sea mat and sponge appeared under the title of "seaweed".

Mac an Iomaire, however, did have occasion to attempt to identify the organisms by their Latin names in some of the articles that he had written for publication in *An Stoc* and on which much of *Cladaigh Chonamara* was based. As he was not a trained biologist it is difficult to accept their veracity at all times. It seems as if the articles in *An Stoc* were based on a supplied list of English and Latin names and Mac an Iomaire matched these names to organisms with which he was familiar as best as he could. For example, in describing the wrasse family he ascribes *an ballach meilsceánaigh* to the scale-eyed wrasse, *Acantholabrus palloni,* a species that has not been recorded in Ireland. After the entry "Spanish Mackerel" he notes "*Ronnach Spáinneach*"; while this is a literal translation these are two distinct fishes – the spanish mackerel belongs to the mackerel family and is the species *Scomber colias,* whereas *ronnach spáinneach* as used today and as recorded by Farran (1946) is the garfish which belongs to the family of needlefishes and is the species *Belone belone.*

There is also an occasional contradiction between what appeared in the notes in *An Stoc* and what was published in *Cladaigh Chonamara*. The angler fish (*Lophius piscatorius*) is said by the author to be *"An Láimhíneach"*, a name recorded by Farran and which in current use denotes the angler fish. In *Cladaigh Chonamara,* however, the author quite obviously describes a squid under the title of *An Láimhíneach.* Another article in *An Stoc* entitled *An Liabhán Gréine* begins by giving the English name "Sun-fish (*Orthagoriseus mola*)" a fish which is described as being seven or eight feet in length. He then proceeds to describe the basking shark fishery. The problem here originates in the use of the name sun-fish in Hiberno-English. It is used to name two separate fish – one the ocean sunfish (*Mola mola*) and the other the basking shark (*Cetorhinus maximus*). When *Cladaigh Chonamara* came to be written the *liamhán gréine* was described as being thirty to forty feet in length and is quite obviously the basking shark.

In spite of these difficulties one cannot deduce that the variety of types described by Mac an Iomaire did not exist, but rather than all being distinct species, some of the variety may be attributed to changes in morphology or colour due to environmental or breeding factors. In the case of the seaweeds some of the plants ascribed specific names are merely different parts or forms of the one plant. For example, *feamainn gheimhridh* (winter seaweed), *scothach* (literally meaning tufted), *ceanna slat* (rod heads) and *slata mara* (sea rods) all refer to the same species *Laminaria hyperborea.* Mac an Iomaire did, however, at times distinguish between various species where no equivalent distinction is made in English. An example of this is the distinction between the different species of the red seaweed called sloke in Ireland (laver in England and Wales) where he describes *an fíorshleabhcán, an sleabhcán cuircíneach* and *an sleabhcán slamach.* He also presented some very precise names for which no equivalent exists in the English language, as for example, the word *bromóg* for a juvenile wrasse.

The late Professor Máirín de Valera and the present translator, respectively, supplied notes on the identification and scientific nomenclature of the flora and of the fauna described in the original book to *An Gúm.* The 1985 edition, however, listed the scientific names of only a few of the described organisms in an appendix; these names were included by the editor on the basis that the Irish names were not to be found in the "normal sources" or were very localised in use.

Where an animal or a plant is common, can be easily identified by the layperson and has a commonly used name in the vernacular there is no problem in assigning a scientific name to it. Problems arise when a name used in the text is not in common usage, when expertise in the flora and fauna among native speakers of the language is scarce and when the description of the organism in the text is insufficient to allow a definite identification. The problem is exacerbated when the name may have been very localised in usage. For example, *feamainn bhoilgíneach* is commonly applied to spiral wrack (*Fucus spiralis)* in Connemara but was also applied to bladder wrack (*Fucus vesiculosus)* in north Connemara. In the Cois Fharraige district fertile spiral wrack is known as *feamainn bhoilgíneach* and the sterile plants as *feamainn bharr-chladaigh.*

The ideal method of collection of Irish names of organisms by showing specimens to native speakers who are experts in the natural history of the seashore is a near impossible task today. There are a number of written sources of names that were of some help and these are to be found in the bibliography. The present translator has taken the responsibility of identifying and assigning the scientific names to the fauna and has based identification and nomenclature of the flora on the notes made by Professor Máirín de Valera for *An Gúm* in the 1970s.

This translation includes a re-allocation of a few of the descriptive articles within the three main groups used by the author and a change in the sequence of the articles. Each article is headed by the Irish, English and Latin (scientific) names of the organism, where known. Not all the organisms have a common name in English, however. Identification to species is attempted but in some cases the name of the class, order, family or genus alone is given. Where more than one species name is given it means that the Irish term encompasses each named species.

Cladaí Chonamara is quite unique in many respects. It is, to some extent, a guide to the seashore and coastal waters for anyone interested in natural history, although it cannot be regarded as a guide in the strict sense of a key to identification of marine organisms. It is also a commentary on the social and economic life of the coastal dwellers of *Maínis* in the late nineteenth and early twentieth century. It includes a description of the crafts in which the inhabitants were engaged, such as searching for bait, fishing, boat building, seaweed harvesting and kelp making. The use of natural materials from the sea and seashore, apart from the more obvious such as food and the production of kelp, is best illustrated in the author's description of one of the wracks – " Children often make balls from the holdfasts and hurleys from the rods to play hurling. Knife handles are also made from them; when the rod is fresh the iron is thrust into it and when it dries it will have a great grip on the blade. They're often thrown on the beach beneath the boat keels when they're being launched or being taken ashore . . ."

The author was not a naturalist in the sense of that word as used at the turn of the century in Ireland; he was not a member of an educated, urban middle class, predominantly Protestant of settler stock, who were active in field clubs and natural history societies. The acquisition of his deep knowledge of the natural history of the environment in which he was reared was incidental to a way of life he and other members of his community practised. The transcribing of this knowledge and experience to paper was what made Séamas Mac an Iomaire different to the other members of the community. *Cladaí Chonamara* is thus unique in that it was written not by a scientist or an academic but by a practitioner.

Mac an Iomaire was first and foremost a very keen observer of nature and in this sense he could be referred to as a naturalist. Some of his comments on the population dynamics of the sea creatures that he observed echo the observations of Darwin that led him to his Theory of Natural Selection. For example, when writing about the lobster he observed "You would often see the young ones swimming on top of the water during fine weather. They're only as big as a shrimp, about two inches long. It's hard to notice them, as they are the same colour as the water; nevertheless, the fish slaughter them. Only a small number escape; indeed, if it happened that all of the seed matured, then the sea would be full of lobsters. Nature prevents this. It's wonderful the way that it can keep the fish under control so that they won't become too plentiful and won't be destroying each other".

[3] For those who would delve further into the historical context of the Irish literature of natural history, *Nature in Ireland – A Scientific and Cultural History*, edited by John Wilson Foster (Lilliput Press, 1997) and *An Dialann Dúlra*, by Breandán Ó Madagáin, (Clóchomhar, 1978) are recommended

On the other hand, he repeats a number of examples of folk mythology that have no scientific basis. Among these are the beliefs that the goose barnacle begets the barnacle goose, and that eels can be produced from animal hairs. At times he presents both the folk mythology and a more rational explanation. In the case of the barrel-fish, he states that the natives were in fear and dread of this fish and believed spirits were involved because sealed barrels containing numbers of the fish came ashore. He does, however, postulate that a mature female could insert her eggs through the narrow gaps between the planks and that the fish could grow and develop within the barrel.

He was also a believer in the concept of creationism and throughout the text he expresses his wonder at the work of a divine creator. It would be an exaggeration, however, to suggest that he was an inheritor of a more ancient tradition of natural history writing, where one's perspective of fauna and landscape are modified by a cultural ethos, such as Christianity.[3]

The editorial work on the original manuscript is of some interest. In the article on the sea belt, the editor drew a series of red lines through a paragraph and wrote in the margin the word "Libel?" The lines in question were (translated) " There was a man in our townland and he used spend the whole fine summer cutting it and taking it ashore. One load of oarweed would be better than three loads of it (sea belt) and he had oarweed and he wouldn't look at it. He would get himself into such a hassle with the sea belt but he was so peculiar that he couldn't tear himself away from cutting it even though the neighbours were always making fun of him"

Another paragraph that was removed dealt with the issue of the landlord's agent who wanted half the proceeds of any weed that was cut for kelp, and with how the political environment created by the Land League spurred the scores of tenants on to stripping the shores with no deference to landlords and their followers. It is not clear why this paragraph was removed – perhaps the tone was too political or militant or there was fear of reaction from descendants of the hated landlord's agent.

A description of a court case where the defendant was charged with not paying his share of the weed cut to the landlord resulted in the defendant giving a demonstration in court of the actions involved in cutting weed. In order to give the demonstration an air of realism, the defendant stripped to his shirt – *"Struipeáil Micheál Shéamais é féin go dtí a léine"* (Mícheál Shéamais stripped to his shirt) became *"Bhain Micheál Shéamais a chuid éadaigh de"* (Mícheál Shéamais took off his clothes). The word *"struipeáil"* was probably too earthy for the editor or perhaps showed too much of the influence of the English language on Irish. Another example of editing which may be the result of this latter attitude was the substitution of the word *gabhal mara* by the editor for *cráifis,* even though the latter was probably in common usage at the time.

Although I found it impossible to do justice to the richness of the language in which it was written by Séamas Mac an Iomaire, I hope that readers of this book will get some flavour of *Cladaí Chonamara.*

Padraic de Bhaldraithe
September 2000

ACKNOWLEDGEMENTS

The idea of producing a translation of *Cladaí Chonamara* was first suggested by my friend Dave Mc Grath, a man whose expertise and interest in the seashore is matched by his enthusiasm for sharing his deep knowledge with anyone who cares to visit that habitat with him. Leo Hallissey provided continuous stimulation when the work flagged from time to time. The following people provided advice and support in various ways: Jackie Chiaráin Mac an Iomaire, Cóilín Ó hIarnáin, Liam Ó Mainnín, Brian Ottway, Pádraig Ó Tuairisg, Máirtín Ó Cadhain, Tim Robinson, Seán Ó Cathasaigh and Criostóir Mac Cárthaigh. I would like to thank Cilian Roden for his encouragement and support and for his valuable personal insight to *Cladaí Chonamara* as expressed in the foreword. Thanks are due to Nuala Nic Con Iomaire for her translation of *An Marcach Tréan*. Sabine Springer's wonderful original illustrations speak for themselves. Finally, I would like to express my gratitude to Anne Korff for researching historical photographs, for the design and layout and for her willingness to publish this book.

Inhabitants of Garumna Island, 1898.

MAÍNIS

There are many islands in Galway Bay on the west of Ireland and I intend to give a short description of one of these islands on which I lived at one stage of my life. I can still see with my mind's eye those cottages and the islands and the beautiful sights that surrounded me that time in *Maínis*. The name *Maínis* suits it well, i.e. *maigh* (plain) and *inis* (island), as a lot of it is a smooth level plain surrounded by the sea. It's about two miles long and a mile and a half wide. Even though it has dune and plain, that does not mean it hasn't a lot of rough rocky places, heights and valleys, big and small cliffs and stony quarries scattered here and there.

The coastline is wild and rough on the south and west sides. The swell of the sea has eaten away the place where the land is soft. Those indentations that stretch in through the land like arms of the sea are called *aircíní* or creeks and great bold hard projections of big granite rocks stretch out to challenge the breakers. Those same creeks are like boat harbours, narrow enough at the mouth and wide inside, high cliffs on either side to give shelter, and landing places here and there. The coastline on the east and north sides is less wild. There is some shelter here from the face of the open sea. Many houses are situated by the sea, as the ocean was the main provider for the people. Their livelihood is hard earned by fishing and burning kelp, early and late, in fair and in foul weather, out on the high crest of the waves, and with one foot on the edge of the grave. As for land, few possess it, small fields are full of stones and in some places have not even a foot of soil. The sandy ground is not much good for any crop. Nevertheless, in a good year the potatoes grow well. Seaweed is the manure and it's said to be a good fertiliser. These people have little in the way of earthly goods, but they work away as hard as they can. During summer and autumn they labour away but have little to show for it the rest of the year. Having been subject to penal laws and tyranny for hundreds of years has left them badly off. As for rent and tax, it's hardly worth talking of them compared to other worse deeds. The place was once cleared as was done in other parts of Ireland. The people were chased off their holdings and their houses knocked down. They suffered much torment at the hands of the landlord's bailiff and from the gang with the iron crowbars whose work is still to be clearly seen; bare old lonely ruins with moss and ivy growing outside and nettles inside. A terrible treachery was done but as the proverb says "treachery brings its own punishment"

There are about eighty houses on this island and they're situated nice and cosily by the sea. Most are thatched houses. They're given a new thatch in November, when winter and the bad weather is approaching, as "the windy day is not the day for the scollops". A bridge was built to connect the island to the mainland a number of years ago.[4] Before that it was an inconvenient place as anything that was to be brought in or out had to be ferried by boat. During the time of the Great War a lot of useful valuable articles came ashore from commercial shipping that the German sank to the bottom of the big ocean. The local people did well that time from the articles that came ashore. There's no accounting for the

[4] This bridge was built about 1893

amount of wood that sailed in, barrels of rum and all kinds of oil, tallow, blubber, packs of cotton and so on. When the vessels were sunk west of *Ceann Léime* the wind was generally west or south-west, and the contents of the ship came from the west on the surface of the sea with wind and current. The proverb itself says " 'tis an ill wind that blows no good". It wasn't only the amount that came ashore on the island, but the boats would go out every day on the sea looking for valuable salvage. They often came across goods that they couldn't take aboard. They would have to tie them with the end of a rope and tow them ashore. They would have a good life sailing about, sometimes with a favourable wind and other times beating, until it was time to come home with the onset of the dark night.

It's a beautiful place in the summer when the sea is a flat board like a big silvery mirror around the islands, the smooth sandy beaches resplendent and glittering under the shimmering sun, everything in full growth, the birds of the air happily singing and warbling up in the blue sky, gulls and other sea birds fishing and swimming in the mouth of the waves, every animal, every insect and all, without worry or otherwise, happy with life, people here and there on the beaches swimming and bathing in the healthy brine.

When winter arrives that's a different story. The south-westerly and westerly winds blowing in terrible gusts on the surface of the big dark green sea; the islands a dour black colour and the small islands looking sombre; the sea in a mess, swelling and rising in white mounds, bending and twisting under the power and control of the big wind; around the edges of the bare lonely islands all that is heard is the grumbling, murmuring and creaking of the fierce violent surf, the remains of the violence travelling and flying in a foamy ferment up to the top of the high tide mark, to get shelter and refuge under the shade of the cliffs and the hillocks. It's no lie to say that it's a lonely, bare sight in winter. The people keep the fire on the hearth all day long; now and then they glance out trying to look through the bad weather at the surface of the sea that looks like white milk away towards the horizon. The view would remind you of the *Beanna Beola* (The Twelve Bens) and their valleys under white sheets after a night's snow. If the fisherman's field is not covered in a white bloom, then there's no winkle on a shore. Big surf rising in high walls drawing back and folding, swelling and running and rushing at each others' heels, doffing their white crests as they approach the shore, bursting and falling on top of one another, mixing and making whirlpools and boiling in one big commotion, until their strength and their pressure is exhausted and used on the hard granite edge of the island which stands boldly against it since time immemorial. The ceaseless noise and roaring and creaking of the wave, every now and then interwoven with the noise and sharp screech of the wind – the big thunderclap the only natural sound that can get the better of the rough sound of the sea.

Often when the weather is riotous, black clouds change their colours as they sail in, turning black and blue, the lightning shining every other minute, making crescents and crosses on the dark blue clouds. Hailstones as big as pullets' eggs arrive. Silence comes and you can't tell from what quarter the wind is coming. The lightning flashes as blue as indigo; the thunder explodes; you would think that a stone quarry and a pebble beach were being mixed together and poured out in the clouds above your head. It's a sign of bad weather to have it at sea at that time of year; it's strange weather. It frightens every living thing on the face of the earth.

That's where I spent a time without sorrow or woe or gloom, and I would love to have stayed there forever. I can see now in my mind's eye the cabin by the shore, the high spring tides accosting me at the doorway, undertows rushing and tumbling on the shingly shore near the side of the house, the healthy salty taste of the wind blowing around me and the continuous pulsing of the breakers reaching my ears throughout the severe winter. I thought there was nowhere on the surface of the earth which bettered it for beauty and adornment, and it was hard to beat for fun and pastime. I can see in front of me now the long white roads, the people working in the fields, the boats sailing and heading out to sea in the evening, and the sun declining in the west and giving a golden sheen to the Bens. I can hear on every side the sweet voices of young and old in the ancient tongue which was fashioned and sung by the Gael; in spite of what they suffered in Cromwell's time and before and since then, they kept their language and customs alive. They never yet succumbed to the enemy, and I hope they will not until "Ireland is free as well as being Gaelic, and Gaelic as well as being free"

A púcán under sail in Cill Chiaráin Bay. This boat is Púcán Bharrett, launched in 1928 and still in commission and owned by the Barrett family in Foirnis, Leitir Mealláin.

FISHING

The way and the form of fishing in this area are very different now to that of long ago. About a hundred years ago or so, there were very few sailing boats. Most people had *báid iomartha,* and they fished mainly with hand lines, except that the odd person had a piece or two of netting.[5]

The women would clean and repair the nets in those days. The boats would head out to the fishing banks at dusk to set their nets for the night. They usually made a fixed cast at that time – that is to set the nets on the fishing ground with a big long four-cornered stone which would have a groove cut around it so as the rope would fit into it. There were about thirty fathoms of strong rope from the net stone with the other end attached to the clew of the net. The boats would head for home then and leave their nets there until the following morning when they would come to lift them, hoping to have a haul of mackerel or herring. They often had. Other times they would have nothing after all their hardship rowing throughout the night, because the nets were often set far out to sea and were often cut by spurdogs. They couldn't go out again until the nets were repaired with a net needle. Fishing was hard, stressful, cold work at that time.

Catching gurnard was a type of fishing that was very common in the old days. Gurnard were usually caught on hand lines trailed after a moving boat. When they're taken aboard you can't remove them from the hook until they're hit against the beam and they die. *A tharraingt isteach is a bhualadh faoin seas – sin é a mharaigh an cnúdán.* (Being hauled in and struck off the beam – that's how the gurnard was caught). The reason for that is that the gurnard has so many spines sticking out when alive that it would injure you; and when it's dead it's not harmful. It's a very nice, sweet-tasting fish. Not many are caught nowadays in any event.

Life has changed a lot between that time and the present. The people of this region now have three types of boat – these are the nobbies, the *gleoteoga* and the *púcáin.*[6] There's a

[5, 6] The *gleoiteog*, the *púcán,* the *leathbhád* and the *bád mór* are traditional wooden carvel sailing craft, which are peculiar to the west coast of Ireland and more specifically to the inshore waters between Slyne Head in north-west County Galway and Black Head in County Clare. They are sometimes collectively referred to as hookers, although the term hooker is more narrowly applied to the *bád* mór and the *leathbhád.* The *bád mór, leathbhád* and *gleoiteog* are gaff-rigged cutters, carrying a mainsail, staysail and jib set on a bowsprit, whereas the *púcán* carries a dipping lugsail and a jib set on a bowsprit. The hull of the *bád iomartha* was much the same as a small *gleoiteog* or *púcán.* It did not carry sails and would have had no weatherboards nor mast beam nor bowsprit. It was propelled by two or three long sweeps.

The nobby was introduced to Connemara in the 1890s by the Congested Districts Board. Instructors were brought over to Ireland to initiate local building of the nobby (the favoured type in Connemara) and of the zulu. The nobby ranged from 13 to 20 tons and was quite unlike the hooker, being double-ended and having two masts, setting a standing lugsail on the mizzen mast and originally a standing lugsail on the main mast, this being later replaced by a gaff rig.

lot of different kinds of fishing also practised. Fishing is done with nets, with long-lines, with trammels and with hand lines. The nobbies usually look for mackerel and herring. Each one of the boats has forty pieces of mackerel net and thirty pieces of herring net. One of those boats with the two trammels is very expensive – up to twelve hundred pounds. There's a big difference between the mackerel net and the herring net.

The mackerel nets are thirty-two fathoms long and three-and-a-half fathoms deep. There are two ropes on the top that are called cork ropes. The corks are very close together on the top – within two feet of each other. There are two other ropes stretched on the bottom that are called the bottom ropes. These ropes keep the net stretched from the top, as the corks on the top are on the surface of the sea. The thread in the net needs to be good. They're also covered in tar and stained so as they don't absorb water, as the thread would rot if the water entered it. The mesh in the mackerel net is about one-and-a-half inches. The herring nets are twenty fathoms long and eight fathoms deep. They have ropes at the top and bottom, as with the mackerel net, but the corks on the herring net are further apart. The reason for the herring net being that deep is that the herring swim deep in the sea, and the mackerel swim at the surface. The mesh in the herring net is about one inch in size.

The boats look for herring in Galway Bay and these herrings are bought in the town of Galway. The boats search for mackerel out west of the Aran Islands. They go out in April. Each has a crew of seven. They leave the harbour at four o'clock in the afternoon and sail until the sun goes down. They then take down the mainsail and sail under the jib and the small sail (mizzen). The crew then starts to shoot the nets to starboard and they don't take long to set them.

There are ropes from the clew of the net attached to the head of the boat. And the corks look nice in one long single line from the boat as far as you can see. As the current then flows, whether east or west, the boat also moves, because no matter how strong the wind, the nets are able to pull the boat with the current. As soon as the nets are set, the main mast is taken down, in case it might add to the windage or that it might sway from side to side in the boat, because out on that deep sea there is always a swell and the boat rocks with the movement of the sea. When the weather is bad and there's a swell you need to be clever and have sea legs or to be well used to walking on a deck, because if a person were unaware of it, he would be knocked down and thrown from side to side and would be in danger also of being knocked overboard and being drowned.

During the time the nets are set, one of the crew is on watch, one person in turn each night, in case the wind changes and the boat were to go into the net and the weight of the boat on it. They don't forget to keep the lamp lighting on the mizzen mast. They start hauling up at one o'clock. The big strong rope is stretched at the bottom of the net and it takes the weight of the boat. The end of this rope is on the capstan and the capstan has two iron handles which two men turn; and as they turn them the rope comes aboard and the boat advances towards the nets. There's a man below deck up forward keeping the rope taut, two other men hauling the nets, and two others stowing them. When they have the last piece in, the mast is raised and the boat sets sail and they head towards the place from where the fish is sent to market. The fish are boxed and iced in *Cloch na Rón* (Roundstone) or *Cill Rónáin* (Kilronan) to keep them fresh until they go to England.

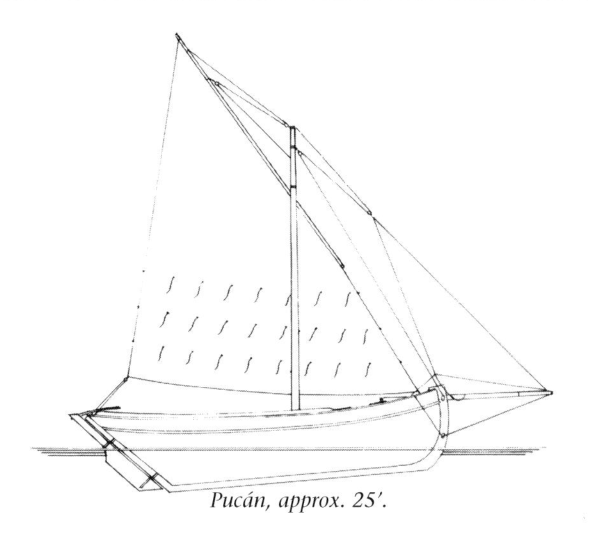

Pucán, approx. 25′.

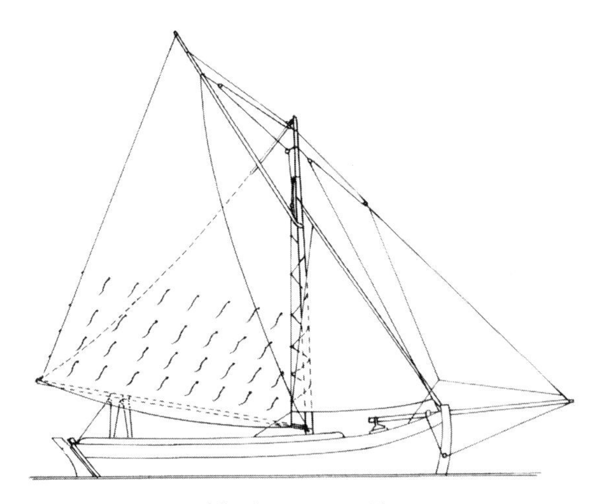

Bád Mór, approx. 40′.

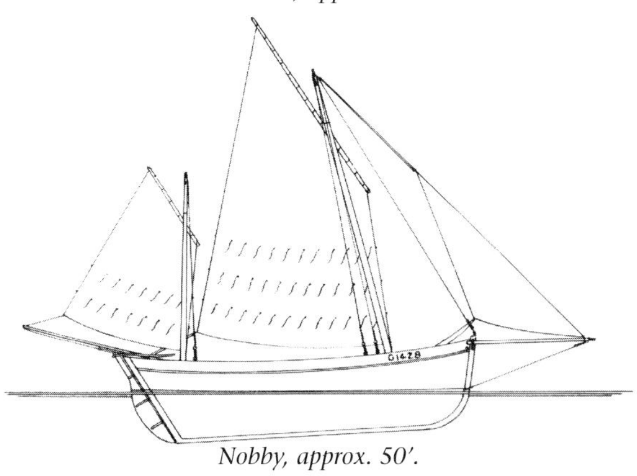

Nobby, approx. 50′.

The *gleoteoga* and the *púcáin* are involved in much the same type of fishing. They're about the same size also – able to carry four or five tons weight and each has a crew of two. They're open boats and the *gleoteoig* has three sails – the mainsail, the foresail and the jib; the *púcán* has two sails – the mainsail and the jib. They normally fish with long-lines and trammels. The long-line is made up of a long hand line that is up to a hundred fathoms long. This long hand line is called the back of the long-line, and attached to the back, three fathoms apart, there's a fathom and a half of a snood that's called a *fortéim* with a hook at the end. That hook has a bait of sand eel, or of a piece of fish such as mackerel, pollack, coalfish, rockling, garfish or a worm that is found in the sand, which is called a lugworm. Baiting a long-line is slow work. When the baiting is finished you start to let it out of the boat. You need to be quite skilful in setting the long-line. You let out the head stone first, as there is such a stone at either end of the long-line that has a long line out of it and a buoy at the surface of the sea. The long-line is then stretched on the sea bottom, around the edge of the weed-covered rocks. It's left there for a couple of hours. It's then taken into the boat and as one man hauls it another removes the fish and another settles it in a basket and fixes the hooks in corks on the rim of the basket. Many kinds of fish are caught on long-lines – eels, rays, skate, flatfish, turbot, halibut, ling, cod, hake, haddock, dogfish and many others.

The trammels are set on the weedy areas and on the bare flat rocks. Wrasse, pollack and sea trout are taken with these nets. The trammels are set on the sea bottom. There are lead weights on the bottom to keep them down on the sea floor and corks on the head rope to keep the net stretched from the bottom. You would often be fishing all day long without catching anything; "if all else fails, go fishing". There are certain days that are better for catching fish than others. Cold weather is not good, and especially northerly or

Fishing net laid out to dry.

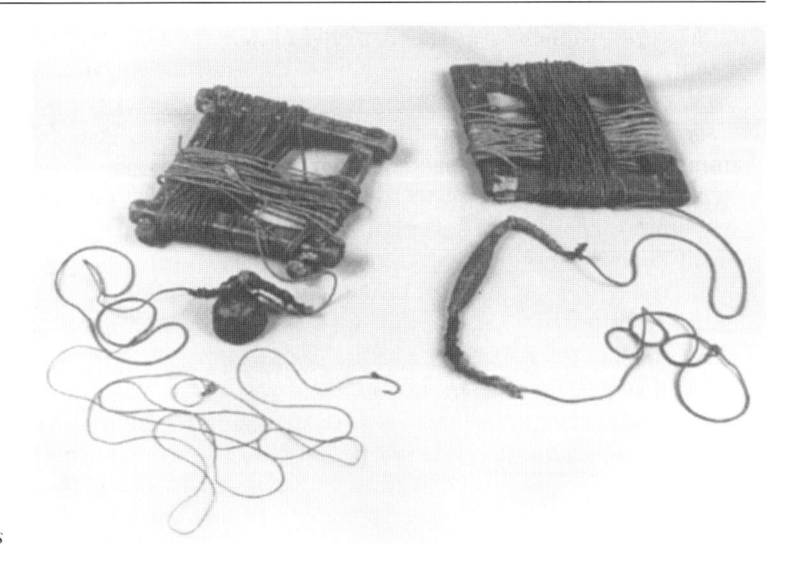

Hand lines

easterly winds. The old folk never thought much of a day that would have the wind blowing from either of those quarters. It's said that the southerly or westerly winds are best. The proverb also says of the west wind *"gaoth aniar bíonn sí fial is cuireann sí iasc i líonta"* (the west wind it is bounteous and fills your nets with fish), and it's probably a true saying. A quiet pleasant day with no damaging swell in the sea is the day to go fishing. As well as that everyone understands that, like everything else, the fish is happy in the sea on a fine day unlike the cold un-natural day that would put numbness in your fingers if you weren't working hard. A day that has any sting or cold in it is not a day for fishing.

There are places on the sea bottom that fish prefer to others, so that it is believable that the hordes with fins that have always lived down under the waves have a certain dwelling place, down amongst the seaweed-covered rocks and on the sand. There are many places in the sea and if you were ever fishing, you might never feel a bite in some places, as if you had your line in a peat bog, and, on the other hand, within two lengths of an oar of such a patch there would be a very good fishing ground. That means that fish feed together in the deep sea, just as every tribe on the surface of the earth does, and that they have made some kind of nesting places in the seaweed-covered bottom and in the gravel to spend the time during bad weather. As the year goes by and the fine weather passes, the fish move out to the deep, and probably stay there for the winter and the first month of spring, because during that time, there are few fish to be caught, except for a few types like eels, rays, skate and sometimes herring and mackerel when they come in.

Lobster fishing is another type of fishing that is carried on here. This fishing is done with *púcáin, gleoteoga* and *currachaí.*[7] The people who wish to do this work have to go off in winter to cut hazel or sally rods to make lobster pots. Every boat crew needs to cut rods for material for thirty pots, that's the allocation of pots for each boat. When the rods are

[7] The *currach* is the traditional canvas-covered and tarred boat. A man by the name of Cloherty built a wooden carvel boat on Inishnee, near Roundstone around the turn of the century. This prototype, which was reputedly based on a tender off a foreign vessel he saw at Cleggan, Co. Galway, became known as a *currach adhmaid* and gradually supplanted the canvas *currach* in many parts of Connemara.

Greasing the sail of a púcán at Más, Carna, before going fishing.

cut, the work starts immediately and it's a lot of work to make a set of lobster pots. A man who would know how to make them would make about three a day; they're made like a basket, quite big, about two feet in height and two feet wide, but round like a keg. They have a flat bottom to place them properly on the seaweed bottom, and they have a crown on top. In the middle of the crown is the *bearach*, a round hole that your hand can go through. The lobster goes down that way, and when it's down it's not easy for it to come up, as the opening is made in such a way that it will not find it. The lobster fisherman needs to get ropes for the pots and corks for the ropes. Each pot needs about eighteen fathoms of a thin red rope. The head of this rope is tied under two ribs near the *bearach* as the *bearach* is in the middle of the crown of the pot, so that when the pot is let down into the sea the bottom of the pot will rest on the sea bed.

There's also a small pile of stones in it to keep it settled. It's necessary to have corks on the rope within one and a half fathoms of each other, about six stem corks and then the buoy at the end of the rope. Four or five corks make up the buoy. These corks that I'm talking about are up to eight inches in width and an inch-and-a-half high.

The lobster fishermen begin to get ready to go to sea in the month of May. They have to go fishing first for bait for a day, as every pot needs to be baited carefully. Every sort of fish is right for bait. They make small pieces of the fish with a knife, every piece about the size of your fist. The bait is hung inside the pot with small branches of rods that have a

Lobster pot, known also as a French pot.

Traditional lobster pot, usually made from sally rods (willow).

Fish drying on the thatched roof of an outhouse in Carna.

barb on one end, to prevent the bait from falling off and the other end of the branch is fastened in the crown of the pot. The pot needs to be on the seaweed-covered bottom when set and to be let down a hole on the bottom if possible, as the lobster is found especially near the caves. When the lobster passes by the place where the pot is set it sees the bait inside and it tries first to get it from the outside but to no avail. It goes up the side of the pot then and down the opening. It doesn't realise then that it's trapped, and it starts to eat the bait, and keeps eating it from night till morning. There is often more than one lobster in a pot and eels and edible crabs often enter also. That's when the lobster fisherman has a dangerous job, taking them out of the pot, if it turned out there were lobsters, three or four edible crabs and an eel. They all flay each other bloodily and often one of the lobsters is killed by the others. Certainly, if there are more than a couple in a pot the third is finished. If a lobster got a hold of a person's fingers with its claws, that are as sharp as a scissors, it would take the finger off quickly; and the crab that's called the (velvet) swimming crab is every bit as bad as any lobster because it's so agile that it can move on its head, and so fast that it would catch you when turning around, and I can tell you there's no grip like it. When the lobster fisherman comes in from the sea in the morning, he puts the lobsters that he has from the previous night's work, whether few or many, in the main pot; that is the storage pot he has for the lobsters on anchor at the mouth of the harbour in which he keeps the lobsters alive for a fortnight or month, when he takes them live to the market. If there is any dead one it won't be accepted from him.

He gets about one pound a dozen for big ones, and according to size for the others. He needs to restrain every lobster when he puts them into the storage pot; if he didn't they would kill each other. The lobster is restrained by cutting a muscle in its claw with a small knife, and it won't be able to do any damage then.

The summer and the autumn is the lobster season, and the last month of summer and the first of autumn are the best for the lobsters around this coast. The shallows are not the best places at the beginning of the year, but they are the best out in the autumn when the lobster moves into the oarweed. The lobsters come in from the deep sea in shoals like every other fish, and it's said there are large numbers of them together.

Hookers sailing around Mac Dara's Island.

Seaweeds exposed on the shore on Maínis.

SEARCHING FOR BAIT

It was a fine afternoon in the yellow month of May, as fine and sunny an afternoon as anyone ever saw. The day was quite warm from early morning to noon, but now there was a fine coolness and freshness, except that there was the odd swarm of the small flies up and I can tell you they were not good friends. They were able, my good man, to send you clean out of your mind with their poisonous stings. The sky was a pale blue with neither cloud nor mist but there was a certain amount of haze on the horizon to the south and to the south-west, a sign of heat and fine weather. The tall peaks of the *Beanna Beola* raising their summits above each other against the sky to the north, changing their beautiful colours every other minute in such a way that would make a painter envious. The sun a big golden globe lowering itself slowly and easily down at the back of *Cruach na Cora* in the west and, as it was descending, the sky around it was changing colour from yellow to tan and to orange, letting the whole country know that fine weather was on the way.

The lonesome murmur of the sea was to be heard on the shore, lapping and chuckling in the rough stony places and running in and out of the irregular clefts. The musical sound of the wave was breaking slowly and evenly on *Trá Mhóir,* pools of smooth white foam moving in the mouth of the tide, a lot brighter than the strand. The poets of long ago who wrote love songs thought there was nothing on earth brighter than "the foam of the wave on the strand". The imagery suited them when praising the young woman – *"is gile a píob is a bráid ná cúr na toinne ar trá"* (her neck and her throat are brighter than the foam of the wave on the strand). That imagery pleased the women, and no wonder, because there's nothing under the sun brighter than it.

It wasn't yet full tide, because there were a few footsteps between the morning's high water mark and the bright lace of foam that was at the edge of the big dark green sea. It was in no hurry to flow, and why would it and the spring tide almost spent and it near a neap tide, and the wind to the east north-east to further prevent it.[8] The birds of the shore and sea were quiet, without a peep out of them, except for two large wrack gulls with black backs that were standing on the crest of *Carraig na mBan* in a plaintive and mournful way. Hunger, perhaps, was the cause of their complaint, and they thinking of the life of plenty they once had. It's a good horse (not to mention a bird) that never stumbles. Wasn't it many the sea beam on which they got a passage in from the deep wet abyss? If so, it wasn't with an offshore wind but mainly with a westerly and south-westerly wind. Didn't they have fun gobbling their way on that lovely free ride on the surface of the big blue sea, swallowing long soft goose barnacles from their shells, while they were being rocked and swayed with the roughness of the waves on the high crests of the long, tough wavering shafts, sometimes down in deep valleys between long curling waves of the sea, craning their necks and standing up on their legs, trying to look over the next wave? Here they are again on the crest of the wave with their wings outstretched to give more speed to their vessel while they sail before the wind on top of the big sea. That was the time

[8] The wind has an effect on the height reached by a high tide on the coast of Connemara – easterly winds having a negative effect whereas westerly winds have the opposite effect, adding to the height reached.

when everything was going well for them, with neither too much nor too little. And if they were sorry and disappointed now, don't blame them.

I was looking for young eels and gunnel that particular evening as I had intended to go fishing pollack the following day if it was suitable for sailing. I went to a freshwater pool on top of the small storm beach that's below the cemetery. There were a few quite big stones. I looked and pondered and I was sure from the look of it that it wasn't completely empty. I thought I saw with my mind's eye the eels asleep and coiled in loops on the shingle beneath the stones. There was a good cupped handful of water there, and since I had a bucket, I thought I wouldn't be long emptying it. I started throwing water out of it as fast as I could but I wasn't reducing it much, because there was a small stream running into it. I cut a few scraws and put them in the mouth of the stream and they stopped it for a while. I emptied about half of it and when I had that done I got a bit lazy and said in my mind that I would turn over the stones, that I would know one way or another. I was so greedy for the eels that I could wait no longer. I grabbed the stone, put the tips of my fingers between it and the red sand at the bottom of the pool, I raised it up on its corner and threw it back, mixing and disturbing the water a lot on the spur of the moment. The small eels came out from it but the water had been so dirtied that they went astray on me. I waited a short while then, quite impatiently, until it settled. I thought I saw the shape of an eel twisting about on the far edge of the pool. I tried to place my open knife on it, as that's the best trick to catch an eel because it's as slippery as you ever saw. But I didn't succeed; devil the bit was under the blade of the knife but rough sand. I waited impatiently a while longer, my eyes fixed, looking at every part of the pool at the same time. The water being mixed again at the far bank, I made another fierce lunge at the place with my knife, but it was the same story, my work was in vain. The pool was quite dirty now, and I was sorry I hadn't emptied it completely at the start. But it's easy to be wise after the event. But to make a long story short, I had to bale it again and not leave a drop in it. But it's said that it's better late than never. And even so, I had great satisfaction; I had the better of them because the eels were visible coiling and twisting on the shingle and trying to hide under the small pebbles on the bottom of the pool, twisting themselves in amongst them tail first. I turned over the rest of the stones with no hurry, and I had six or seven heads of eels going home at dusk.

Early next day, before the clear white light of dawn had disappeared from the sky to the east, we were ready to go to sea, Máirtín Mhicil Sheáin Phádraig from *Bóithrín na Trá* and Labhcás Pháidín Ó Nia from *Garraí na nGéabha* and myself.

"Did you get many eels yesterday evening?" said Máirtín.

"Indeed, not many" said I. "Five or six. On my word they're scarce commodities"

"I caught a handful of sand eels on the *Ard-Trá*" said Labhcás.

"Good for you" said Máirtín, "We have plenty of bait if there's anything to be done"

When we had the hand lines and bait, three trammels and anchor stones in the boat and sails raised, the sun was rising up in the east at the back of *Leitir Móir*, showing the world that another day was at hand. The sky was without cloud or mist, and the sea was like a mirror. The odd piece of floating wrack ashore and floating seaweed going slowly and lazily out the bay with the ebbing tide; gulls and terns gliding and flying back and forth with the hunger, looking for the morning's meal and their reflections to be seen below in the big silvery mirror. To crown the beauty of it all, you would swear that there was another sky and birds down at the bottom of the sea, the image of the one above. The

most skilful painter that ever turned a brush at home or abroad could never do justice to that beautiful picture at the beginning of the day.
The odd boat moving out of the sheltered bays from the shade of the tall bare rocky places and of the sandy headlands and making their way out to the wild rocks. The sound of rowing to be heard from far and near, mixed with the lonely musical sound of the wave on the shore, and as the tide was falling and the shore was being exposed, the seaweed was being moved back and forth and mixed together by the small lapping of the undertows. The knotted wrack in a golden lace shining brightly under the shafts of sunlight; lines of fine white foam at the edge of the green sea as a boundary between it and the seaweed. Up to the top of the shore there were all other kinds of seaweed growing and they were many shades of brown and black and so on until the twisted channelled wrack that was at the high tide mark of the high neap tide.
We had to put out the oars, because there wasn't a puff of wind but the ebbing tide was a great help. The wild rocks of the sea were making strange sounds. *Carraig Iolra* and *Carraig na hEilite* like sailing vessels between us and the mouth of Galway Bay. The islands of *Árainn* were off to the south and they were as blue as indigo and the boundless sea off to the west and south-west with neither end nor boundary, out to the horizon. Big heavy waves coming slowly after one another in from the west, three long curling waves in succession and six other waves increasing between them. Isn't it wonderful how the waves of the sea are regular, and the surface of the ocean is at the mercy of nature, just as is the surface of the earth? The *Sceird* rocks like big buildings on the horizon to the west and fishing and lobster boats here and there heading out to them; the crews rowing as best they could in contest, and hoping to God in their hearts that they would have the fruits of their labours when they came home in the evening.
When we were off *Leathrach na mBran*, drawing towards *Stopóg an Táilliúra*, a gentle north and north-westerly breeze came up. "Thanks be to God" said Máirtín, shipping his oar and drying the sweat from himself with the sleeve of his shirt, "It's better late than never".
"You've said it", said Labhcás, "he who waits for a fair wind will get it. Ease off your sheet".
"I think", said I, "that it's eased enough. The wind is far to the east, coming over your aft beam"
"If so, let it be" said Labhcás. "In any case it won't be long before we're at journey's end with this light wind".
"Don't eat it", said Máirtín sarcastically. "Don't speak too soon until you see what happens.
I wouldn't put it past it to die off again and leave you there rooted to the spot".
"Now you're talking", said I. But to make the story short there was no need to put an oar in the bed of a rowlock again, and we reached the fishing ground.
"Throw out your anchor stone", said Máirtín, when we were within an oar's length of *Leic na bhFaoileán*.
Labhcás looked down below him, and as the day was bright, he was able to make out the sea bottom clearly, and when he saw an arch between the clumps of sea rods he let down the stone that was in his hands. It certainly had a good grip now. He eased off the anchor rope, giving it a few pulls as he made a hitch on the *mullard.* [9]
"Has it caught?" said Máirtín.
"You can say that", said the man forward.

"Take down her sails then", said I.
He let down the jib, and folded it on the bowsprit and lashed it with the sheet. He let off the peak halyard and the throat halyard from the cleat and let down the sail into the boat; he folded it on the spar and lashed the sheet around it firmly and gently, he raised the throat a couple of feet out of the boat and tied the halyards to the cleat again.
"Where do you think, in God's name, we'd better set those nets?" said Máirtín, and he on the aft beam skinning an eel for bait. "What about setting one of them in *Glaise na bhFoiriún?"*
"*Glaise na bhFoiriún* is not much good on a low tide like this", said Labhcás. "Not only that, but it is cleaned out by the boats from *Aird Mhóir*. I had better set one of them under the foot of *Maidhm Mhicil Bhuí*, near the low tide pools, and another at *Mullán Domhain*, a good place for wrasse before, unless it has changed".
"Isn't it a good place for wrasse out near the *Mulláin Dubha*?" said Máirtín.
"Between them and *Carraig na Meacan*?" said Labhcás, looking out over one shoulder.
"Not quite", said Máirtín, taking the smoking pipe out of his mouth and pointing the shaft of the pipe out towards the rocks that were being exposed with the ebbing tide, "west of them".
"That's right", said I, "that much is settled. We'll set them, whether there's fish in them or not. We can't run them down and put them in the meshes".
Labhcás hauled up the boat and Máirtín was fixing the thole pins in their beds on the gunwales.
"Let's set the first one at *Mullán Domhain*" said I. "Keep going up to it".
When we reached the *Mullán* a good part of it was exposed.
"It's almost beginning to flow now", said Máirtín, and it's necessary to keep it set until it's nearly full tide".
I was setting and the other two were on the oars. I threw out the buoy rope and let down the head stone at the bottom of the *Mullán*, at the south south-easterly end. I was letting it out gradually and the other two were rowing the boat from the south south-east, until I let out the other end of it and let off the slack rope. I gave the rope a few tugs before letting it off, so as the net would be a straight wall without hollow or fold, down on the bottom.
"That mixed bottom shouldn't be empty, and it's not either", said Máirtín, and it's set just as you'd wish with its side to the current".
We set the other end east under the foot of *Maidhm Mhicil Bhuí*.
"There's the odd wrasse there" said Labhcás, "or else it's not what it looks like".
"There should be pollack and cod there", said Máirtín. "There was no place at *Carraig na Meacan* in the old days better than this patch. But fish were plentiful everywhere a long time ago. In any case, today is very sultry and lovely for fishing".
When the trammel was set at the *Mulláin Dubha* we were ready to go looking for pollack.
"Indeed, this place hasn't much of the look of fish", said I. "There isn't a single shag here. Maybe it may improve with the beginning of the flow".

[9] A *mullard* is a timber head on the boat – there are two in the bow (the tops of frames) and two at the stern (the tops of the transom frames). The *mullard* is used for making fast mooring and anchor ropes. In addition a bow *mullard* is used for hitching the tail of the bobstay of the bowsprit and an aft *mullard* is used for hitching the mainsheet on each tack.

"There are two maybes," said Máirtín, as he let off the hand line from the frame.
"We may as well take a run out now to the edge of *Leic Mhóir*" said Labhcás. "On my word, there's a flock of birds off *Leic na bhFaoileán*"
When the lines were taut behind the boat, Máirtín said "we'd better not have too much speed until we go down past the *Mulláin*". Labhcás and I were rowing at this time.
"I've a bite", said Máirtín, "don't go any faster".
"Keep going! A big pollack. Put the hook in it" said Labhcás.
"You can say that", said Máirtín and he hauling as fast as he could until he hauled it aboard. Indeed, it's a shoal pollack. They're in".
Labhcás had the oar shipped across the boat and he and another pollack were eyeing each other. Turning in from the shoulder of *Leic Mhóir* Máirtín hit another pollack and we caught five or six more of them on the way in.
"There are some fish there", said Labhcás, "if we can keep that course. We may as well decide to take some markers for it. The big shingle beach on *Oileán Lacha* is to be seen on the west side of *Dúleic*, and when opening it out, that white house to the east on the side of *Leitir Calaidh* will be lined up on the high rock on the north *Foiriúin*."
As the boat turned out again Máirtín struck a big pollack, and when he had a few fathoms taken in, he had to let off; he was letting off and letting off until he let the line into the weed bottom and got stuck between the heads of sea rods. The boat had to be brought back until it was over the place that the line was caught in the sea rods.
"Easy and carefully now", said Labhcás. "See can you coax it in to you. Let the boat aft a little"
"Even so, it's no good; I feel it's twisted around under the holdfast of a sea rod".
"Ease it up and down," said I, "and you might bring it with you".
"But there's no might about it". He had to break it off board. "Pity that we didn't turn her out before now".
"It's not only that", said Labhcás " but you have too much line out".
"I need it all", said Máirtín "Fourteen fathoms is little on a depth like this, but we were too far in on the shallows".
"It's time we lifted the trammels now. It shouldn't be long before full tide", said Máirtín.
"Keep going up towards the *Mullán Domhain*". He took in the head stone and was hauling it in gradually. Out near the deep there were a few wrasse in it.
"I'm surprised", said Máirtín "that there were no pollack in it, but they're not in here yet".
We rowed down to *Maidhm Mhicil Bhuí* as Máirtín was cleaning the net.
"Hadn't we best set this first?" said Máirtín, when he had the last wrasse removed. "But I don't know where. What would be wrong with the *Muráite Dhomhain*, it used to be a good place on an ebbing tide?"
"Whether there's something there or not, we'll set it there; it's not known where the best place is" said I.
We let it out near the low tide holes and kept going until we hauled the one at *Maidhm Mhicil Bhuí*. There was a good lot of pollack and wrasse in it, and as there was, we set it near the same patch again. By the time we had the trammel at the *Mulláin Dubha* hauled, it had ebbed quite a bit, and if it wasn't the best, it was no worse and when we had that set on *Maidhm an Urláir* we went looking for pollack again in the exact same place we were at the start. We weren't doing any good.

"On my word" said Máirtín, "I have no faith in today's fishing any more. But it might improve in the afternoon. There's no catching them now; it's too sultry." We were tacking back and forth for a while and our work in vain. A small breeze rose soon and as long as it lasted, there were pollack to be caught. It was getting late by now, and we had to leave the fish there, even though it was heartbreaking to leave. Nevertheless, the trammels had to be hauled.

"Start hauling in" said I.

"Indeed, it's time to go home ", said they.

We hauled the trammels then and there was a good lot of fish in them; we didn't set them any more. We raised the sails, and if we did, the oars had to be put out. There wasn't a puff of wind again, and I can tell you that we weren't making much progress against an ebbing tide.

"Indeed, and it's a long steadfast piece of sea between the tip of *Maínis* and us and we'll lose sweat unless some small breeze comes up" said Labhcás, and he on one of the oars on the aft beam, lighting his pipe.

"Don't worry", said Máirtín, "Do you see that *gleoiteog* in from *Dún Ghudail*? Wouldn't you notice that she has her sail filled, and she has too? He who waits for a fair wind will get it; isn't that a breeze over your quarter?" The sail soon started to fill and there was a small lapping to be heard from the nose of the boat as she cut her way slowly and smoothly through the sea.

"Take this tiller", said Máirtín, when the oars were shipped "until I put a grain in this pipe". I sat on the aft platform, and he took out his pipe and filled and lit it. Soon there was a cloud of smoke above him and when there was he caught the baling bucket and threw a few gallons of saltwater on the boat and washed and cleaned it.

The evening was beautiful, and it didn't take us long going in. We had a fair wind; a south south-westerly wind and the sea good and flat. The sun was a good way to the west by now, and the sky to the west as red as a sloe; a sign of more good weather. We reached the pier with a little sunlight and when we had the sails taken down and pleated we threw the fish out on the pier.

"Put out the trammels" said Máirtín to me " and I'll divide the fish".

We were sharing. He made three even shares of them in such a way that you would not know which share was smallest or biggest.

"Cast lots, Labhcás" said Máirtín.

"I have three winkles increasing in size in my two hands", said Labhcás.

"I'll have the small winkle", said I.

"The medium winkle", said Máirtín.

"I have the big winkle then. Cast them. Let the first choice of the two casts have this share, the last have that share over there by the hand line and the solitary hand have the middle share with the pouting." Labhcás opened his two hands and threw the big winkle on his own share and correspondingly with the other two winkles. We were happy as each one had the result of his draw.

When we had the fish opened and gutted, the dark clouds of night were falling and the day was fading. A flock of gulls glided above us noisily complaining in their own strange conversation. But when we went home with our own lots of fish, everything was fine with them as they walked on a small pebble beach at the edge of the sea, and as sure as there's sand on the shore, they had lots of fun, gobbling and eating fish gills and intestines. When we also had eaten supper and the fish was split and salted in barrels, it was time for sleep. And since it was, and us in need of it, we slept soundly from then until morning.

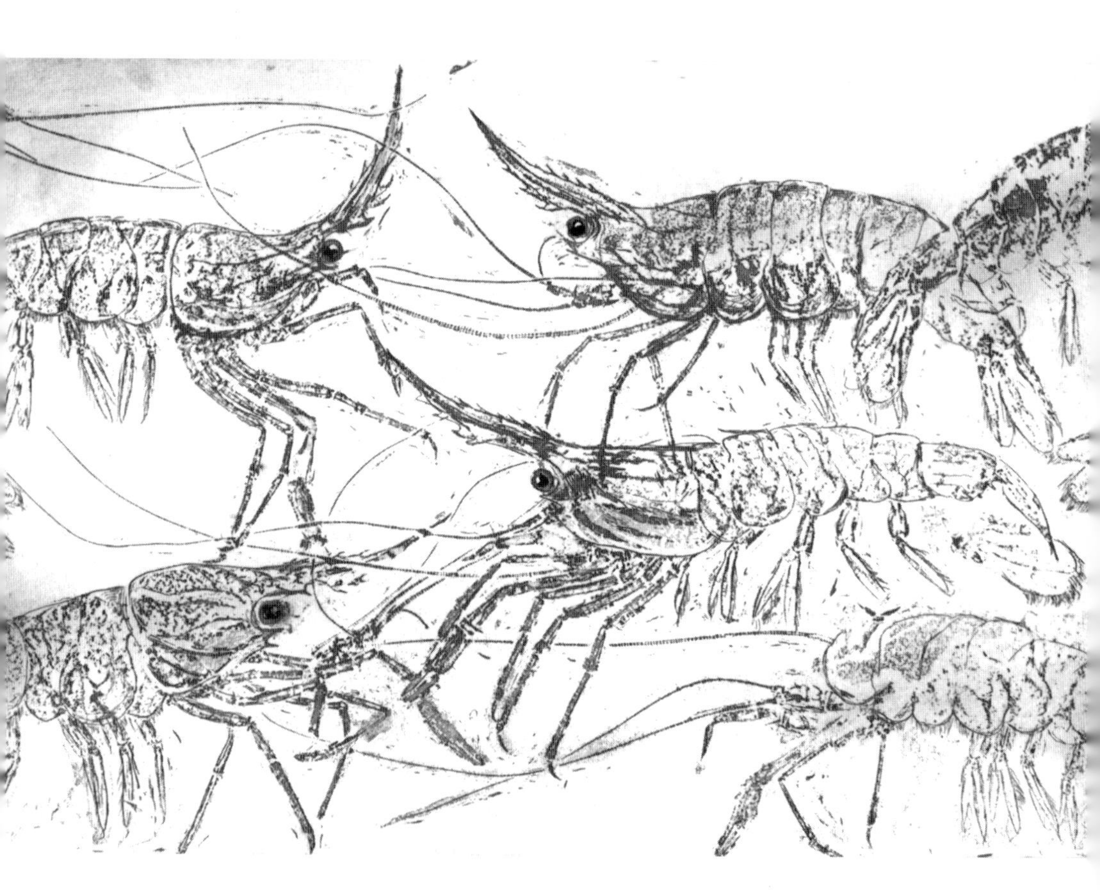

"Ribe ribe róibéis, tabhair dom greim ar bharr do shlata bige agus tabharfaidh mé duit arís amárach é." (Give me a grip of the top of your little rod, shrimp, and I'll give it back to you tomorrow).

SHORE CREATURES

An Smugairle Róin | The Jellyfish | Class: *Scyphozoa*

The sea is full of jellyfish in summer. They are in no way independent as they are at the mercy of the elements with the power of the ebbing and flowing tide. There are many sorts but they are nearly all the same shape, the shape of an umbrella, the convex side uppermost, some of them a foot wide and from that down to the size of a halfpenny. One day that we were looking for wrack near *Sceirde*, I remember seeing ones that were two feet across. It was a dark kind of day and you would swear that they were coming up from the deep competing with one another as they beat fast with the edges of their backs. Those ones rarely succeed in coming near land as they are pulled east and west with the tide. When there's a big wind and a swell in the sea in summer many of those near the coast get thrown ashore. They wither out of shape with wind and sun, as they are nearly all water. There's a small type the shade of water with a blue cross in the middle called *sceitheanna róin* (seal vomit).[10] They have exactly the same shape as the others. Some of them can sting a person who catches them gently. It's hard to get a proper grip of them, as they're soft lumps of jelly. They're only shadows. It entices the little fish with its many coloured hairs on top of its tentacles that sway to and fro. The little creatures think that what glistens and shines is something to eat until they are caught and in no time at all are in the belly of the tempter.

On moonless nights as we looked for seabream on the fishing grounds, the luminescence on the jellyfish would amaze us. There's no colour in the rainbow that wasn't mixed together in one beautiful light. Some of them would also get caught in the boat's anchor rope and when the swell caused the anchor rope to be hoisted out of the water, there would be iridescent lights in one straight line out from the bow, appearing and disappearing every now and then with the lowering and rising of the boat on the crest of the wave. Without a doubt it was a lovely sight in the quiet of night out on the boundless sea, but strange things and beautiful sights are in store for the seaman from time to time. The jellyfish aren't used for anything and you would think to look at them in the water that they are very nice things, but when they come ashore on the strand they don't have much of an appearance. When there are many of them rotten they have an awful smell and even the seagulls don't like them, and the crabs wouldn't look straight at them. There's no account of their whereabouts in winter, wherever those that don't get thrown ashore go.

An Bundún Leice [11] | The Sea Anemone | Order *Actinaria*

The anemone is very like a small keg, sitting on a rock, the top removed, and as it were a little tankard inside. The exposed rocks are full of them near the high tide mark and they

[10] *Aurelia aurita,* the common jellyfish

grow in deep places that never dried out. There are many types but they're all much the same in structure, even if their colours are different. Some are a couple of feet in height, and others not more than the size of a wren's egg, some with strong vigorous tentacles and others with only a weak plumage. There's a split across their top and as it were small narrow fingers rising out and sucking in from time to time. With these it kills the silly little things that don't keep away from it. In a way they can't help it as it entices them with a kind of beautiful radiance on top of its tentacles. When it works its little fingers it spouts out and sucks in water fast, and when it draws in it pulls its little mass of creatures that look and wonder at it, and those that it doesn't swallow at once get stuck in bright little drops of slime on its short hairy beard.

On clear sunny days when I would be on the fishing grounds, the sky without a cloud and the bottom clearly visible, I would spend my time looking down under the boat at the sea bottom thinking and studying the life of the fish. I would think the anemone was a right traitor when I'd see the little creatures shaking and turning themselves trying to get out of its bondage. Very few shore and strand creatures don't have some smart trick to confuse the others that are weak and foolish. They (anemones) are most plentiful in summer and autumn. It looks as if they make their way in from the west during the fine weather like the other shoals. The gulls are very keen on the small ones. They carry up skywards the one they remove from the rock and let it drop on the hard surface of a rock so as to break it and be able to eat it without bother. If the gull sees it won't make the rock, it's clever enough to catch it again before it falls into the sea and to make another journey upwards. There are many small chambers within the anemone and thin shelly walls dividing them; weak films of skin, the shells, gills and intestines and other parts all in their place.

But the gull prefers a soft yellow type of stuff. None of them are any good for fishing bait, nor for any human food; they are things without much good for anything. That doesn't mean they aren't as beautiful as any other thing on the shore in their many colours and brightness. There are little purple ones to be found in pools and on top of the shore that don't migrate or move about very much. Like the big ones on top of the shore, some of them are seen throughout the year. That's the life of the anemone on the shores of Connemara.

An Bláth Mara **The Daisy Anemone** *Cereus pedunculatus*

The daisy anemone is yellow and resembles in many ways the land daisy. Some of them can be seen on low spring tides in the pools on the lower shore. It's a strange creature as it can change colour when it so wishes. It's not used for anything. If you were hanging about the lower shore on the day of a big spring tide in summer you would encounter many the strange creature and plant. You would say that many wonderful things are covered by the sea at high tide, not to mention all that is out on the deep that is never uncovered.

When first I would go to the shore there were many things that I would notice. It was a long time before I noticed the daisy anemone. In the end I would look carefully between the stones and in the pools gradually identifying things. One needs to keep a sharp look out to notice the creatures and sea plants on the shore.

An Chíoch Charraige **The Sea Anemone** **Order *Actinaria***

The *cíoch carraige* is much like the shape of your finger, fat at the bottom and narrowing towards the top and if you didn't look carefully at it you would think it had no life or feeling in it. But alas, it is alive and sprightly. Look at it when it's covered at high tide and you will see it moving with agility and the little fins surrounding the mouth waving to and fro, darting out and sucking in fast trying to catch and swallow the tiny little fish. Small and all as it is, it often makes a big kill, and it's no wonder as it needs something to eat. It looks as if it has good hearing – if their tentacles are out and they hear the slightest noise, they can withdraw them very suddenly, I can tell you. They grow abundantly on exposed shores between half tide and low water. They are usually coloured red or yellowish-red. They are not used for anything. They are neither good for eating or for bait; they're useless things. The crabs don't even like them, and very little else can be said about them.

An Lugach **The Lugworm** ***Arenicola marina***

There's no beach on the islands that isn't full of lugworms. They are very like the earthworms found in the soil. No wrasse bait is as good as them and there is no better way to bait a flatfish long-line. They are found about a foot deep and they feed on the sand leaving a pile of it as a mark directly above them. They are strange worms, between six inches and a foot in length, and there are few places between half tide and low tide where they can't be found – some of them black, some red, some yellow and some purple. The red and yellow ones are best for fishing. The black one isn't much good as it's full of water. It lives near the low tide.

Often during the wrasse fishing season in autumn I would get up to collect a load of them, especially on a neap tide, as the neap tide is best for wrasse. Up to forty men would dig the strand at the end of the night, working away furiously under their soft coats of sweat. You may think, reader, that they wouldn't see them at that time of night, but what about their glow? [12]

We would have a good area of strand upturned by the time we had finished as we would go hard at it. It would take about one and a half hours to collect enough. Anyway, we would be ready to go to sea by sunrise. We would often collect enough bait on one day that would do for a week – because the lugworm would stay alive in dry turf dust for a fortnight if necessary. There aren't many of them to be found in winter – they bury themselves deep in the strand, but indeed, they're plentiful during the rest of the year.

[11] There are numerous species of sea anemone found on the shore and these include colour varieties and various forms. Although the name *bundún leice* is most commonly associated with *Actinia equina*, the beadlet anemone, the author's description is sufficiently broad to include other anemones. The anemone, however, has a simple structure and does not contain any "shelly walls", or "shells, gills and intestines" and would not reach a length of "a couple of feet in height". It is not clear what the author was referring to when describing the gull's habit of breaking them on the rocks; perhaps he was thinking of purple sea urchins.

[12] The author is referring to bioluminescence that is produced by microscopic organisms that are disturbed by the digging of the sand.

An Ruarámhach **The Rag Worm** *Nereis sp.*

The rag worm lives under stones low on the shore. It's red-coloured with a blue shine from the bristles that grow on it. It can swim very fast through the water by moving those bristles as it comes out from under the stones when the tide floods. I often upturned a stone that had one under it. It would bend and twist itself with agility, raising its head up now and then as if it were trying to stand up on its tail. Indeed, there are few worms on the shore as ugly as it, and it can twist itself into knots when it wishes. Some are about a foot long and like other classes of worms they beget young. I often noticed wrasse nosing around and trying to thrust their lips in under the stones to try and get at them. The fish and all can be seen on the sea bottom if the day is clear and sunny. Not many of the worms can be seen in winter. It looks as if they emigrate somewhere else. They're good bait for wrasse, that is to say those that aren't too big, but otherwise they're not used for much as they aren't widespread. The fishermen prefer to collect lugworms than waste their time with these; not only that but they dislike these ugly worms. It's no wonder that the poet himself thought of it when he was writing his song, comparing the rag worm to the untidy well-to-do woman. He spoke rudely and wickedly in any case, when he said:

'Twas easily told, Seán, that is was cupboard love
When you married the ragworm and left me to pine,
That you may sooner have your coffin than your shirt so fine,
After that won't the whole human race say what they will

Another poet, who was giving advice, said

If you marry the rag worm you'll regret it forever
Your brows will be cut and you'll be always in danger
You'll have no friend in the street who'll help you in a tight corner
Your heart will be broken whether you live longer or shorter

An Luch Mhara **The Sea Mouse** *Aphrodite aculeata*

At first glance the sea mouse is an ugly imperceptive creature to look at, as its beauty is not obvious, but if you get a clump of seaweed and rub it to remove the bits and pieces that are stuck to it, you will see a many-coloured radiance in the spines, which are growing from its skin, that change colour under the sunlight. One can notice small legs on its belly with which it attaches to seaweed or to anything else in the pools. The small mouth opens and closes every now and then. With what are like hairs around its mouth it gathers its food. It's about a few inches long. It's nearly as wide as it is long. It swims about on its belly in a slow lazy fashion. They are most common in summer and autumn. They head off to the deep in winter. They are no good to eat; they are a soft and slobby kind like the land snail. Nevertheless, they are used for bait in times of need. I remember well a day long ago when I didn't go to school. I headed off in the morning to *An Trá Rua* and from there I went picking blackberries and when I was tired of them I made a dash to the lower shore. I watched my reflection in a pool and you never saw such a smearing of blackberry juice. What did I see sidling about on the bottom but these two strange things.

A friend happened by with hand line and bait, on his way to fish at *Carraig Fhada*.
"Look" I said to him, "what are these things called?"
He took the pipe from his mouth and began smiling faintly.
"Don't let anyone see the state of your face, because you're beyond recognition. Go and throw a dash of water on yourself".
"My face is fine" said I, "but what are these?"
"Is it that you don't recognise them?" he said, pointing the shaft of his pipe towards one of them. "That's a sea mouse, a creature that's no good, but there was another type to be found around these parts a long time ago, the *cat mara*, but I've seen none since the year the paraffin came ashore. I'm sure it was the smell of the oil that drove them away, as the barrels would often be broken with the swell of the sea, and the oil would scatter all over the shore. Indeed, you could walk out on barrels from where you are to *Oileán Lachan* that year".
"I have no memory of that time" said I, "but what about the *cat mara*?"
"O, yes" said he, "indeed there was no other creature on the beach or the shore as mischievous and irritable as it. It could sting you like an ant. It was twice as big as that one and covered in spines like a hedgehog. On a dark night it was beautiful with its glistening colour due to luminescence. You often heard 'the *cat mara* has got hold of him' said to an accursed, irritable person."
"Well" said he, going off, "the tide won't wait for me. I must earn the price of the tobacco. Good day to you".
"And to you" said I.
I pondered awhile and the *cat mara* reminded me to take home the mouse and I'd have a bit of fun with it and the cat. I brought it and put it in front of him. He pointed his ears, smelt it, walked around it, put its paw under it and turned it around. It didn't like it but before long the dog came around and took it away where it butted it about in seclusion.

An Bairneach — The Limpet — *Patella* sp.

No shellfish is as widespread as the limpet. The rocks of the shore are covered with them, from high tide to low tide and it's they who have a firm grip on the stones; it often prefers to let the shell be broken on top of it rather than lose its position. During fine soft weather it rises up on its flank so as to look around. One must come upon it without being noticed to remove it, because, if it hears any noise it fastens its grip. It is removed with the tip of a knife or any iron object with a sharp point. It is said that the limpet with the most rings in its shell is the best to eat. Fishermen make great use of them as wrasse and seabream bait. No fish in the sea is as dangerous for the sailor. It lives always on the rocks of the shore, a dangerous place for ship and boat. Therefore, it is necessary to avoid the limpet.

An Bairneach Iascáin — The Common Limpet — *Patella vulgata*

These live on rough exposed shores beside low tide. They are the biggest of the limpets. They don't mind being always beside the water, as the pools of the lower shore are full of them – smooth shells with the same colour as the place they frequent. Often, as the day brightens, it rises up on its flanks and stretches out its horns from the edge of the shell. When the tide covers the stones they wander about collecting food for themselves.

The tough yellow flesh attaches to the rock, and the part near the back of the shell is softer and blacker. It is a nice mild fish to eat and the juice is healthy. Winkle and limpet soup is recommended for those suffering a cold. Many limpets are picked in spring in *Maínis.*[13] The limpet has good hearing, because if you make any noise, no matter how slight, it will clamp onto the rock.
There must have been people in the old days for whom the limpet had little appeal, as some woman poet said;

It's not on limpets and winkles my child was reared
It's with cup and saucer my child was reared.

And another, giving sound advice to the drunkard, said;

Avoid the drinking house or the limpet will be your food.

But don't mind them, a batch of limpets is a sweet healthy food beside the hearth on a cold spring afternoon when one is hungry. They are good wrasse and bream bait as well if one ties a piece of crab with it and attaches it to the mouth of the hook. They often grow on the backs of crabs and lobsters. I suppose they like being taken for a ride from place to place.

An Bairneach Mín — The Blue-Rayed Limpet — *Patina pellucida*

This type grows abundantly on the stalks of oarweed and sea rods on the deep in such a way that they are exposed at low spring tides only. They are the smallest of their type. They're no good for eating or for fishing. The shells are smooth and slippery and there's no colour in the rainbow that isn't in them. They eat a small hole into the rod, or the stalk, of the oarweed where they attach.[14] They move around from place to place gathering food. Wrasse love them and therefore play havoc with this mild fish from time to time. They aren't as big as a shirt button. You would often find them in the stomach of a wrasse without even being chewed. They grow also on crabs and on other shells on the seaweed-covered bottom. I suppose they like being carried from place to place on the sea floor. There are lots of shellfish that have that habit. Who would blame them? As they say *"Is fearr marcaíocht ar ghabhar na coisíocht dhá fheabhas"* (A ride on a goat is preferable to walking at its best).

An Fhaocha Bhiorach — The Tower Shell — *Turritella communis*

These are commonest in the deep, especially on a red sandy bottom. They are between one and two inches in length, with a sharp whorled tip, like the top of a gimlet. Few winkles are as beautifully coloured as these. Nevertheless, they are no good for eating and fishermen have no use for them as bait or anything. When the weather is very rough in winter, an enormous number of them get thrown up on the high tide mark. During the ebb tide a flock of seabirds gathers to feed on them. That's where there's an awful commotion and noise, each one looking for the fattest, clearing them away with their feet and trying to remove the food from the shells, not such an easy task. They break those with a good strong tap against the stones to get at the food. Hunger and necessity are a good source of inspiration. The winkles and other shells are a lovely sight on top of the shore with the sun shining on them at the beginning of the day, every sort of radiant colour strewn here and there. Schoolchildren often gather and keep them, especially those rare glistening ones. They swap them for such useful objects as balls, little knives, buttons and the like. In any case, as everyone is satisfied, what harm is it; isn't it as lawful as anything else?

An Finicín The Cowrie *Trivia monacha*

No matter how low the tide, it's not easy to see the cowrie on the shore. It seems as if they live out in the deep. But one can get some of the empty shells on top of the high tide line, as the swell of the sea throws them ashore when the weather is rough in winter. They are very nice shells. They are not very big but they have a strange shape where the mouth is, the two shells are curled in and as it were overlapping but there's a narrow slit in a kind of a way in between them.[15] They're about as big as a wren's egg, or even bigger. But it's their nice shape and lovely colour that entices the eye. You would swear they are made from ivory. Children love to look for them and they are a rare item. Not many are found on the beaches of Connemara.

An Feannadóir The Sting Winkle *Ocenebra erinacea*

This is a cursed winkle because it destroys many shellfish whenever possible as it drills them with its sharp poisonous mouth and it sucks the food out instantly. It's about one-and-a-half inches long and of a round shape, with a sharp whorled tip at one end; it's coloured mainly white or yellowish white or sandy coloured. I would see them mainly amongst the eel grass. I remember one occasion when we were lobster fishing, a bad night with a south-easterly wind came and the storage pot that was anchored amongst the eel grass came ashore on the beach. There were up to six-dozen banded lobsters in it. But to make a long story short, when we reached it there was nothing there but the shells, the fish was eaten or sucked out. Thousands of them had entered between the battens and they cut the twines of the trapdoor to make even more mischief. There's no doubt but that the prisoners (even though banded) escaped when they saw the door open, but the sting winkles had done a lot of damage by then – there's no doubt but they had a feast that night. They spawn in spring and they attach the eggs to seaweed close to the rock. They're no good for eating, but they're occasionally used as reserve bait for wrasse.

[13] It was customary to pick them after the first rain showers in April as they were deemed to be at their best then.

[14] They are also commonly found on the fronds of the oarweed.

[15] These molluscs have only a single shell and the author has possibly interpreted their distinctive shell as a fusion of two shells.

An Seilmide Cladaigh [16] — The Periwinkle — *Littorina sp.*

During the summer and autumn the stones on the top of the shore are covered with periwinkles. There's no colour in the rainbow that isn't in their shells. They feed themselves on the fronds of seaweeds and any rotten rubbish they chance upon. When the day is mild and pleasant they wander about. The yellow ones are the most widespread although they're found with all colours. They are no good to eat, as they don't grow as big as other types. During an ebb tide one can hear a musical murmuring from them. Few shellfish are found higher than them. Birds play havoc with them in the autumn. It's very easy to break them on the stones and fill one's belly. Birds often fly with them in their beaks and drop them on the stones to break. They are very clever in the way they can extract the fish from the shell without much bother or hardship

An Fhaocha Faoileáin — The Topshell — *Monodonta sp.*

This is one of the tribe that lives on top of a sheltered shore. They are very like the *faocha con* in shape and size except for their silvery shine with narrow golden stripes mixed with brown surrounding it. The food they contain is no good except for the birds of the bay. Now and then fishermen pick them for wrasse. When the tide covers the shore they sidle about looking for a bit to eat. In winter few of them are seen alive but there are many empty shells on top of the beaches, and when they're tossed about by the surf they make a kind of music; there are, however, many other types of shells in their company. They come in contact with the pebbles and the rough sand in a strange sort of way and with the agitation one hears a fine musical note.

An Miongán — Class *Gastropoda*

When the starlings arrive on the coast late in the autumn they play havoc with this one. You would hear the cry of the birds from afar and they beating the shells against the stones looking for the food. Apart from that, they're no good for eating; they're not very big and there's no colour under the sun that's not in their shells. They're most common in spring and summer. If you were wandering about on the top of the shore on a fine soft day, you would hear their murmuring if you kept an attentive ear open. When the bad weather comes many of them are washed ashore, and get mixed up with the other types, and that's the new crop for oystercatchers and gulls. Often two of them start fighting over the food, and another starts, followed by another, until the whole flock is at each other, and a cloud of sand and feathers rising above them from the encounter. The fight peters out eventually, as is normal, and there is peace among the birds until another time, but often it's a small thing that causes a lot of trouble between people as well as between birds.

An Fhaocha — The Edible Winkle — *Littorina littorea*

Indeed, there are many kinds of winkle on the shores of Connemara. These black ones are the best to eat. They normally live between half tide and low tide. They feed on seaweed and any other rubbish – like rotten fish, or fresh fish – but they prefer rotten bits and pieces. In spring and early summer, the stones and pools among the weeds are full of

them. They are a sweet healthy food when in the proper condition. Many are sent off to market. The pickers get a good price for them in winter and spring and it's a great help to these poor people to have this work at their doorstep. They're very plentiful at the end of spring when the seaweed comes ashore. They feed on it most of the time. They're mainly black and grey in colour. There's a small hard scale on the soft part as a lid on the mouth of the winkle. It attaches itself with that to seaweed and other things.[17]
Many of them live beneath stones and in shallow pools, especially where there are seaweed fragments. They can live for a long time out of water; you would often see bags of them on a pier for a couple of weeks belonging to winkle buyers. They throw some salt water on them now and then to keep them alive. I wonder how they manage to live without anything to eat; I suppose they get nourishment from the brine and dirt around them. Here's a song I often heard from the old people:

'Tis a shell I am that sleeps under the sea
Forever sportive without worry nor care
Among my friends I do always be
Or playing with my brothers beneath the waves

I'm always dawdling back and forth
Along with the crabs 'neath the wave crest
I've no enemy and no one I'd best
But I'm always welcome on mountain or shore

And those that aren't happy let them come with me
And they'll never be sorry beneath the sea
Goodbye my dear folks that's the end of my tale
That your life's not a joy let you never say

An Fhaocha Chapaill **The Dogwhelk** ***Nucella lapillus***

This one resembles the *miongán*. They are exposed at about half tide. They're not much good for eating; they normally grow on stones in pools and when the tide floods they move about looking for something to eat. They are not too abundant on exposed shores. They like shelter. Not many are seen in winter as they emigrate elsewhere. That's the way of many types on the seashore.

[16] There are several species of periwinkle commonly found on the shore. The small periwinkle (*Littorina neritoides*) is found highest on the shore and is coloured blue-black. The rough periwinkle (*Littorina saxatilis*) is variable in colour but often a red-black and is found on the upper shore and the upper part of the middle shore. The flat periwinkle (*Littorina littoralis*) is found on the lower middle and upper part of the lower shore and it varies in colour from brown to red to green to orange and yellow.

[17] The horny lid or *operculum,* which fits tightly in the mouth of the shell when the animal withdraws into it, is not used to attach to rocks but is used to keep the animal from drying out.

An Chuachma — The Buckie or Common Whelk — *Buccinum undatum*

This type is not abundant but nonetheless there are some of them amongst the other winkles. They're bigger than the black winkles, usually coloured grey or whitish-grey. The female has a lot of spawn and it has a greater volume than the whelk itself. It attaches to seaweed with a kind of slime. It is often thrown up on the high water mark in bad weather in batches that look like wax around honey in a beehive. The food is picked out of a whelk with a needle; it's a sweet healthy food when garnished and mixed with other dainties.

An Cluaisín [18] — The Variegated Scallop / The Queen Scallop — *Chlamys varia* / *Chlamys opercularis*

They're shaped like an ear. They're not as big as a cockle, even though some are big enough, but usually they're about three inches across from hinge to mouth. They live about a few inches below the surface of the sand and when the day is soft and fine they jump out onto the surface. The valves are half-open when it appears in the light of day. It takes another few leaps and then closes for a while. Indeed, it doesn't get left long as men, women and children search for it, especially in spring, and it also has many enemies – gulls and terns. They fly continuously to and fro above the strand looking carefully for their chance to devour a piece and since they have sharp eyesight they can see them while flying high in the sky and come down swiftly and grab them. The crabs hide beneath the sand with nothing visible but the stalks of their eyes, so as they can see for a distance in any direction. If they see a scallop open, it doesn't take them long to shake themselves out of the sand and catch their piece if they can.

The scallop, like all other shellfish, is usually boiled, or, as they say parboiled for the purpose of shelling. The hot water causes the flesh to come out of the shell. The shell can then be discarded and the fish boiled and garnished in such a way that it will be a sweet and tasty meal for the company. It seeds profusely. The eggs are often attached to the eel grass and the seaweed with a kind of jelly, but when it grows to the stage when the shell can be seen they fall on the sand and stay there. Often, during days of low spring tides at the end of spring, the eel grass is surrounded with lots of them. But like all other shellfish, they like the incubating heat of the sun and the softness of the wind. During cold unnatural weather it's hard to see one. They stay under the sand until the day is suitable for them. Then, boy, you can see them jumping all over the place.

An Ruacan — The Cockle — *Cerastoderma edule*

The cockle resembles two saucers with their mouths together. It has a flexible muscular hinge at the back so that it can open the two valves when necessary, and another strong muscle inside to close and lock them if it hears an enemy approaching. Don't think that it's not sought after. Its keen sense of hearing is an advantage, as it can hear the slightest noise.

[18] The name *cluaisín* refers to the prominent anterior "ear" of the shell, which is much bigger than the corresponding posterior "ear". The "ear" is more pronounced in the variegated scallop than in the queen scallop. The active swimming behaviour described by the author is a characteristic of the queen scallop.

They live on sandy beaches near low spring tide, in the same vicinity as razor shells, queen scallops, sand gapers and other shellfish. They like soft fine natural weather with westerly or south-westerly winds. They are found in plenty during that kind of weather. They rise out of the sand with the heat of the sun and the beauty of the day. But, on the other hand, if there's cold unnatural weather, even in spring itself when they're in season, few are taken as they stay at home under the sand.

Everything looks for its own share, so it is with these. Many are picked in spring and at the beginning of summer. Even so, they are a sweet and tasty fish when boiled and garnished properly. They are big and small, but when mature, they're about four inches wide from back hinge to mouth.[19] When the rims of the two arched valves open away from each other it thrusts out the muscle that's as fat as your finger. That's the best part to eat, and with this it bores into the sand and uses it as a support as well to make a jump when it feels like it. It seems as if the poet himself had a good regard for them when he said

King's food a cockle,
Peasant's food a limpet,
Hag's food a winkle
And she picking it with a needle.

They're usually yellow, pale, or dark, or rust coloured, but change their colour if they go somewhere else that's coloured differently, and the same applies to nearly all fish and shellfish.

There are a couple of types to be found on the beaches of Connemara, the smooth kind and the rough kind.[20] I often saw a young crab that formed inside two shells of a rough cockle. It feeds on the flesh of the cockle until able to fend for itself. Isn't God's work wonderful? Often when a cockle shell is open, a crab can be seen throwing a small stone between the two shells so as it can have a meal for itself, as the cockle can't close when the fingerstone obstructs its closing mechanism.[21]

One day I saw a gull with a cockle in its beak. It flew up in the air, released the cockle, caught it again before it fell, flew up again and went further upwind this time. It released it, it fell on top of a bare rock, the shell broke in such a way that it was easy to bolt and swallow the food. That's a clever little trick of the gulls.

An Muirín — The Great Scallop — *Pecten maximus*

In deep pleasant bays, where there's rough sand at the bottom, the scallops are most plentiful, but it's a great wanderer and it's no sooner in one place than in another. By opening and closing its shells it can travel far by hopping. When food is scarce where it is, it can go elsewhere. It likes the shelter of the land and it's often found near rocks.

[19] The size is exaggerated – a good-sized cockle would be up to 2 inches in length.

[20] The author refers to two types, one smooth and the other rough. The rough one is probably *Acanthocardia*, the spiny or red nose or prickly cockle. The word *ruacan* is nowadays commonly ascribed to any one of a variety of bivalves of commercial value such as venus shells and carpet shells.

[21] The crab referred to is the pea crab *Pinnotheres pisum* that lives inside the shells of bivalves and feeds partly by intercepting food drawn in by the bivalve and partly on the soft tissues of the gills.

Great Scallop, 5 – 8 cm

When I was dredging a long time ago, they were plentiful in a certain place in the morning, and the afternoon of the following day there might be none there. They love rust-coloured sand, and if there's a layer of small stones mixed in with larger stones, they crown it all, and although the dredge often gets stuck in the rocks, the scallop fisherman nevertheless catches a worthwhile harvest. Indeed searching and nosing about the rocks pays off. He has landmarks for the area in which he gets the best catch. Even though fast moving, they (scallops) take up residence in certain places on the bottom. The weather has a lot to do with their travels and that doesn't go unnoticed by those who fish scallops.

They're usually coloured yellow, dark yellow and white, but like all shellfish they take the colour of the sea bottom on which they live. One of the shells is flat and the other is arched and ridged – about twenty ridges and the same number of furrows. They're nearly like a saucer, some of them about five inches across. They're small or big according to their age. It's said that over five years is an old age for them. It seems that they keep close to shore when they feel themselves getting weak, as one can see many empty shells between the stones on rocky shores. Maybe they are some sort of graveyard. Sting winkles make the most of them. They drill into them and use them as breeding places when the time comes. Many things also grow on the empty shells. There's a thin sinewy hinge joining the two shells together at the back. It can open and close them with a strong internal muscle that expands and contracts as needed. This muscle is the sweetest part of the scallop. Many of them are caught in winter and in spring and they fetch a good price. It's a great help to the poor people to have this work. When I was at it before the Great War, they would fetch a shilling a dozen, and if there was a promise of a good fine day for us, we would take in about forty dozen. Lots of other things would be taken with them in the bag of the dredge, strange sorts of fish and shellfish, encrusting seaweeds and other things.

An tOisre — The Oyster — *Ostrea edulis*

The oyster lives in quiet bays, especially near the mouths of rivers. It seems as if it likes brackish water. It has the shape of a saucer, about four or five inches across, one of the shells arched and the other flat. The arched side is usually underneath and attached to something in the grey mud with a kind of lime. There's a sinewy hinge connecting the two shells together at the back so that it can open and close as it wishes. There's another strong muscle inside which contracts and expands to close and open the shell.
At ease in its bed, its mouth is open most of the time, as it needs to provide its own food. There are little hairs on the gill that attract the food. It has a gill and intestine like any other shellfish. The female has a lot of roe and spawns in summer. The seed is often attached to seaweed until the shell is heavy enough to fall to the sea floor where it remains from then onwards. Indeed, little of the spawn survives as it has many enemies. If they all matured the sea floor would be covered with oysters.
They're taken with dredges on the beds. Few fish are as valuable and there's a great demand for them on the markets. They're sweet and smooth to eat and very healthy altogether. Pearls are found in some. They're very valuable but are said to be very scarce, maybe one in a million. It's said also that the precious jewel is formed from a grain of sand. Many is the person who made his fortune by finding one by some fluke. Maybe while preparing his tasty meal of oysters, and while removing the fish from the shell, he would find the pearl within, even though they're mostly found in empty shells. It seems as if many were fished in the old days, and the people were nourished on them. One can often see many of the empty shells in the soil when people are sowing and digging potatoes, especially near old houses that were occupied during the time of the Famine. I suppose the oyster did its own share, as much as any other shellfish, to keep the people from death's door, on the shores of Connemara.

An Sligín Slamach — The Saddle Oyster — *Anomia ephippium*

The saddle oyster is attached to stones on the bottom at very low tide. Some are found exposed. They're not unlike an oyster, but not as big nor as tasty to eat. It's neither as valuable or as much in demand on the fish market. People living near the shore pick them during big tides in spring. Many are found around stones on which oarweed grows, especially where there is red sand and some current. The fish is between two arched shells with a sinewy hinge so it can open and close at will. In the shell which attaches to the stone or whatever it grows on there's a small hole with a muscle out through it; with this it attaches itself. It has a strong grip indeed. They spawn in spring near the shore. They are of a type that does not wander much. They don't wander as much as many other shellfish, and maybe they're better off as well.

An Breallach — The Sand Gaper — *Mya arenaria*

I often picked a bucket of gapers with a small loy on the gently sloping beach on the east side of *Maínis*, and if they're not abundant there in spring and summer, then I tell a lie.

On a big low tide the place is full of men, women and children picking razor shells, gapers, cockles and scallops. The gaper is usually found about a foot deep in the sand, but with the brightening of the day and the heat of the sun, it rises up higher than that. But if the day turns cold again it lets itself down the hole again as it always has a smooth path before it – the windy day is not the day for the scollops.
If it hears the slightest noise nearby, it releases a stream of water from the top of the hole and runs down as fast as possible. You need to be quick to take it with a loy. Often, after removing a spadeful of sand, you would have to put your arm down to your elbow and let a whistle in order to catch it. When it hears the musical sound it stops suddenly, maybe with wonder, but no matter. The fish is in between two arched shells. It can open and close them gently with a sinewy hinge at the back. There's another muscle that contracts to close them and expands to open the shells. There's a delicate slimy filmy mantle around the two shells and it overlaps where the edges meet at the seams. They are a fine tasty fish when boiled and prepared properly. Many are eaten in the west of Ireland when in season. The big fish muscle, which is normally visible sticking out between the shells, is the sweetest part to eat. With that it also bores into the sand. It's six or seven inches long, much longer than the shells, some even a foot long. Few are found in winter. They go deep into the sand. The cold does not agree with them at all. Such is the case with most shellfish.

An Scian Mhara — The Razor Shell — *Ensis sp.*

I suppose the reason it was called the razor shell was that it resembled the handle of a knife or razor. Some are about a foot long but they're mostly less than eight inches long and one and a half inches wide. They're generally various shades of yellow or the same colour as their surroundings. A thin filmy mantle covers the shell outside, overlapping at the seams so that no sand or other material can enter and there are other films inside between the fish and the two shells, with the shells either side and the fish in between. They can open when necessary. I may as well tell you that one needs to be accustomed to pick them; often if you don't succeed in taking them on your first effort your work is in vain as it goes down on its flanks in a flash. One needs to whistle musically to catch it and to sink your arms to the elbow in the hole you cleared. It also often leaves its large muscle in the hole and leaves you with only the shell and the guts; unless you are gentle and careful when pulling that will be the case.
Many of them are found together where it lives, usually near eel grass, and like the gaper they squirt up water and run down the hole if they hear any noise about. When the day is fine and with heat from the sun, part of them is often seen protruding up through the sand. You would see terns and gulls trying to approach them unawares. Sometimes they would succeed in getting a bite. The razor shell itself becomes clever as it heads for home when it sees the slightest shade on the strand.
The razor shell finds it hard to escape during the big tides of spring because people of all ages, men and women, search for them armed with loys and forks and creels and buckets to carry them home when the tide has turned. The mark above them resembles a keyhole in the strand and those people with the knack and experience can recognise which side they are facing. Therefore, they place the loy quickly in front of it and bring

it up first time. They're a smooth tasty fish when properly boiled. They must be shelled first, that is put in boiling water until the fish leaves the shell, the guts then removed, the fish cut into small pieces, onions and other things added and boiled and it's a fine meal for the household.
The female spawns in summer beside the eel grass so as the young fish can hide there from their enemies. Not many are found in winter as they go deep in the sand away from the cold and the frost until the spring returns, when the sun rises in the sky and the day becomes milder, finer and longer. They winter in their own dark kingdom under the sand and water.

An Diúilicín — The Mussel — *Mytilus edulis*

The mussels are found abundantly near the mouth of a river. It seems as if they like brackish water. Such places are full of them, back to back and on top of one another all over the place. They are bigger than those growing on rough exposed shores. They're nearly egg-shaped, some as small as a wren's egg and from that up to a goose's egg. The part attached to the rock is narrower than the point of the egg and the top end likewise. There's a smooth tasty fish between the shells. When it's properly prepared it's a smooth tasty dish for anyone. The wrasse have a great liking for them; during a flood tide they leave the seaweed bottom and go in amongst the rocks eating mussels. I often caught wrasse on the bare rocks and their bellies full of them. Without a doubt they're good bait and therefore the fishermen pick lots of them from time to time. They are very plentiful in spring and summer and are abundant from half tide to low tide. Dulse grows on some of them; that's why it's called mussel dulse. When they're covered by the high tide they release the threads that attach them to the rock and they loiter about finding their food with their valves half open. They (the valves) are attached to each other with a flexible sinewy hinge, but if it hears a noise it can close them suddenly with a muscle which contracts inside. Few shellfish are unable to do this. A filmy mantle covers the shells and when it closes them the edges of the mantles overlap slightly at the joints. There's a piece missing in the mantle as if it were torn at the overlap by something trying to thrust in between the valves. But that's the place where it naturally receives food or inhales or expels water when the valves are locked. It spawns on the rocks and many of the young ones, which are as small as a pinhead, are to be seen at the beginning of summer densely packed in the same places where the big ones were the previous year. They go somewhere else and hand over possession to the young ones. They are quick to release the threads, go away and cast anchor somewhere else. I will leave them like that for now and close this small chapter on the dark blue mussel.

An Cudal — The Common Cuttlefish — *Sepia officinalis*

People often argue about the cuttlefish, some saying they're young squid and more saying they're not, that they're a class unto themselves, that they are not bound to the squid or *láir bhán* by ties of kinship or affection. Many of them are found swimming near eel grass especially in autumn and the *cudal méarach* ('digitate' cuttlefish) is very similar to the squid as regards structure except that it's only about two inches long. The *cudal sceitheach* ('spewing' cuttlefish) is smaller than that and it lets off its ink every now and then. [22] Therefore it's hard to make out exactly what it looks like. When the weather is about to break is the most common time to see it. It's a good sign of rain. There's no doubt but it encourages kelp makers to make stacks of their seaweed in time before the rain. You can't say they aren't clever little fish with the way they have of defending themselves when an enemy is after them.

An Láir Bhán — The Cuttlefish — Order *Decapoda*

This fish is abundant on the coasts of Connemara. They can be seen on low spring tides among the eel grass. [23]

An Láimhíneach [24] — The Squid — *Loligo sp.*

There are a few of these types to be found around *Maínis*. Although the squid is the most common, the type called the *láir bhán* is plentiful some years. It's a strange thing to say, they often disappear for two to three years from the coast without trace, and the old people say that they remember them disappearing and that they heard the same story from their ancestors. This emigration, therefore, has been going on for a long time. Indeed, they are strange creatures – between one and two feet long. The squid would remind you of a cat in a small bag with its head visible at the mouth of the bag. There are nine or ten limbs, erect as rods on top of its head and circling its mouth, which resembles a bird's beak. The legs are three-cornered and some are longer than others, and when in danger it doesn't stop shuffling, thrusting and looping them about.

This bag that surrounds it is not fastened to its body; you would think it doesn't suit it at all and that it would slip off when it swims, but it normally swims backwards through the water like a lobster. It goes very fast in small spurts. It is made for speed, the end which cuts through the water being shaped like the tip of a spear and at the other end are the mouth and the big eyes and the long fingers. The legs are folded into each other when it ploughs the seas; a stiff slippy skin and there's no colour of the rainbow which it hasn't got, and it can change them at will and can also mix them cleverly.

[22] The *cudal méarach* and *cudal sceitheach* may refer to the other common species of cuttlefish such as *Sepia elegans* (up to 12 cm in length) and *Sepiola atlantica* (up to 5 cm in length).

[23] The cuttlefish are the most common of the cephalopods found among eel grass.

[24] It is quite obvious from the description above that the author is talking about a cephalopod mollusc and most likely a squid. The word *láimhíneach*, however, has been used widely in Galway and Mayo as the name for the angler fish *Lophius piscatorius*. In the latter use, the name seems to have originated from the shape of the hand-like pectoral fin. It is curious that, in an article published by Mac an Iomaire prior to the publication of *Cladaí Chonamara* he states the following "*Monk-fish* nó *Angler*. *Lophius piscatorius*. Láir Bhán (nó Láimhíneach), Láireachaí Bána. Bíonn said fairsing ins an áit seo. Ar thráigheanna móra is féidir iad a fheiceáil i n-aice leis an meallsgeanach" (....... They are common here. On exposed strands they can be seen near the eel grass). Although the title of this short note is "Monk-fish or Angler" the habitat described is not that of the monkfish, which is found mostly at depths below 20 m partly buried in sand or mud, but more likely to be that of the squid.

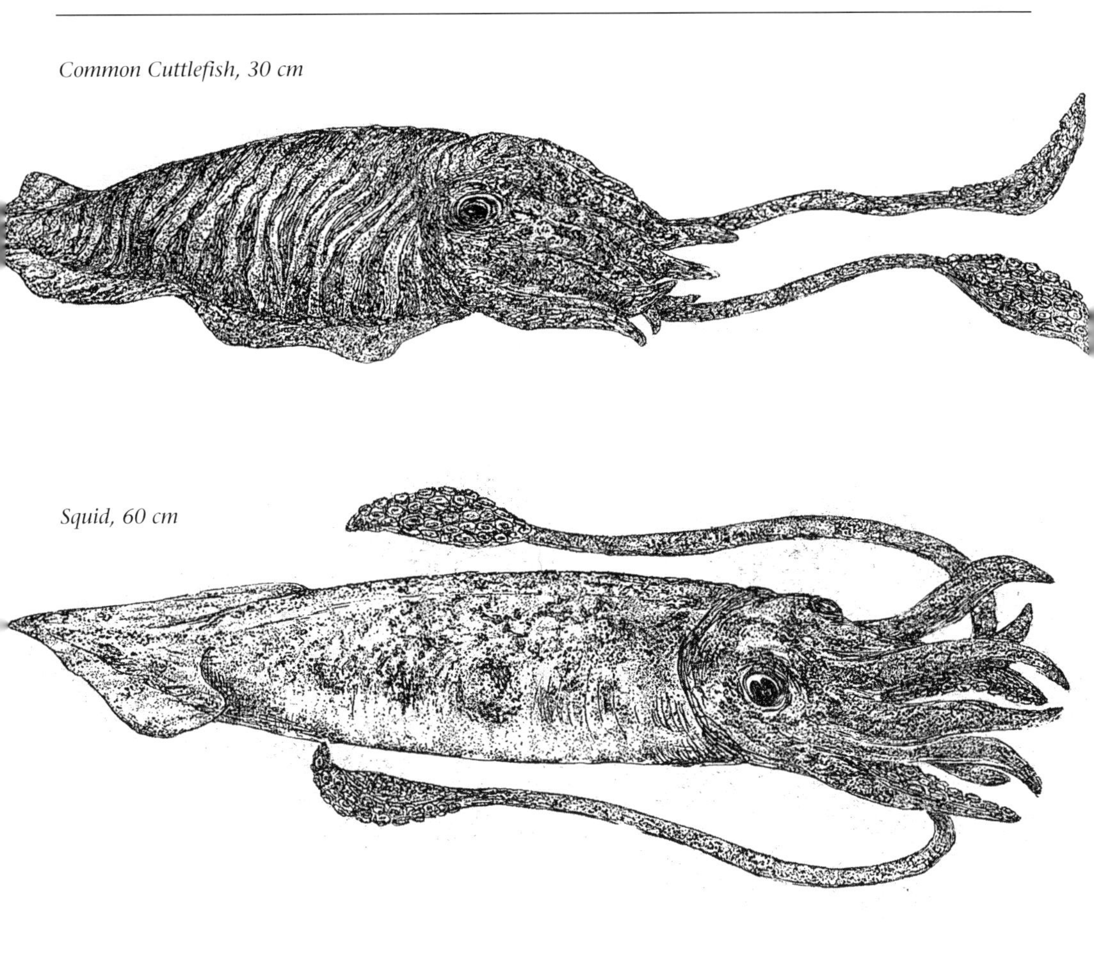
Common Cuttlefish, 30 cm

Squid, 60 cm

One day when I was alone in the *currach* lifting the trammel net, what should I find but one of them, but when I was taking it out of the net – its legs were tangled in the mesh and stuck also with a kind of slime and some of the threads in its mouth and the mesh cut by its sharp teeth – it let a kind of sigh and in a flash let out a dart of ink into my face. That was my reward for releasing it from captivity. I had to laugh at the look of me when I saw my reflection in the water in the bilges. Around my mouth was spotted and one half of my face almost completely black. I can tell you it was no easy job to clean off either. When I came ashore I took the squid and threw it in a saltwater pool so as I could see what it would do. It thought for a while; the small fish that were swimming about darted suddenly into the clefts. I suppose they never saw the likes before. It started to fold in its legs and soon changed the colour of its jacket to the colour of its new surroundings. It now had its head down and was thinking of its strange new life. The small fish that had hidden in the cracks plucked up some courage and started to come out. A blenny came across from the other side and started to examine the stranger closely. It approached gradually. It came within six inches of it. The squid closed one eye cleverly. During this time the stranger played dumb. The blenny came closer and started sniffing its rear end;

a crowd of its own tribe in a row behind him, as if waiting for something to happen. Their expectation was rewarded, as in the blink of an eye the show-off was caught by the nape of the neck by the giant who came upon them. But they didn't see him close his eyes as he swallowed the fish, as they were in such a hurry to go and hide in the clefts of the rocks. The rogues! When I tried to catch it again it blackened the water with another squirt. That's its trick to hide from its enemies. But it didn't succeed this time as I got the boat hook from the *currach* and when I lifted it from the water it was thrashing about in a fit of anger.

I often saw some of them come ashore during a full moon and a full spring tide. It's said that they're under some strange spell during the full moon and they're so playful and excited that they prance about backwards until they land on the shore unknown to themselves. Isn't it a strange way they let themselves die, but perhaps they're aware of it.

An Garbhán Carraige — The Acorn Barnacle — *Balanus sp.* *Chthamalus sp.*

The acorn barnacles are very like small limpets except for the small holes on the top of their shells.[25] To notice the hole you can see what looks like a small feather rising out and being sucked back into it again and little hairs around the edge of the hole continuously vibrating; with these it catches its food. Indeed, it needs little, but, however little, it must catch it just as the whale must do.

They are so densely distributed that you would think they are part of the rock and there's nowhere from low tide to the top of the high neap tide that isn't covered with them. They grow on top of one another from year to year and often when there's a thick covering of them on the shore, the swell removes them.[26] They're not used as they're no good for fishing or anything else.

An Giúirlinn — The Goose Barnacle [27] The Shipworm [28] — *Lepas sp.* *Teredo navalis*

This worm does a lot of damage to wood. I often saw beams, spars, planks, boxes, barrels and other such things that would be a long time in the sea completely full of their holes.

[25] The barnacle is a crustacean and has many separate plates in its shell unlike the limpet, a mollusc, which has a single shell.

[26] They are also likely to be removed by the dogwhelk that feeds on them.

[27, 28] The author is describing two distinct types of invertebrate here as one animal. One of these is the shipworm *Teredo navalis*, a bivalve mollusc that bores submerged wooden structures such as boat hulls. It has an anterior shell, each valve of which functions as a drill and encloses only a part of the wormlike animal. The other is a crustacean, the goose barnacle *Lepas*, which normally attaches to boats and driftwood and is not a boring animal. Legend has it in European maritime countries that the goose barnacle hatches into the barnacle goose. This is reflected in the species name *anatifera*, meaning goose bearing. The first written record of this myth is in *Topographiae Hiberniae* written by the Welsh monk Giraldus Cambrensis who visited Ireland in the 12th century. He stated that the barnacle goose began life as an excrescence (later identified as the goose barnacle) on floating logs. For Giraldus the barnacle goose was both fish and fowl and therefore could be eaten by Christians on fast days.

In my youth much salvage would come ashore in *Maínis* from time to time; when vessels would be sunk way back in the wild sea, anything which floated would escape when the storm and swell shattered the hull of the ship, and if that flotsam came ashore safe, it was worth a lot to the coastal people. But often it wouldn't be, as it isn't long being tossed about with the unfavourable winds and tides when small scales begin to grow on it. They grow and strengthen gradually until they're mature and during that time they bore and sharpen planks and the holes increase as they grow in size. In about four or five months they have done a lot of damage. You would scarcely recognise the mouth of the hole, it is so narrow, but it is so wide inside in the wood that you would put your finger in it; part of the worm is inside and part outside, and the two parts joined together at the mouth of the hole with a foot which is as slender as a hair. You would think they are two, but they're not; it's the one in the wood that does the boring, but the other one probably helps and gets some of the food as well. They make crooked tunnels which are as near to each other as possible, as smooth as glass inside and lined with a thin coat of lime from the work of the barnacles on the long journey on the high crest of the waves. Though strange to relate, those crooked little burrows are clear of one another; this means that these aren't an unintelligent lot, the way they can do their boring without crossing each other, as clever as any sinner. Normally, when they go in a small bit they turn, and go along the length of the wood with the grain, and quite carefully also to avoid the knots, so that those same paths aren't straight. They give themselves a good turn to avoid any knots in the way. They would remind you of a road gang who would meet a great big cliff of granite and who would prefer to turn about rather than attack it.

They grow a few feet in length in time; in seven to eight months they're four or five feet in length, that is away out to sea. They have two big shells made from small slates, like a case around the worm, or on the tip furthest from the wood. The worm is yellow and the shells pale blue. It is said that birds come out of them and if so, it's no wonder, as they resemble each other besides, as regards feathers and plumage that dart in and out every now and then between the valves of the shell. Gulls often get a passage across the ocean on sea planks, and there's no denying that they get a feast of the barnacles. I often saw one giving another a prick, another doing likewise, and so on until the whole flock attacked each other. There are two groups of barnacles, those with black backs and those with grey backs. It's said that the first covering of them does little damage at times of the year as they haven't got their teeth, nor are they sharp enough, but the second covering does the damage. I have no idea where they seed; I suppose it's way out to sea.
I often saw a beam come ashore and you would swear to look at it that it was sound, because it's not easy to see the holes, as they're so small.

I have to remind you, before I proceed any further, that much wrack comes ashore with no sign of barnacles, but nevertheless it's bored. Such beams are bored as they've cast off their covering (of barnacles). That kind of salvage you can sound, that is give it a light tap of a small stone on one end and let someone put his ear to the other end, and if it's sound a sweet musical note will travel to his ear, and if it's unsound an empty deaf noise will reach him. The wood that's badly perforated falls apart when it comes ashore in an exposed place. It's no good for a fire, neither is anything which has as many worms and snotty things or as much water.

Maybe if it were split into small pieces and it to get a dry summer, it could be put to good use. Yes, red deal wouldn't be bad. But I often used stand a long while listening to the sweet music coming from a bored beam on top of the shore as the result of the sharp wind scouring the crooked burrows which were shaped and bored by a host through hard work over a long period, while being tossed about mercilessly on top of the boundless sea, and maybe even their enemies, the seagulls, amongst them.

There are two tiny shells on the end which does the boring and they overlap each other; they are the teeth, and even if they are, the work they leave is a great credit to them, but I suppose it's hard to blunt them or notch them. In the two big shells there are thin muscles, so that it can open and close the valves as it wishes. That's how it provides its food. They grow on glass, on iron and on other such things, but no matter how sharp the teeth, they can't make any headway.

Below the waterline of wooden vessels they're covered with copper to protect them from that cursed tribe. I found a barrel of paraffin oil once on the grassy land above the shore, and they had it surrounded by a thick coat and they a good length as well. I scraped them off with a knife, and even if I did, there wasn't one piece bored through to the oil. I was grateful to them for that. I suppose they didn't like the smell of the oil as they left a quarter of an inch between themselves and it. Not one drop of it was wasted even though all the cants were bored, as usually they go with the grain. One day, as a friend and I were out looking for wrack, we found a barnacle goose out near *Stopóg an Táilliúra*. It was alive and barnacles three inches long growing out of its big broad beak and out of its wings. We took it ashore and the village people were amazed at it; none of us had ever seen the likes of it before.

I saw them growing on a whale that came ashore on *Trá Dheiscirt* during the Great War, proving that they grow on living things as well as on the dead. It is said that they beget the barnacle goose.

An Fhaocha Ghliomach — The Hermit Crab — *Eupagurus bernhardus*

It has the shape of a lobster, except for its small size like a shrimp. It has rough skin instead of a shell except for its claws and the top of its head. It spends its life inside a winkle – or inside a winkle's shell to be more precise – carrying it on its back from place to place in the pools throughout the shore, and I can tell you, it can also get around under that weight. It often has surplus weight on its hump as small limpets and seaweed grow on it at times of the year, that is, if the winkle is empty for a while before the new tenant occupies it. Seaweed, green slime and sea anemones grow on shells or on winkles that don't move, like stones, but no slime or anything grows on moving stones.

One day that I was cutting weed on the shore east of the house, however I managed to glance in a pool of water, I saw one of them walking carefully until it reached an upturned winkle shell. It turned it over; and apparently it was to let, as in a wink of an eye, it suddenly darted out of its own small house and into its new dwelling, tail first. That's one of its tricks, because when the little cabin gets too narrow for its body, it gets a bigger one and therefore doesn't spend too much time in any one house.

This strange creature is coloured reddish yellow and the tail is hook shaped to get a good grip on the inside. It's not very big, about two inches long, but in spite of its size it's mischievous enough, to tell the truth. When its cabin gets too small for its size and there's no vacant lodging in the neighbourhood, it gets cranky and impatient and takes the law into its own hands, goes off on the spur of the moment and when it meets the first suitable winkle, what does it do but drag out the occupant by the nape of the neck and settles itself comfortably in its place. It's a real tyrant, without pity or compassion for the weak, but treachery brings its own unmerciful punishment, as it gets mistreated by gulls and other birds who break its little house against the stones and swallow it back in one gulp.

If you break the winkle shell you will see it properly, the twists in its back half to make it suitable for the whorls in the back of the winkle. The front half is more attractive as it has a shell. It twists back around into the shell a little distance in from the door of the house, and the two eyes on stalks between claws. It must keep its eyes open all the time, as it is a nice tasty morsel and there are many enemies on the lookout to swallow it if they get a chance. Often when they are in danger, they jump out of the winkle altogether and even if the first shell they meet is tiny and not big enough for the crab, they shove the tip of their tail into it. They prefer that to being without any shell. It seems as if they like to protect the tip of their tail; maybe they're afraid some enemy will creep up on them from behind and cut it off.

They don't live long ashore. When winkles are gathered it happens that some hermit crabs are amongst them and the buyers don't like them as a few will rot a whole bag. Any ones that are noticed are thrown away, but they're not easy to notice. They're no good for eating but they're often used as wrasse and bream bait.

I remember one day in autumn that I was looking for bait. However I managed to glance into a rock pool by my side, I thought I saw something that looked like the bowl of a pipe walking around the bottom. I rubbed my eyes as I thought I was imagining things, that perhaps I had some sickness. I looked more sharply; it was there. It was no hallucination. But when I tried to catch it, it ran in under a clump of seaweed. It didn't escape and what was in the small pipe but a hermit crab and the tip of its claws sticking out through the lid made from a shell that was fast in the mouth of the pipe. Well, I thought, the lid was in it when it fell into the sea, as many a person had a lid like that. "There's no use talking", I thought to myself, "but one shouldn't wonder at anything in this world". There were strands of seaweed and limpets beginning to grow on it in such a way that it wouldn't be easy to notice. It seems that many shellfish make bits and pieces grow on them to confuse their enemies. When I rubbed off some of the growth "Déanta in Éirinn" (Made in Ireland) was engraved in chalk near the mouth of the pipe! Maybe it had no hut available when it came by the pipe, or maybe it was interested in it to be out of sight. Anyway, I left it where it was.

One night a long time after that I was somewhere there was music, song and drinking. When the company in such a situation gets a bit tired of witticism there's nothing they like more than a bit of arguing. Often, if the argument doesn't come easily, a way is found to start it. One man lost his pipe and was looking around for it:

"Is that it?"

"It is indeed ", said the other man.

"That came in from the ocean on the back of a fish"

"Nonsense" said the other man, placing it under his heel and making smithereens of it. The fat was on the fire. *Báiníní* were thrown off and jerseys pulled over heads. The fun was starting, lots of noise and people setting to each other. But that doesn't concern us here; as that wonderful pipe is broken I can't add any more to this chapter

An Portán Glas — The Green Crab — *Carcinus maenas*

There's nowhere between high and low tides that the green crabs can't be found, and the more rocky and clefted the area the better for them. When the tide ebbs they hide in their crab holes. If a stone were overturned you would see them rushing out and taking cover under seaweed and other stones. They don't like people's company. It puts up its claws to fight if cornered but usually discretion is the better part of valour as far as the crab is concerned. Its back is coloured dark green mixed with yellow and its belly is pale yellow, with a wide girdle under the female's belly to cover the eggs. A fine plumage grows on the legs and on the mouthparts. The eyes are on stalks so it can look about afar. It likes to take the shortest route to its food, as no matter how difficult the way it doesn't like to go the long way around. The more putrid and rotten the food the more it seems to like it. It can stay out of water for a good while without any concern; it often goes up the dried strand in search of sand-hoppers and flies. Indeed it does that in a clever way. It moves about slowly until within a foot of the small creatures, it gives a sudden impetuous dash and does the damage. If it cannot hunt on the shore it goes up on the land. It can stay out of the sea for the night without any harm to itself, because with the type of covered gills it has, it can keep the seawater humidity for a long time.

Once, a man who was coming home from a night visit saw a lot of confused lights at the bottom of the sand dune. He was sure it was the fairies prancing about. He became quite frightened. But he met someone else on the way and the two of them went to the place in question and what was there but a group of crabs eating a piece of dead ray. It was the luminescence on their bodies that this man saw. They made their way down to the sea as quickly as possible – their meal was ruined.

One evening as I sat on the boat at the top of the pier, however I looked around I saw a group of them around an old shoe, trying to lift it, one coming one way and another coming the other way to help; they went about it with vigour, lifted it and headed off fast. I nearly called after them "more power to ye, as ye all helped one another eagerly with no dodging or laziness!" A piece of fish lodged in the shoe was the cause of their hard work. They took the whole lot into a trench in the rock to have at a later date. They often migrate from place to place with wind and current on floating seaweed. They are not easily noticed, as they are the same colour as the weed. They remain as quiet and still as you've ever seen in case they'd be seen as gulls and terns are often hungry. In winter they go into the sand under stones and when spring comes with a stretch in the day, there are many young crabs among them. It's mostly in summer and autumn they cast off their old coats so as to get new ones. They stay in the dark; they must do so as they are tasty morsels when exposed. They are not much use as human food, but they are good bait and therefore you would often see a fisherman turning the stones on the shore, or fishing with a rod with a piece of fish on it to collect a load of them for a day's fishing on the wrasse grounds.

An Luaineachán — The Swimming Crab — *Macropipus sp.*

None of the crabs is as fast and supple as the swimming crab. As well as being quarrelsome, it often fights with the green crab. There's not much difference in size between them, four or five inches across the back. They are nearly as wide as they are long. The swimming crab is coloured green on its back, and has as it were a thin satin cloak with hair growing on it covering its shell. Its belly is coloured light yellow, its flattened legs coloured a mixture of blue, red and yellow with a growth of hair on them, the pincers raised on the ready when it hears a noise. The girdle that holds the eggs on the female is wider than that of the male. Apart from that one can detect little difference, but that's the way with all the crab types. The swimming crabs are not much good to eat but they're not bad bait. The female's eggs are excellent bait on the hook. There's nothing wrong with the carcass if the jacket is removed and it's chewed between your teeth before you attach it to the hook. The fish itself likes it among its food. As the carcass itself is full of thin little bony walls, with, as it were, small chambers between them, one needs to break up those bones so as those who are watching the tip of the fishing line can get a smooth soft grip of the bait. Wouldn't you think you could grind them with a stone? It's possible, but not as good for fishing.
Often, and I out on the wrasse fishing grounds chewing them, I would swallow lots of them as they are very sweet to eat. I think, also, they must be excellent in preventing the teeth from decay. Anyway, the wrasse have a great liking for any sort of crab and therefore the fisherman must have a number of them if he wants to go fishing. The swimming crabs are very abundant on rough shores that have a dense cover of knotted wrack and bladder wrack. They stay in their crab holes when the tide ebbs. When it's full tide they come out and wander about looking for food. They prefer rotten rubbish to anything else; they can smell it a long way off. That's when there's a rush. As there are birds and other enemies watching the sand-hoppers during the day, when night falls they come out of the rotten seaweed at the high tide mark and start prancing and frolicking about all over the place, some of them going down to the edge of the tide, and if they succeed, good luck to them as the green crab and the swimming crab are on the dry strand ready to slaughter them. One late evening I was watching one of each type of crab pinching the other, but with all the fumbling about they strayed too far from the water as they paid no attention to anything else with their determination; but soon a gull descended suddenly, lifted one up in its beak in the air and the other decided discretion was the better part of valour. In winter the swimming crabs are buried in the sand under the stones. Many of them go to other places out on the pleasant shores near the small islands. In spring one can see many of the young ones under stones on the lower shore – that's where the female spawns.

An Portán Rua — The Edible Crab — *Cancer pagurus*

During very low tides in summer and autumn the strange droning of the edible crab can be heard and it comfortable in its hide between the rocks, and the more uneven and difficult the shore, the better for it. There's no doubt that it has a protected place and it's not easy to dislodge it as it's the same size as the cleft and always faces out, its mouthparts half open and it letting off its noise – this is the source of the droning. If you look at it unawares you will notice that its claws are crossed above its mouth and its eyes on stalks – three joints in each claw. I often thought its eyes were in a dangerous position, that perhaps if it fell asleep it would close its claws on its eyestalks and become blind. It can lose its legs and grow new ones later but if it loses its eyes there's no cure for it but to remain in the dark in its own kingdom. Perhaps it's as intelligent in its own way as any other living thing; even people can often do strange things. When I was teaching Irish in Kildare I was travelling east along the road from Castledermot when I saw a man sitting comfortably on a strong branch of a tree and him doing his utmost to cut it with a saw. It wasn't long before I got a fright and a laugh when I saw your man and the branch falling to the ground.

Lobster fishermen catch a lot of the edible crabs in their pots during the season and many are sold on the fish markets throughout the country. They are a sweet tasty food to eat. Fishermen use them for bait. No bream or wrasse bait is as good as the red roe of the female in autumn, as a piece on top of the hook to deceive the wrasse and entice it out of the seaweed bottom or off the bare rock.

It used be said about a girl who was very fashionable and brightly coloured *"go mbeadh eochraí ar bharr an duáin aice"* (that she had roe on top of the hook); more often it was said behind her back – what a person doesn't hear doesn't upset him or her too much.

As long as the crab is growing it must change its coat from year to year. During this time it stays in a cleft, because if some of its enemies got a chance at it without a hard shell that would be the end of it. Limpets and seaweeds grow on those old ones that don't change their coats. In any case they don't wander much when they are old. They eat small fish and any rubbish they come across. They don't mind it being rotten either. There's a wide girdle under the female belly and the eggs are underneath. One cannot approach her during this time as she has her claws at the ready all the time. They spawn in summer and in autumn and they go out into the deep in winter. There are few fish that don't do this.

An Portán Clismín — The Masked Crab — *Corystes cassivelaunus*

There are not many of this type around the islands. Rarely would you come across one buried in the strand or it would be more correct to say that all that's visible are the eyes on top of the stalks. It's a bit timid and does not like fighting or such. It's always quiet and calm unlike the green crab. It's nearly the same shape but its shell is not as hard. It stays hidden in a cleft or in the sand most of the time and feeds itself on the tiny fish that it entices into its trench with tiny little many-coloured hairs around its mouthparts. It usually doesn't wander much as it's very lazy. You would think it had very little feeling and at a certain time of the year it's covered with a strange mantle. They make bait for wrasse and seabream. Apart from that they are not much use. The female carries a lot of red roe but often does not succeed in protecting it as many are on the lookout for it. Any crab's roe is sweet and pleasant and therefore it's no wonder that creatures have a liking for it. If it were not for the destruction of the roe, the shore would indeed be full of them.

An Portán Iarainn **The Spider Crab** *Hyas araneus*

This is very similar to the spiny spider crab except for its smaller size; it has a round body like a ball and long crooked legs with a growth on them; it has a very hard shell on its back and a brown-red colour like iron rust. The young ones look exactly like spiders. During that time the shell is soft but gradually it hardens during its life until the crab is mature. They are no good for eating but are sometimes used as wrasse bait. Indeed there are not many to be found on the shores of Connemara.

An Portán Faoileann **The Spiny Spider Crab** *Maia squinado*

This is a crab that has little life or feeling. It moves about very little. Its hard shell is full of hard sharp spines and limpets and seaweeds grow densely between the spines with the result that it's difficult to see it in its own surroundings. It lives near and below low tide. Like the other crabs it likes a clefted rough rocky shore. The male is found in a cleft out of sight, especially in summer and autumn. It is said that it plants the seaweed and limpets on the back of the female so as she's always hidden from her enemies. The strength of the shell defies description. I remember once cutting exposed oarweed on the south side of *Maínis*. One of them was in the way where I was carrying the weed. I stood on its back many times as I thought it was a stone at first, as it was so similar to one in shape and had the same growth as a stone on it, and not a budge out of it and it wedged as firmly between the stones as you ever saw. (I left it as it was, as I had no time to be fooling about; the boat was to be loaded and a flowing tide waits for no one, and never did).
It does this in such a smart way, as the limpets and seaweed are the same colour as the surrounding shore. It's no good for eating and fishermen don't use it much for bait. It's round shaped, about five or six inches wide with very long legs. It would remind you of a giant spider. They are not as widespread as the edible crabs. Lobster fishermen catch them occasionally in their pots. Indeed it's an ugly creature with the different growths on its back, but it looks well when shaved of it.

An Gliomach **The Lobster** *Homarus gammarus*

Few people have not seen a lobster in a restaurant or in a fish shop and therefore little needs to be said about its shape. It changes when cooked. The blue colour, with yellow, red and white spots, that was on the shell when in its own home amongst the rocks fades to red due to the boiling and unnatural death. It didn't think of that when the bait lured it into the pot. When it was in, it wasn't easy for it to come out. It left its kingdom for ever; its death was due to its hunger, as happens to many. Many are caught in pots in summer and autumn. During that time they come in large shoals in from the strange deep. That's a great help for the fishermen who make a living for themselves and their families during the season. They are big and small depending on age. The buyers don't accept any smaller than eight inches long. When I fished before the war, we would get six shillings for a live dozen of them. Indeed, it was a cheap food at the time. I once remember catching a lobster in a wrasse net, a lobster that was four foot long from the tip

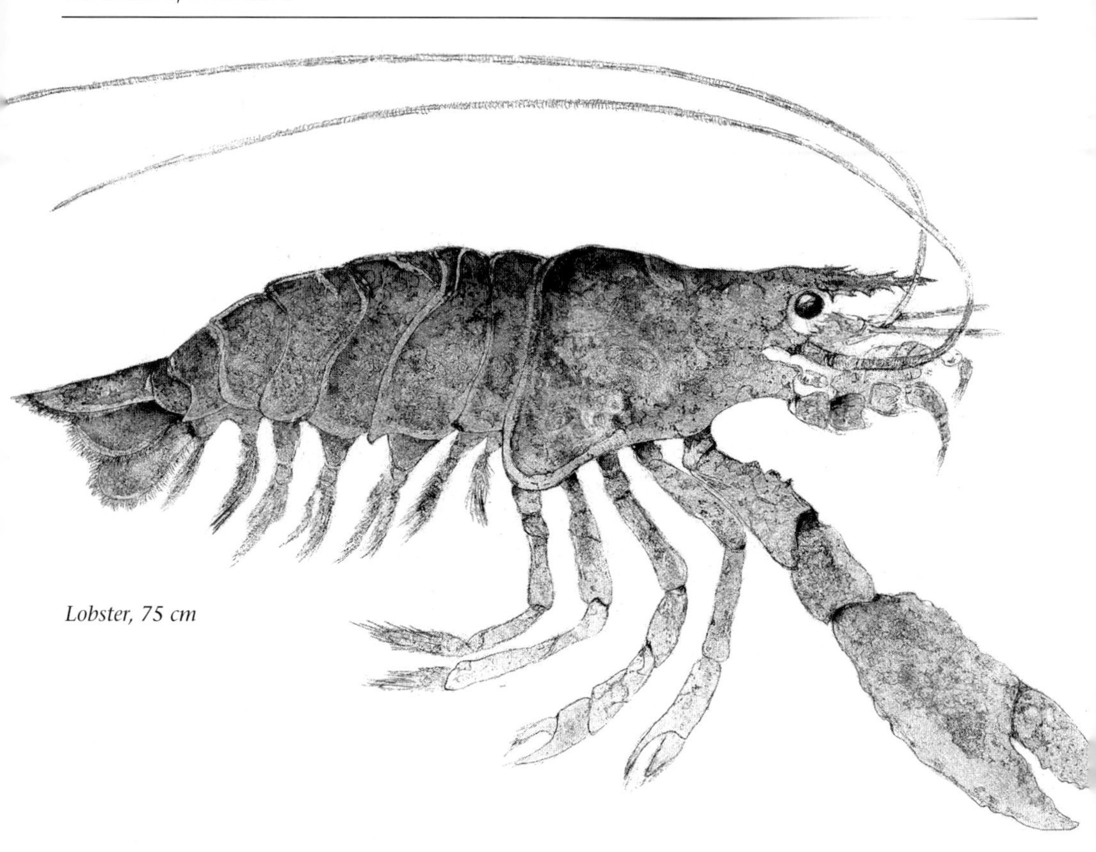

Lobster, 75 cm

of its tail to the sprit of its head. It was up to three stone in weight. It was amazing, like a pole and it covered with oarweed and sea belt and limpets in such a way that it was unrecognisable, and when I cleaned it of the assorted growth it looked more like itself. It wasn't much good for eating as there was quite a lot of water in the fish. The flesh was also quite soft. This type wanders very little. They stay near the rocks from year to year in such a way that the heavy growths of seaweed and limpets grow on it. There are thousands of eggs attached to the belly of the female. They're like turnip seeds. You can fill a cup full from a lobster ten inches long. The lobsters are very sweet and therefore other fish seek them out. It tries its best to protect the roe. It fights diligently and keeps its tail folded from time to time over the roe, sometimes as long as a year. The lobster generally moves backwards and it can also move very fast. It contracts the tip of its tail to make a dash or more correctly to jump.

You would often see the young ones swimming on top of the water during fine weather. They are only as big as a shrimp, about two inches long. It's hard to notice them, as they are the same colour as the water; nevertheless, other fish slaughter them. Only a small number escape. Indeed, if it happened that all of the seed matured, then the sea would be full of lobsters. Nature prevents this. It's wonderful the way that it can keep the fish under control so that they won't be too plentiful and won't be destroying each other. There are few types in the sea that can match the lobster for viciousness. It goes berserk altogether when it hasn't a scrap of food. It has neither pity nor compassion for any other creature. I remember a fine afternoon in the autumn that I was fishing crabs in the *Aircín*. A lobster was annoying me a lot as it was keeping the crabs away from the bait. But, to make a long story short, it eventually stole the piece of fish from my fishing rod and you never saw anything more like a burrowing pig the way it made a hole at the foot of a rock. It buried the chunk of fish as a dog would and buried it nicely with its tail with sand and seaweed. It went back into its hide seemingly happy. It wasn't long before the crabs got a smell of the rubbish and started digging, three of them hard at it, but they didn't succeed as the lobster came at them in one quick jump from behind and laid its heavy claws on the first one of the trespassers it met, and for the others it was a question of discretion being the better part of valour. He didn't leave his lot there now but took it into his den. I think the crabs had the final feast on him, because I brought the defender home one afternoon in a bucket. When I had it on the plate with the blue coat changed to red I began thinking. "You poor creature" I said to myself, "weren't you the greedy one not long ago! Isn't it easy to satisfy you now! Pity to be in such a bad way at the end of it all. Maybe if you had stayed in your hide from the start you might have won the day. It's easy to be wise after the event".

Fishermen aren't their only enemies. Dogfish, skates, rays, pollack, cod and others play havoc with them. I often saw one six or seven inches long in the stomachs of some of these I mentioned. The lobster fights diligently and bravely and it's easy to see that he takes part in some big fights, with the scars of the wounds on its body and claws. If it loses some of its legs or even its claws, new ones grow to replace them without much delay. Not only that, but if they get stuck in anything all they need do is leave them behind and head off if they've any limb left in their body.

The fork of the claws is not the same – small little sharp teeth on one, which is called the scissors, and big teeth on the other, which is called the pincers. Fishermen must cut the strong muscle that is in the angle of the claws when they are being put in the storage pot, or bind them before they kill each other. More lobsters are caught in a fine year when the sea is calm than in a rough year. It's said that when there's a swell in the sea they become very restless and that they don't stay in any one place but wander about all over the wide sea. Even when plentiful, if boats are fishing for a long time in any one place they are cleaned out and none remains due to the continuous activity. Every area must be given some time and no area should be over exploited. For a few years now, big fishing boats from France and other countries have damaged the lobster and crawfish stocks off the west coast of Ireland. They catch a lot; they are well adapted to it as they have the best of instruments and means and big seaworthy boats. The lobsters can't come near the coast because of the shores of pots those boats have set out to the west, and not only that but trawls often comb the deep. Notice that the poor man near the coast with his *currach* or *púcán* has little chance. Isn't it a pity that he wouldn't get a chance with a seaworthy boat that would tack out in all weather to the fishing ground and that could set and lift nets and pots when the day is rough or calm. It's often bad enough for the small boats near the shore and during bad nights the pots are thrown ashore and broken on the rocks; and as well as the cost there's work in making a set of pots, but when the fisherman has to go to the wood to cut rods, make new pots and fit them out, then the story is much worse.

An Gabhal Mara — The Crawfish — *Palinurus elephas*

The crawfish and the lobster are very alike in structure. The crawfish is usually red and bigger than the lobster. We often caught them in wrasse nets around *Sceirde* rocks; they're also quite plentiful in the deep areas around *Carraig na Meacan*. They have a sweet tasting and strong flesh. It would be a big family that would not be fully fed by one of them. I remember well when I was a child how I was amazed at one we caught at *Sceirde*, because of the music it was making when taken aboard. A loud quivering sound that lasted for the whole journey home eastwards. The female carries a lot of roe and spawns out on the deep.

An Tonachán Trá — The Sand-hopper — *Talitrus sp.* *Talorchestia sp.*

The sand-hopper is a type of creature like a wood louse or a shrimp.[29] It works ceaselessly during an ebbing tide making little burrows under the surface of the sand. It's not more than two inches long and lively as well. It sticks up its hard pointed head from time to time to look around and see how the work is progressing. I have no idea why it works so frantically like this. It never rests at all. Large numbers of them help each other diligently and faithfully.

An Ribe Róibéis — The Shrimp — *Palaemon sp.*

"Ribe ribe róibéis, tabhair dom greim ar bharr do shlata bige agus tabharfaidh mé duit arís amárach é," (Give me a grip of the top of your little rod, shrimp, and I'll give it back to you tomorrow). That's what we'd say long ago when trying to deceive this little creature which would swim to and fro in the pools on the bottom of the shore. It wasn't easy to see them as they are the same colour as the sand on the bottom, but if you put your hand in and leave a small gap between your thumb and index finger saying at the same time *"ribe ribe róibéis . . ."* it would not be long before a group of them gathers around your hand looking as if they are amazed at the piece of flesh, and before long, one of them which is bolder than the rest will put its antenna in the wrong place. I suppose it thinks the fingers are to be eaten, but if you close them quickly it will have a different opinion, as it will be caught between your thumb and index finger. I can tell you that in spite of its small size it will make a great effort to escape from captivity. It fights courageously but to no avail as its rear half is so sweet to eat raw or cooked. A lot of them have a sorry end as they are cut in two while still living and quivering. The tail is eaten and the head is thrown away as it contains only guts and skeleton. They look very like the lobster as regards shape and otherwise. They're generally between one and three inches long. They're a fine pleasant fish and they're much sought after in fish markets. Many are caught in some areas with a kind of small meshed net, but not much of this is practised in Connemara yet. The female has many eggs and spawns naturally when the time comes. They migrate to the deep in winter according to their nature, as do many others.

[29] Although both creatures are crustaceans, the sand-hopper belongs to the order Amphipoda which are *laterally* flattened whereas the wood louse belongs to the order Isopoda which are *dorso-ventrally* compressed.

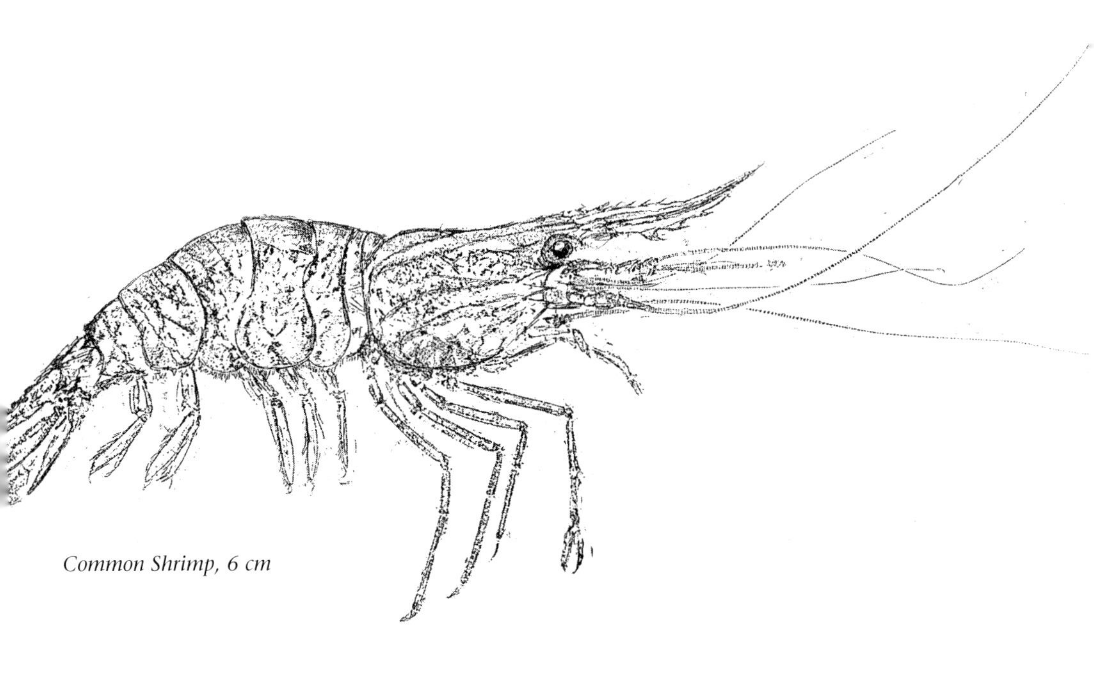

Common Shrimp, 6 cm

An Slobán [30] Sea Mats, Sponges, Algae

There are many kinds of *slobán* but the small grey *slobáin* that grow on seaweed and on rocks on the deep and the small ones that grow on sea rods are the most abundant on the shores of Connemara. The grey *slobáin* are good as manure and for that reason a lot are harvested in the spring in deep quiet holes with a type of dredge. Sometimes they are exposed on low tides and are loaded into the boat from a creel. They contain a lot of water because the small branches are full of holes and are therefore very heavy. They are no good for kelp. The red ones that attach to the sea rods wither a lot in such a way that only their shape is visible when the burners put them in the kiln. There's another type of the grey one that's called *buirlín (*purse sponge*)* and it's also good for manure. Indeed, there's no great difference between it and the other types. They're nearly all much the same.

They grow in little round clusters, almost ball-shaped, and have what seems like a type of fur growing on them; they're the grey types that grow in quiet places. But the type that grows on the sea rods are flattened and thin like a skin around the sea rod near the holdfast. If you remove them you can see they're made like a ring. They have a strange heavy odour when fresh.

Big ones that you would never see growing often come ashore. They probably grow far offshore. Anyway, they are strong and vigorous and full of holes. A person can use them when he wants to wash his face or hands, because they don't break up as easily as the ones I mentioned earlier.

[30] The name *slobán* probably encompasses a variety of organisms, more especially the green alga *Cladophora sp.* and encrusting animals such as the sea mats and sponges.

An Teanga Chait — The Sea Mat — Order *Cheilostomata*

Indeed, this rough red tuft resembles an animal's tongue. They grow on sea rods and on other types of seaweed during the summer and the autumn. They're no good for kelp but when they're thrown ashore mixed with other types during bad weather they're let pass in the fertiliser. That's not to say they have any good or vigour, but it's not easy to separate them from the rest of that stuff. It's not unlike *slobáin* except that the *slobáin* are better material for fertiliser. They wither a lot with the sun as they contain a lot of water and they're full of small holes. There are many strange things on the sea bottom which people who don't live beside the shore find hard to believe exist at all. But if you happen near the sea any time visit the shore on a low tide and you'll see some of those wonders.

An Súmaire Cladaigh — The Sea-cucumber — Class *Holothuroidea*

It's hard to say if this is a fish or a worm with its strange appearance. Indeed, it is not a pleasant sight. Some of them are six inches long, reddish yellow on their backs and white on the belly. They live near the level of low spring tide. Sometimes they are found exposed on the shore, but they prefer the depth. They're of no use to lobster fishermen, they are not much good for bait. They're things without much feeling or life but they can attach themselves to other things and get a passage from place to place. They're not abundant and it is rarely you would come across one. They often attach to other fish and they look as if they suck them and once they get a grip it's often difficult to remove them. I often saw a wrasse and one of them attached to its navel and it trying desperately to shake it off.

An Cuán Mara — The Sea Urchin — *Echinus sp* *Paracentrotus sp.*

There are two types of sea urchin to be found on the shores of Connemara, the smooth one and the spiny one.[31] They're very similar in shape, that is oval shaped. Some of them are as big as a goose egg and others bigger or smaller. One of them has a covering of many coloured spines and the other is as smooth as silk. If you were to go down to the lower shore during a very low tide in summer and look among the weeds in the pools you would see them opening and closing their mouths from time to time, providing for themselves amongst the tiny little fishes. Indeed, they're content with very little; they're clever in the way they fish with delicate little many coloured hairs around their mouths that they wave about continuously to deceive the little creatures and to entice them towards their death. It's said that treachery brings its own punishment. The same is true for the sea urchins, as seagulls and terns often give them a beating as they have a great liking for the food inside the shell. It would remind you of the yolk of an egg except for its strong heavy smell of the sea.

[31] The two most common urchins to be found on the shore belong to the genera *Echinus* and *Paracentrotus*. *Echinus* is the larger of the two (shell generally up to 10 cm in diameter) and its pale coloured spines are about 1.5 cm in length. *Paracentrotus* is smaller (shell up to 6 cm in diameter) and its spines are longer (up to 3 cm) and darker (dark green to purple). When the author states that one is smooth he is probably describing the spines in relative terms and is referring to *Echinus*. *Paracentrotus* is the urchin favoured by gourmands in France.

An Crosán Ladhrach — The Common Starfish — *Asterias rubens*

There are a lot of this class to be found in the shallow rocky weed-covered sea beds of Connemara. They come in from the deep like every other shoal at the beginning of summer and stay until the end of autumn when they set off for the deep again. As the female has a lot of roe they reproduce profusely, too profusely perhaps, as they are no use for anything. Not only that, but they do a lot of harm to lobster and long-line fishermen as they make the most of the bait, that's to say they cover it in a tight embrace with their rough arms and they suck away until there's nothing left but the bare pins in the pots and the hooks on the long-lines. Neither the lobster nor any other fish, however keen their eyesight, can see a scrap of the bait while the starfish is in possession. This type has five arms between three and five inches long. You would think to look at it that it's not alive at all, but alas, it is, and if you look closely you will see it opening and closing its mouth, which is in the middle, from time to time. Other times it bends and turns its arms with agility, as if to get a grip on something. I often saw them moving about on the bottom and they're well able to move fast as well. During fine weather in November when we would be out on the deep with long-lines, their luminescence made a great spectacle. [32] When the top of the long-line was raised out of the water at the break of day you would swear that it was a light that stretched out in a straight line under the boat, shining like the stars above. The starfish, attached to the snoods and the back of the longlines, helping the rays and the eels, the ling, the turbot and the cod that were on the hooks, to make one big lantern before the break of day – yes, reader, perhaps they knew they were leaving their own kingdom behind forever.

An Crosán Faoileán — The Cushion Star — *Asterina sp.* *Anseropoda sp.*

Maybe, reader, it would be as well for me to give you an example, before we proceed any further with these, of the shape, the size and the colour of the starfish. A round shape like a cartwheel without the wale or like the wheel of fortune that the trickster would have at a fair or a market or at the races. They vary in size from a shirt button to a parasol and they have every colour under the sun. They're a beautiful sight, indeed, on a clear starry night when they glisten with the magic of luminescence. It would be worth your while to go out of your way to see such beauty. I often took one aboard on a hand line and it with a strong grip on the bait with its rough muscular arms and I can tell you it wouldn't let go until it had its fill. There's no doubt but that lobster and long-line fishermen hate them and they have good reason. They're not a good lot at all. Often, when I was lobster fishing, I would hear the others talking to each other as the boats passed each other.
"Isn't it a fine morning, Mícheál?"
"It sure is, praise be to God. Did you do any damage?" "Not much, as the pots were full of starfish"
"Aren't the devils plentiful."

[32] The luminescence referred to by the author is a product of minute organisms that would adhere to the starfish as it was raised out of the water.

"O bad cest to them, they're a cursed lot, boy," and so on.
The cushion star has many limbs and a type of web in the angle of its arms going about one third of the way to the tip almost like the sunstar.[33]
They come in from the sea in summer like any other shoals and settle in the weed-covered bottom where pickings or dainty titbits can be got. Fishermen would prefer not to have their likes in the boundless sea. But it's not up to them, but to God, who directs everything in the world.

An Crosán Mín (an crosán grianta) — The Sun-star — *Solaster sp.*

The sun-stars live on the deep. The upper side is smoother than on the other types but the other side is rough.[34] They're yellow coloured. They're not as long as the others; nevertheless they ruin the lobster fishermen in the autumn. One day when I was fishing wrasse behind *Oileán Lachan*, a fine calm cloudless day, and I could see the bottom clearly, I saw the one that's called the brittle star bending and twisting itself as fast as you ever saw. It was in danger as a crab was cornering it, but the brittle star was equal to the occasion as it released a couple of its limbs and off it went when its enemy started eating them. It knew that new ones would grow in their place again. But the starfish is not alone in this respect, being like many others in the deep sea.

[33] The name *crosán faoileáin* may derive from the resemblance of the cushion star to the webbed foot of a gull (*faoileán*). It has, however, only five rays, unlike the sunstar, which may have up to 13 rays.

[34] The purple sun-star (*Solaster endeca*) is relatively hard and smooth on its upper surface, giving rise to the name *crosán mín* (smooth sun-star). Its colour varies between purple and orange.

SEA FISH

An Siorc The Shark [35]

There are several different types of these common on these coasts – the blue shark, the tope, the smooth hound and the basking shark.

An Liamhán Mór The Basking Shark *Cetorhinus maximus*

The basking sharks are very common on this west coast in summer. During fine calm weather they bask in the sun at the surface of the boundless sea. Their fins are like the small sails of a boat when they raise them. It's very large – between twenty and forty feet in length and between one and two tons in weight. It's a vulnerable fish because of the oil that's extracted from its liver. It's worth a lot.

In the olden days, a long time ago, basking sharks were caught on this coast.[36] The fishermen would have big *gleoteoga*, boats of six or seven tons. They would go to sea in May when the weather was fine and settled. The prow of every boat had a big coil of strong cable and a spear at its end. There was a small keg at the other end of the cable, not quite at the end but within a few fathoms of it. The keg and the spear bore the name of the fisherman. The boats would go very far west, south-west of *Árainn Mhór*. The *Beanna Beola* disappeared and *Árainn Mhór* was just like a spindle of a spinning wheel on top of the big sea out there on the strange abyss. When a boat encountered a shark there was a certain way to kill it. It has a white patch on its back and when the spear was laid on that patch it would push itself upwards against it as if it had a tickle or an itch. When the spear pierced it there was an opportunity to open it inside. Then it would take off in anger dragging the cable with it. The cable was hitched to the *mullard* and a man standing on the forward platform with a sharp axe in his hand to cut the cable if it happened that the shark took the boat too far, as there was no time to loosen it when the slack was taken up; it would be too late and the boat would be in danger of sinking. Even if the cable were cut

[35] In addition to those listed above, the spotted dogfish and the spurdog, described below, also belong to the sharks or selachimorphs.

[36] In the eighteenth century a number of extraction plants for fish oil, which provided the basis of locally significant industries, were set up in Irish ports. Government bounties were introduced to encourage the industry and a number of fish species were used, but the basking shark contributed by far the greatest proportion of oil produced by the Irish fisheries in the latter half of the eighteenth and the early decades of the nineteenth centuries. As well as a number of uses for domestic purposes it was used industrially for the hardening of cast steel and for public street lighting. The Connaught Journal (29 May 1828) listed "Pale Seal, Sunfish and Spermaceti Oils" among the inventory of goods obtainable from Mathew Healy's General Assorted Warehouse in Galway. The fishery deteriorated for various reasons in the second half of the nineteenth century. Joseph Sweeney established an inshore fishery in Achill in 1947 and this continued until the early 1970s.

the boatman had a chance to catch the shark as his name was on the spear and on the keg, wherever it would come ashore. As soon as it was speared the blood came in strong streams until its strength was wasted and then it would drift with the tide and current and perhaps it would be finally thrown in on wild rough shores or on fine sandy beaches.
I often heard the old people say that any boat that caught three of them would have that year's season finished, as there was a lot of money to be got from their livers. It's clear from the poetry itself that it was very important long ago as Raftery said in that song *Condae Mhaigh Eo "Tá an liamhán ag triall ann ón bhfarraige mhór"* (The basking shark is making its way there from the deep sea). It appears that the fishermen used welcome it into the bays. That was no wonder, as it was wonderful to see it coming in close to shore from the west to give help and assistance to the *Gaeil*. Isn't it often since that help has come across the sea from the west?

An Fíogach **The Spurdog** *Squalus acanthias*

The spurdog, except for the spotted dogfish, are the smallest of the shark family. They do a lot of harm to fishermen, especially in summer and in autumn when they come in plentiful shoals from the deep open sea. The spurdog clear out areas where mackerel, haddock, cod and other fish live, as there's no telling how widespread they are. You can feel the boat sailing through them and it would take no time to load them into it with a gaff. When they wander about at the water surface they are so hungry that they would often jump clean out of the water to catch a piece of a rope or anything else hanging overboard. One of them can break a piece off the blade of an oar with its strong sharp teeth and with the continuous rubbing of its rough skin. They can scour the outside surface of the boat. They go mad for mackerel and herring and they tear and eat nets to get at the small fish caught in the mesh. That part which isn't cut by their teeth is worn away and in bad shape due to their rough skin.
Its back is dark brown and it's pale grey on its belly. Some of them are about three feet long. They often give birth to their young after being taken on board. These are strong and healthy also – about five or six inches long and able to swim immediately. It doesn't spawn like other fish. The female gives birth to the young, like the shark, the tope, the spotted dogfish and others of that family, just like a land animal.[37]
A lot of spurdog were caught during the Great War, as there was a big demand for them on fish markets in big cities. Indeed, fishermen have little interest in them except for pot bait. Few are eaten in Connemara although the oil is taken from them to put on shoes or on boat halyards or some such thing. The skin is fairly useful also to scrub furniture or to put on the handle of a knife for a better grip. As it's rough a piece of it is often stuck to a piece of wood in order to light matches with it. So they have some use. More of them come inshore during years when the weather is fine than when the weather is rough. They follow other shoals inshore and plunder them on the journey eastwards. There's no doubt but they're a wicked mischievous ravenous race. One evening my father (God rest him) and I were sailing out to sea in the *púcán* on a broad reach – the wind from the west south-west and the sea flat. A little distance west of *Árainn Mhór* it looked as if there were fish

[37] Most sharks give birth to live young but a number of them lay eggs that are protected by a horny shell or "mermaids purse".

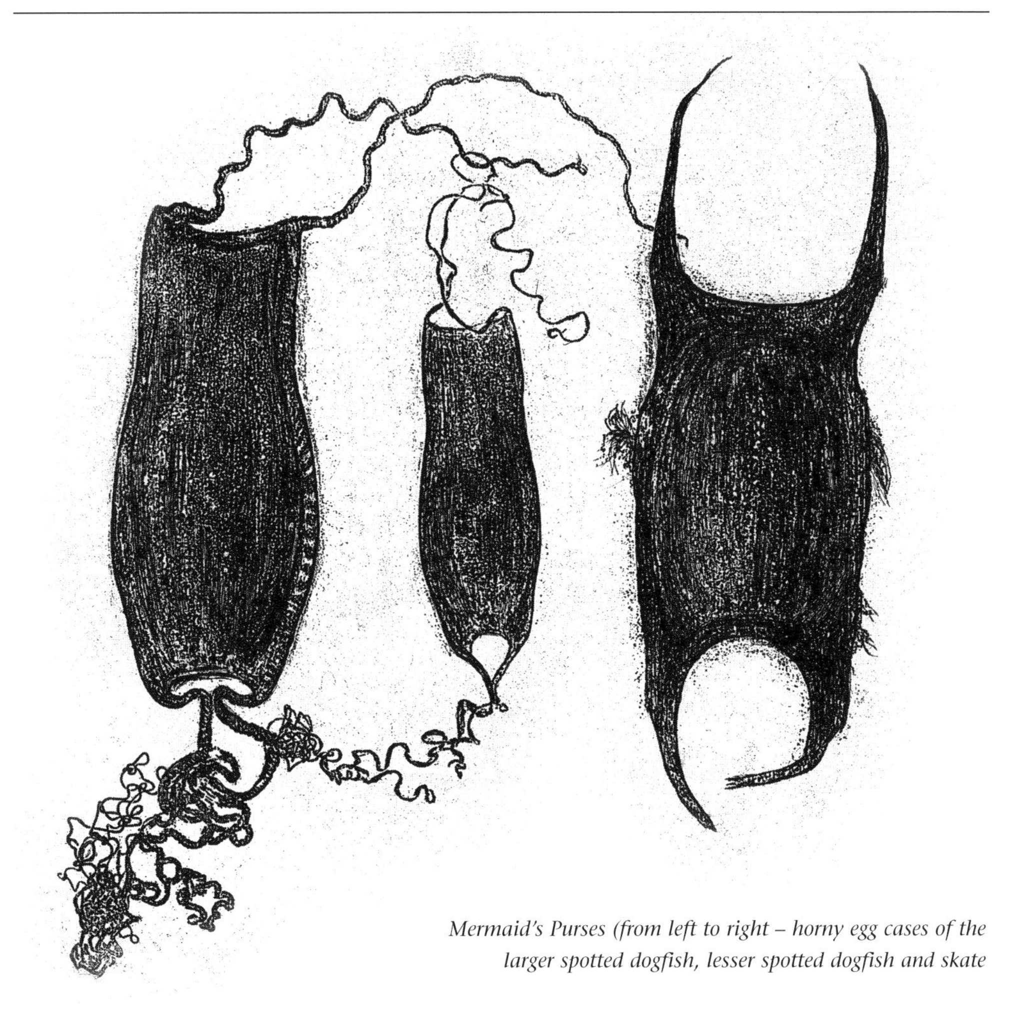

Mermaid's Purses (from left to right – horny egg cases of the larger spotted dogfish, lesser spotted dogfish and skate

about from the number of small gulls and black birds and gannets diving and sending up spouts of water. As well as that there was a heavy odour of oil from a smooth slick to the west. "Take down the mainsail", my father said "we'll shoot them here". When the nets were in the water the ebbing tide pulled us westwards against the wind, *Sceirde* to the north-west and the cliffs of *Árainn* to the east rising hundreds of feet out of the sea. Darkness fell shortly so that all that was visible were the lanterns of the lighthouses and the lights from other boats to the west.

There wasn't a puff of wind. It wasn't long before we heard the splash of spurdog about the boat. We took the nets aboard as fast as we could. They jumped out of the water to catch the fish that were caught in the net coming aboard, some of them wrapped in the net, gnashing their teeth and stretching themselves with all the fish they had eaten. We knew they had done a lot of damage though we couldn't see the holes nor the tears in the darkness but we saw the damage soon enough and I can tell you it took a good part of a day to repair it with the needle.

The remains left over by the spurdog, between mackerel and herring, were no use as most of them had chunks taken out of them, some with only their heads left, not to mention the amount of net they had chewed and a small amount that they had no time to use. I noticed that there were some fish with milt. It's said the spurdog prefer those with roe as they have more juice and oil and they're eaten first. Indeed, they don't leave any kind after them if they have the time, not even the net. During nights when we fished seabream on *Maidhm Mháirtín Thaidhg*, no sooner were the seabream underneath and us thinking that we'd have a good night of them than a shoal of spurdog would come by. The seabream would be raised out of the water and would you believe it but one of the spurdog would jump and cut it from the middle and perhaps another would jump up to take the rest of it. There's no use trying to fish where they are. Sometimes you can chase them if you cut up a few of them and hang them over the side of the boat in the water. Another time if a hundred of them were cut up it would make no difference. They would gather around to drink the blood. It's hard to know what to do with the same cursed lot.

Lesser Spotted Dogfish, 75 cm

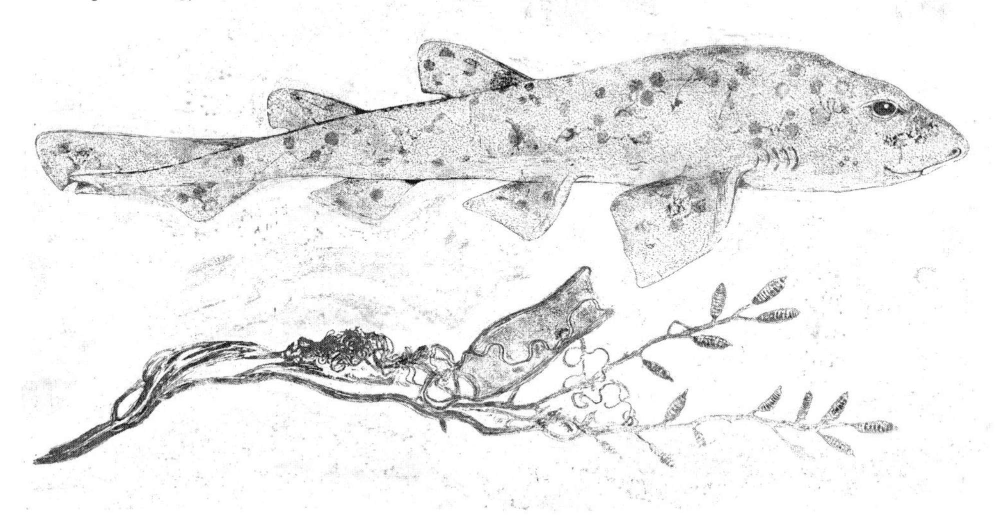

An Freangach — The Spotted Dogfish — *Scyliorhinus canicula*

The spurdog and spotted dogfish belong to the one tribe and they also look alike except for the rough brown skin of the dogfish which is speckled with black and yellow spots. It's not as big as the spurdog and it goes closer to the rocks and stays nearer the bottom to feed itself. Some of them stay throughout the year in the calm bays with the result that some places are named after them – *Carraig na bhFreangach* behind *Fínis*, one of them. It has a big group of them always around it. Fishermen don't like them as they often get into wrasse nets without warning and do a lot of damage to the thread. Not only that, but the hooks of the long-line that are so carefully baited to entice rays, skates and plaice are taken over by the hungry accursed and uninvited dogfish. They pay dearly for it as they get an unmerciful thrashing on the gunwale from the fisherman who hates them.

An Ghobóg — The Tope — *Galeorhinus galeus*

The tope belongs to the shark family and therefore the same traits are found in it, that is, it destroys and kills other fish. It's bigger than the spurdog. Some of them are five or six feet long, dark coloured on their back and paler below. It's not possible to fish anywhere near them as they catch hold of the bait and cut the hand lines and the snoods. Often when we'd be on good seabream fishing grounds we'd have to haul up and go home from them. When we'd haul one aboard she'd often release five or six young ones that would be strong enough to swim in the water in the bilges. It's an irascible wild fish to haul from the weedy bottom especially. They're no good to eat and therefore fishermen don't like them at all.

An Roc [38] — The Ray — *Raja sp.*

It's said that the ray, seal and mackerel are the three fastest things in the sea.[39] There's no doubt that the ray can hurry away when frightened. When it moves on the smooth sandy bottom it's difficult to notice it at all. All that's visible is a type of cloud around it due to its raising the sand with its speed. It leaves behind a trail of this cloud in a line. It would remind you of smoke from a ship ploughing the sea with speed. There are usually two types of ray around the coasts of Connemara – a smooth one and a rough one. They're nearly the same in shape – wide, thin, diamond shaped, a long tail and many spines on the back of the rough one. It is usually coloured brown, with black and white spots on the upper side and coloured white below. Often, on rust-coloured sand they are yellow-spotted on their backs to merge with their surroundings so as it will be difficult for their enemies to see them. They're nowhere as abundant as on red sand between the weed-covered rocks on the bottom. They come into shallow water in winter. Many other fish do the same thing, as there's more food to be got during the fine day near the rocks.
Some of the smooth ones are very big. I often saw them four feet long and four feet wide. They are better food for people than the rough one. The females generally have fewer spines. The male has most of them. The female is the better fish for eating. The head, tail and entrails are discarded. The two wings are the best part of it and they are attached at the backbone. The ray has soft bones. Someone with good teeth would find them very sweet to eat. The young ray has a kind of case around it. When the female spawns, this purse is about three or four inches long and two inches wide. They are often cast ashore when the young rays have left them. The sea hag's purse is what it's called. There's a small cleft in one end of it. This is the way out for the young ray. It's bar-shaped and hard like a shellfish.

[38] There are several common species of ray belonging to the genus *Raja* off the west coast. The larger species of *Raja* are commonly referred to as skates while the smaller ones are called rays. Skates and rays can generate weak electrical fields and the *roc garbh* (rough ray) that is mentioned in the text is *Raja clavata,* the thornback ray, which can generate an electrical potential of 4 volts. The stingray *Dasyatis pastinaca* can inflict painful wounds with its long tail. The author's description of the pain inflicted, however, resembles the effect of a jolt from the electric ray *Torpedo nobiliana,* but this fish is easily distinguishable from other rays by its round head and it does not have the long tail as described above.

[39] This has no scientific basis but is based on the use of alliteration in Irish, the three organisms being *roc, rón agus ronnach.*

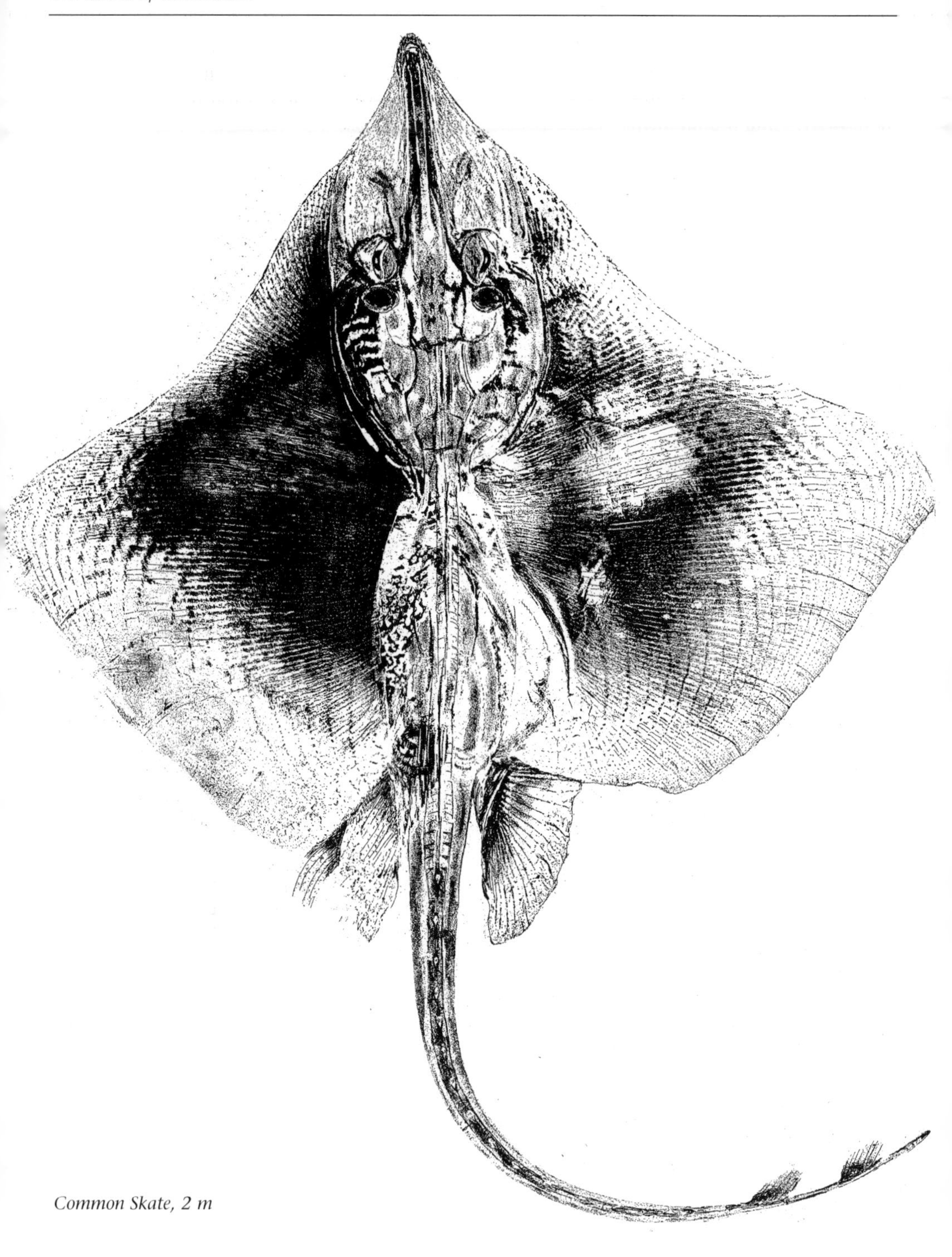

Common Skate, 2 m

A lot of rays are taken with long-lines and trawls in Connemara and most are sent fresh to market. When many boats spend a lot of time fishing them in one place they clear the area and there aren't many to be caught for a while again. But all fishing is like that. And fishermen know it well also.
One day that we were lifting longlines out from *Oileán Barra*, between it and *Carraig Iolra*, we had the three long-lines set – four or five hundred fathoms of line on the bottom, up to a thousand hooks – there was a good catch of ray, skate, eels and plaice on it, but there was one ray that astonished us.[40] There wasn't much difference between it and the others, except for the tail being longer and narrower. We mightn't have noticed this difference were it not for this thing that happened. I was hauling the long-line from the bottom, Ciarán was rowing and Pádraig Choilm was removing the fish from the hooks. The tail of this ray was twisted around the back of the long-line (that's often the way with any type). I tried to unravel it, but as soon as I touched it, it gave me a sudden sting in my arm as if I had pins and needles running up to my shoulder. My hand shook so much that the ray was shaken off the hook; it fell on the gunwale and away from us into the sea. The pain did not last long in my hand. Nevertheless, I didn't like to see any of those stinging rays from then on.

An Scolabord — The Skate — *Raja sp.*

The skate has a thin diamond-like shape like the ray. They're very alike. The skate's back is brown, spotted yellow and black and the underside has a more bluish shine than the ray. The ray is also more slimy when taken aboard. The two tribes live on the one sea bottom and they approach the shore together in summer and they move off again before the bad weather. It's not a good neighbour to the ray as it wreaks havoc on them when it gets the chance. Some of them are very big. I myself saw one that was two hundredweight. It was taken on a long-line in three fathoms; it had swallowed a ray. That's what it always does; it swallows other fish that lure it without as much as putting a tooth in them. It's kept on anchor on the snood as it hardly moves at all until it's brought aboard. It's not a nasty fish. It's said that when it has the other fish swallowed that it doesn't move until it has digested it. There's a type that's called the *scolabord tintrí* ("flashing skate") but it doesn't wander in much from the big deep, as that place happens to be very dark at times. Nature has bestowed on it the capability of making its way through the forests of sea rods that are in the valleys between the high arches, as there is light shining from its eyes that shows it the way ahead. It's said that it's much bigger than the other skate. A boat from our townland caught one of them on a long-line off *Leic Mhór Charraig na Meacan*, but they threw it overboard because they thought it wasn't a real thing at all. There were people who didn't believe the story, but that's their own business. The truth is often bitter. It's not the only type that has a light shining from it on the bottom of the deep sea. There are many types out there that have never been seen near the shore.
The female skate spawns like the ray, that is the young is inside a case that's called a sea hag's purse, when it's thrown ashore after the young skate is released.
Many skate were caught on longlines along with rays during the War. The fishermen would get between a crown and eight shillings for a stone weight for them gutted. They

[40] *Oileán Barra* is more commonly known as *Bior* (Birmore Island on the Admiralty Chart).

would often give a good pay. Fish were scarce then and you would get a good reward for them. They were sold fresh. We often had skate and ray in boxes on anchor off the pier head for three or four days when we had no way of getting them to market. They would stay alive also. We would have to feed them fish every day as food.

An Scadán The Herring *Clupea harengus*

The herring is called "king of the fishes" as it's difficult to lure it with any bait, however good. A lot of them are caught in nets in autumn. They come in from the sea in big abundant shoals and as the weather gets worse the quiet bays are filled with them right up to the face of the rocks. They provide a lot of work throughout the season and thousands of people, fishermen and those who gut and salt, take part in the work. It's a great help to have this valuable abundant fish coming in from the sea twice a year. There's not much difference between autumn and spring herring as regards shape and size. There's up to a cup full of roe in the female's ovary, maybe up to fifty thousand eggs. That's the best time for them, when they're full; the male is full of milt at the same time – in autumn, the autumn race, and in spring, the shoals that come in spring.

There's no need to say much about it, as there are few people who haven't seen it sometime. It's covered with thin flimsy scales which overlap each other from the tail like shingle slates on the roof of a house. The fins have no sharp spines – a fin in the middle of the back, two small fins on its flanks beside each other in the middle of the belly and another fin near the tail. There are thin films covering its two eyes and they're probably interfering with its eyesight. Spurdog, dogfish, tope, sharks and other fish make a meal of them and gannets, gulls and shags watch for their opportunity to steal away the remains of the hunt into the air.

The herring season is very important on the coast. They come in from the strange abyss each year without fail – and fishermen are surely full of joy – they give many thanks to God for having driven this valued harvest towards them.

An Breac Geal The Sea Trout *Salmo trutta*

The sea trout and the salmon belong to the same tribe. It has a shiny silvery colour on its belly and little black spots through the yellow on its back. It's a beautiful fish without doubt. They're plentiful in summer and in the fine evenings they jump out of the water and catch flies that fly about. I remember one evening I was out in the bay fishing mullet. There was a mass of quarreling flies beside the boat above the water. It wasn't long before I saw a sea trout moving about below the surface. I got the gaff as I thought it was watching the flies and that perhaps it would jump to catch them and if it did I would sink the iron gaff hook to the hilt in it. But it shortly sent up a spout of water from the surface of the sea from its mouth. It knocked down some of the flies and took off after swallowing them. I thought it was a smart trick. Maybe it was afraid of me and that was why it let off the spurt of water. It and the sturgeon have a trick. When porpoises and spurdog corner them, if there's any boat sailing near them they hide themselves by the keel or near the front of the rudder until the enemy goes away; as it is in such a hurry and the rest of it that it thinks they're out in front of it all the time.

Sea Trout, 80 – 100 cm

There was a time when England had a law prohibiting the placing of any net near a town as they thought that the fishermen were catching salmon and sea trout. I placed nets hundreds of times in the bays and I never caught as much as I could eat of salmon or of sea trout. That government also declared war on shags and cormorants. They paid three pence a head; perhaps many of those birds never saw a salmon or sea trout. It was a terrible injustice, they being killed in innocence and not being in a position to defend themselves.

Fishermen aren't very interested in sea trout or in salmon. They would much prefer a pollack or a cod. Indeed, they had no idea what was behind those stupid laws and when the bailiffs used bark at them they would try and explain the story to them, which is that neither the sea trout nor the salmon would ever go into their nets. There was no use talking; they would have to give in to the law if they didn't want to be taken to court and to pay a heavy fine, or maybe a long imprisonment. On the same subject, neither would they pay any attention to the fishermen as regards the sea birds that were slaughtered as they slept in the night out on the bare lonesome rocks.

An Luathóg — The Eel (young) — *Anguilla anguilla*

The *luathóg* belongs to the eel family and a certain type is found in freshwater pools or in streams or in any place where there's some freshwater, and another type is found in saltwater pools on the shore. They're not any one colour; those nearest the sand are whiter than those found in mud. Some of them are about seven or eight inches long. They are good bait when the skin is peeled off, especially the bright yellow one that's found near the sand; it attracts fish no matter how clever the fish are. There's no easier way to catch them than this; if there's a stream flowing into the pool where you wish to catch them, stop it flowing by placing scraws and other such things in it and baling it dry. You will then see the young eels exposed, writhing and making rings of themselves and trying to hide under the sand and the small stones. As they are very slippery, you need to place the blade of a knife gently on them to catch them or to have some sand so as they don't slip through your fingers while putting them in a container.
They're often given to calves as a cure for the murrain. Nine or ten are put swimming in a bottle. The neck of the bottle is then placed in the mouth of the animal and they go back into its mouth with the flow. Sometimes they do no good and in that case the animal is given another bottle. I often saw them curing animals. It's said that the fish are best in spring for that sort of thing.
During dry weather some pools often dry up and the young eels are very clever as they leave them at night and swim through the grass to the pools that have water. But they can live a long while without being in water at all. It's said that they are created from the hairs of some animal. I often saw those hairs with eyes on them writhing about under the stones in the pools. There's no doubt but it's a strange thing. These small ones are not eaten in *Maínis*. Indeed, the people have a fear of and an aversion to them, and maybe without reason. A traveller who came around once said they were good for sick people as well as for animals. Not much notice was taken of him. I suspect fear prevented anyone from trying them. They are also used for long-line bait. They are cut into pieces and put crosswise back to back on the big fishhooks for the deep. They're excellent for attracting cod, haddock, pollack and the pollack could attract a skate or a halibut.

An Eascann [41] — The Eel / The Conger Eel — *Anguilla anguilla* / *Conger conger*

It's said there are few fish in the sea that don't go asleep at night except for the eel. It can be easily recognised, as it's long slender and slippery with a long dorsal fin stretching from its neck to the tip of its tail and around under its belly as far as its navel, dark above and pale yellow below, a wide mouth and a mouthful of sharp teeth that can cut anything it meets on the sea bed. Some are quite big. I often saw some seven or eight feet long.
When we were out with long-lines we'd catch a lot of them near the rough ground. They like rocky places with clefts. They ruin much of the long-line because of their continuous coiling and twisting about. They add and remove twists to and from every snood and line with their prancing about and some of them take away the hooks and snoods. You need

[41] The name *eascann* includes both eel (*Anguilla*) and conger eel (*Conger*). Most of the description above refers to the conger (length of seven or eight feet, long-line fishing at sea and entering lobster pots)

to shove a stump of a stick into their mouths when removing them from the long-line. It's a strong cursed fish and it wouldn't be in the least bit surprising if it caught your hand with its sharp teeth, but as long as the stick is in its mouth it can't do any harm. They're a good tasty fish fresh or salted and there's a great demand and a premium price for them on fish markets.

They're very difficult to catch with nets, as it's said that they can pull their whole body through any space where their tail fits. They often go into lobster pots and when they've eaten the fish bait they pass out cleverly again tail first and they prise the battens apart leaving a window on the pots as a sign for the fishermen that they've been around.

They also kill the lobsters in the pot and therefore the lobster fishermen hate them because of the damage they do. They can often be found on low tides in clefts on the shore. They are very difficult to chase out of their hides as the mouth of the hole is very narrow and it's far back in the cleft. You would need a spear or a gaff to wage war on it. There are few hides in which it is found that there isn't an escape exit for it if cornered. It's a very intelligent fish when it comes to saving itself and when put to the test is a cursed cross fish to fight.

It appears they can stay alive for quite a while out of water, as many of the hides haven't a drop of water for an hour of the ebbing tide and another hour at the start of the flowing tide. There are several types of them but the one called the conger is the biggest near the shores of Connemara. They are all a slippery tribe of fish. It's often said, *"Is é greim dhriobaill na heascainne a bhí agam air"*(It's a grip of an eel's tail I had on him)

An Ronnach Spáinneach [42] The Garfish *Belone bellone*

Many mackerel are found on the coast of Connemara. They're taken with nets. There are spring mackerel and autumn mackerel. It's said that the spring mackerel are blind because they don't take the bait. They have some film on their eyes.

An Breac Eitill [43] The Atlantic Flying Fish *Cheilopogon heterurus*

It's wonderful how nature bestows upon some of the fish a way to defend themselves from their enemies. This facility was not denied the flying fish. It's my opinion that it's the winner when it comes to confusing the enemy, as it can spread its long wide fins and make wings of them and fly like a bird in the air if any enemy tries to corner it under

[42] Though the author gives no description of *An Ronnach Spáinneach* above, everyday usage and historical references identify it as the garfish. The name *ronnach spáinneach* literally means Spanish mackerel. The Spanish mackerel (*Scomber japonicus*), however, is a member of the mackerel family and is rare in Irish coastal waters. The garfish, on the other hand, is a member of the needlefish family (*Belonidae*) and is common.

[43] Records of flying fish in Irish waters are very rare. Although *Exocoetus volitans* has been recorded off the coasts of Cork and Waterford in the 19th century it is thought that these were more likely to have been examples of *Cheilpogon heterurus*. The author's description of the action of the flying fish is very accurate – the fish begins its launch below water and comes through the water surface at about 60 kmph using its tail to give it additional momentum. It then expands its broad pectoral fins and these are kept stiff while it glides through the air. When it begins to lose speed and drop back tail-first towards the surface the caudal fin is vibrated rapidly on the water surface to give it another lift-off.

water and it has no other means of escape. One afternoon when I was off *Na Sceirde* in the *púcán* looking for wrack, I got a good view of one of them. It rose up under the bow of the boat on the lee side. It rose in the air and moved forwards at the same time until it reached about three yards high and it started coming down until it fell in the sea about twenty yards from where it arose. I didn't notice it moving its fins at all, they were stretched out from its side in one position for the duration of the journey, but I seemed to have noticed that the tail quivered and moved as it arose. There was a slight south- westerly wind and it moved with a following wind. I think that if there were a strong wind it would be a great help, and it could stay longer in the air. It's not big – that one was about six or seven inches, white, and looking very much like a gurnard. I saw some of them again near the coast of America when I was out on the sea during the evening.
Old fishermen told me that they often jump clean into the boats as they have no independence and no means of steering themselves. Killing themselves on the deck of a boat when escaping from the enemy under the surface of the waves is akin to going from the frying pan into the fire.

An Ghlasóg — The Coalfish — *Pollachius virens*

The coalfish resembles the pollack a lot as regards shape and structure. The coalfish is blacker in colour and it's bigger. It's a hungry voracious fish and there's no time it prefers to take a bait than at night. The flesh isn't too good to eat, as it's a bit rough. Some of them are salted for the winter and when they're dry and preserved they're not as untasty. Often when we were fishing off the shore we would catch the odd one and it's a wild irascible fish to haul from the weed-covered bottom. They arrive from the west in plentiful shoals in summer and they feed themselves on mackerel and other small fish. So many of them arrive in some places that they are named after them, as *Aill na nGlasóg* and so on. The female spawns at the beginning of summer a good bit off the shore.

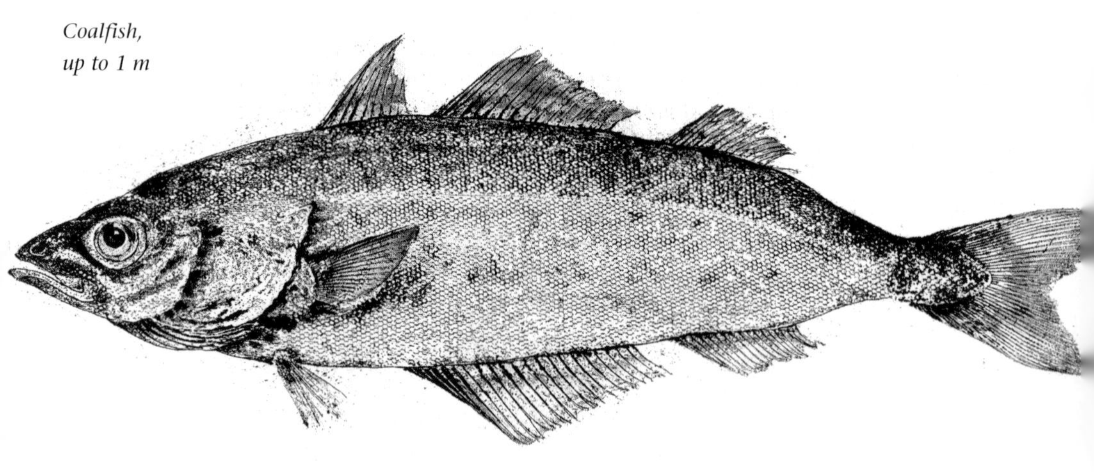

Coalfish,
up to 1 m

An tSnáthaid Mhara — The Pipefish — *Syngnathus sp.*

These come in from the deep at the beginning of summer. They're often found amongst the mayweed when it's thrown ashore by the churning of the sea. Indeed, it's a strange fish, four or five inches long, narrow like the dragonfly, a hard and shell-like skin, especially towards the front. It's good pollack bait and during the period when it's found a lot of other shoals come in from the sea. They follow each other, and not from love of one another, because during the journey, there's plenty of fighting and killing, one living off the other. The smaller ones lose out. The strong have no pity on the weak.

An Colmóir — The Hake — *Merluccius merluccius*

When we were out on the deep with long-lines we would catch an odd hake on the hook. They're not very abundant on the coast. It appears that itself and the cod and the haddock are all members of the same family as they have several similarities. They all live on the weed-covered bottom a good bit offshore. The hake has a coat of wide scales. Its back is coloured brown spotted with black and its belly coloured white, two dorsal fins, a small fin beside its neck and a long fin from there back to the tail and another long fin from under its belly which goes back to the tail also. It has a set of sharp teeth and it often wreaks havoc on other fish with them. Mackerel and herring get a bad time from it and from cod and spurdog also. No hake is as good to eat as a cod. Not many are caught off the islands of Connemara.

An Langa — Ling — *Molva molva*

The ling is not unlike the eel. It's a long narrow slippery fish with few scales, two dorsal fins, a short one forward, another long one back to the tail and another on its belly going back from its middle. They are normally coloured yellowish brown with a white belly, though their colour depends on the sea bottom where they live, as with other fish. We often caught ones on long-lines that were five feet long from the barbel on its chin to the tip of its tail. They're found quite commonly off *Carraig na Meacan* and west of *Carraig na Meacan* and *Dúleic*, in up to and above forty fathoms of water. It's a good fish and sweet, fresh or salted. They're in great demand on fish markets. The crew of a boat which would catch a few after a night's fishing would have no cause for complaint. There's no doubt that cod, eels, halibut and other fish are found where the ling lives. There are two types of ling common on the coast of Connemara – the *Langa Gorm* ("Blue Ling") and the *Langa Carraige* ("Rock Ling").[44]

[44] The author may be referring to the blue ling *Molva dypterigia,* which is normally found offshore in deeper water on the continental shelf and slope. The rock ling referred to may be one of the species of rockling or forkbeard found in inshore waters and on the shore, such as *Gaidropsarus sp., Ciliata mustela, Enchelyopus cimbrius* and *Phycis blennoides*. Any one of these, however, is normally called a *donnánach.*

Hake,
up to 1 m

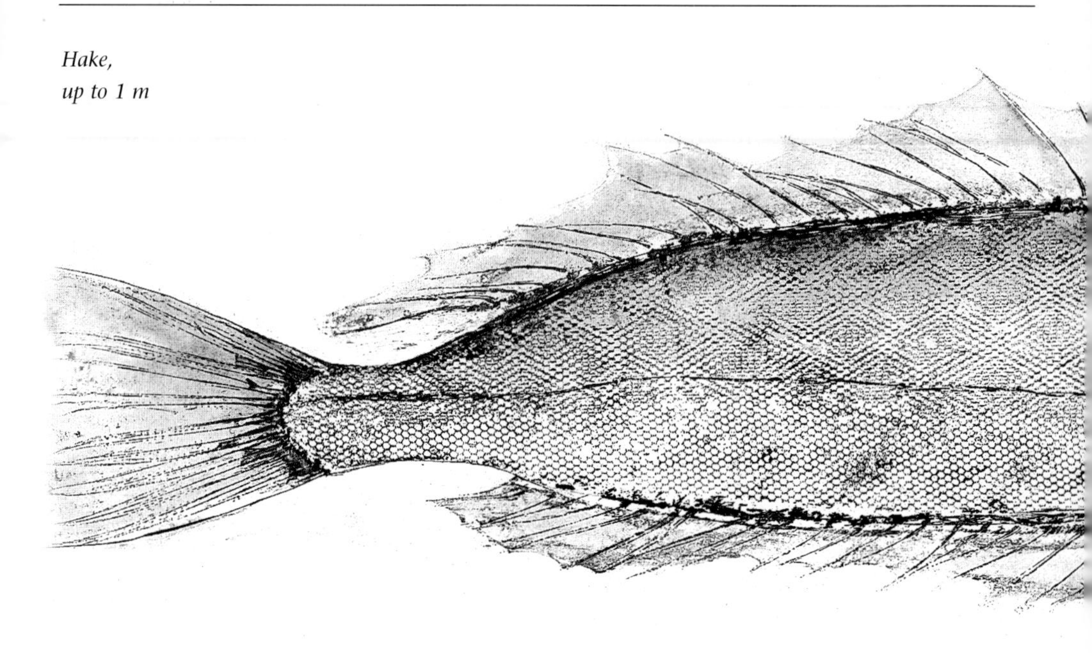

An Chadóg The Haddock *Melanogrammus aeglefinus*

The haddock is not unlike the cod, but there's a black spot as if you placed the centre of your thumb on the shoulder of the haddock and a narrow black line back on the side as far as the tail, its back yellow-brown and its belly white.[45] The haddock is very sweet to eat. Many are caught on longlines and in trawls and some are also caught on hand lines. They are often salted and dried for the winter. It's said that it's the mark of the top of St. Peter's thumb that's on the haddock from the time long ago when he was fishing. The haddock feeds itself on other small fish and on shellfish. There's a lot of roe in the female and she spawns at the beginning of summer. Indeed, if every grain of it matured, haddock would be plentiful, but they have many enemies. But that's the way with all sorts of fish. There's another type called the Norse haddock.

An Trosc The Cod *Gadus morhua*

There are few fishes in the sea better or more beneficial than the cod. It's said that they used be fished in olden times a long way to the west, and that was no wonder, a fish as valuable as that which has such strong healthy tasty flesh. Not only that but the oil which is extracted from its liver which has a balm and healing qualities in it for those of the human race who are unfortunate enough to be stricken with asthma and coughing and other such illnesses.

The big boats that scrape the sea bottom take a lot of them in their trawls and many are also caught out on the deep with long-lines and hand lines. "Fishing from land" is what fishing with hand lines is called. The boats which search them are hove to, that is to say

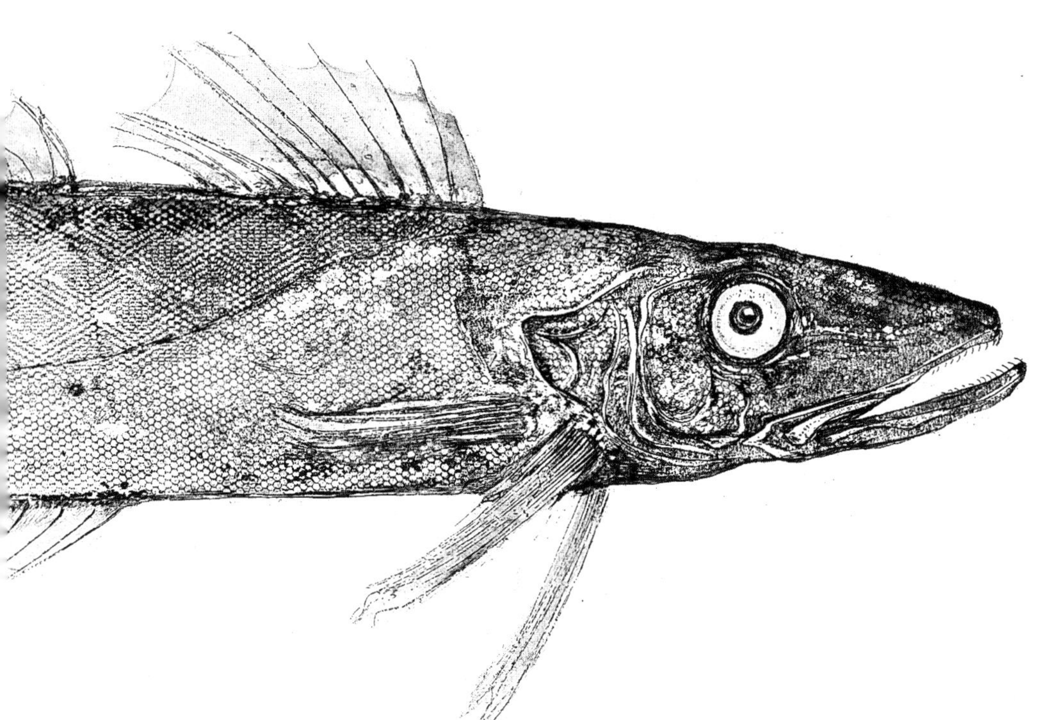

the sails hauled in tight and the head of the boat very close to the wind. But if there wasn't much wind the head of the boat wouldn't be that close to the wind, the sails would be let out a bit and they would lay off the wind so as the boat would have a small amount of speed. If there were three people in a boat "fishing from land", one of them would be on the helmsman's seat, one on the aft beam and one on the mast beam. The cod normally lives between thirty and forty fathoms deep at the edge of a weed- covered reef or between the reef and a rough sandy bottom. They are often to be found beside arches, that's to say the holes between the reefs, some of them ten fathoms deeper than the top of the reef. The head of the hand line has a ball of lead about two pounds in weight, three fathoms of snood from the ball, a hook and a bait of sand eel or a young eel or a gunnel. When the boat arrives at the fishing ground the fisherman removes the snood from the ball of lead and puts a bit of grease (butter or lard) on the lead. He then lets out the lead into the sea and lets out the line until the lead reaches bottom and when it does he hauls it up again. He'll know then what kind of a place the sea bottom is, because if there's sand attached to the lead it's a sandy bottom. He'll know whether it's rough or smooth sand, red or light coloured or black. On the other hand, if the lead comes in clean it's a seaweed-covered bottom or a rocky place. He feels too with his hand whether it's a soft or hard bottom, that is, when the lead hits against it. When they're fishing they let down the line at first to the bottom and then take it up a couple of fathoms and they pull it up and down at the side of the boat like that until the cod takes the bait. It's quite a nasty fish to pull in, and if there's a big one it's necessary to gaff it on the surface as it's heavier when hauled out of the water, and there would be a risk of breaking the snood or the knot and that it would take off.

It's said that when bad weather comes the cod takes on a ballast of small stones to keep itself settled on the reef when the weather is very rough, in winter at least. After a bad night, a sea swell or a thunderstorm a cod is often found ashore and when opened its belly is found to contain lots of small stones.

An Troscán Stopóige | **Pouting** / **Poor Cod** | *Trisopterus luscus.* / *Trisopterus minutus*

This is another type and it's like a cod except that it's neither as big nor as fat. It's often taken in nets on deep seaweed-covered reefs. Indeed, this fish is not as good as the fish with the big mouth.

An Mangach | **The Pollack** | *Pollachius pollachius*

The pollack is a widespread fish and a lot of them are caught on the shores of Connemara. It's a good fish, both fresh and dry. The pollack resembles the coalfish a lot. Its back is coloured a dark green, and its belly a white mixed with yellow. Indeed, it's a nice fish after being taken from the hook, but its colour changes after death like every other fish. Many are caught on this shore in summer and autumn. It's a nice tasty fish when fresh and it's not bad either when salted. Many are caught in trammels and they're also caught from boats moving with a little speed. They feed on sprats, pilchard, sand eels, gunnel and eels and they also eat mayweed in May. They spawn during spring on the deep – in about fifty fathoms. Oil, which is very useful for many things, is extracted from their livers. It's put in wool and it's said there's nothing as good as it for putting on shoes to give the leather long life. It's also said that it's good for curing cows of illnesses such as coughs and the like.

An Faoitín | **The Whiting** | *Merlangius merlangus*

The whiting is silver coloured except for a small dark spot on the pectoral fins. They come in from the sea in plentiful shoals at the beginning of summer. They're very voracious fish and do a lot of damage to herring and mackerel. They normally live near the bottom and therefore a lot are taken in trawls. They're also caught on hand lines. They're nice tasty fish to eat and they're much sought after at fish markets. It seems as if they were highly regarded even in the old days as the poet sang their praises. Here's a verse:

The basking shark's a good fish for the fishermen of Galway
But the whiting's much better for it earns good money always
And it's whiting tooranoo and it's whiting tooranarum
It's whiting tooranoo, it earns good money always.

[45] The "thumbprint" on the side of the fish resembles that on the John Dory (*Zeus faber*), to which the legend associated with St. Peter normally applies. The John Dory is called "Saint-Pierre" in France and the haddock is called "faux Saint-Pierre" in parts of France. The 'Norse haddock' mentioned is possibly the Norway haddock or Red Fish, which is not a member of the cod family.

An Bolmán | The Scad or Horse-mackerel | *Trachurus trachurus*

The horse-mackerel is almost the same shape as the mackerel except that the horse-mackerel has a lot of scales and some of them standing on their edges. They arrive on the coast in the mackerel shoals and many are caught in mackerel and herring nets at the end of summer and the beginning of autumn. Many are salted for winter and they're a good and nice fish, fresh or salted. They have a lot of roe and spawn from June to the beginning of August. They have very big eyes and someone with big eyes is often addressed as *"a shúile bolmáin"*.

An Bran | The Red Seabream | *Pagellus bogaraveo*

A large amount of seabream is caught on hand lines at the end of summer and the beginning of autumn on the breakers off the shores of Connemara. They stay mostly around the shallows after coming in from the deep sea because it's there that food is most plentiful for all sorts of fish as well as the seabream. Some of them are about one foot in length and others are even longer than that. There's more than one type of them. They can be recognised from the large number of scales on them. There are few fish more scaly than it, as it has a couple of layers and they're as dense as you've ever seen. Its back is usually yellow brown and its belly a shiny white, yellow rings around its eyes and soft thick lips. Its fins have a lot of sharp spines and the fisherman needs to be careful removing it from the hook and if he isn't he'll know all about it. When they arrive below a boat many of them can be caught. They're very hungry and voracious for the bait and it will be swallowed as soon as it hits the water. You must be very careful when hauling it in because if you haul it too strongly you'll break it's grip due to its soft thick lips and

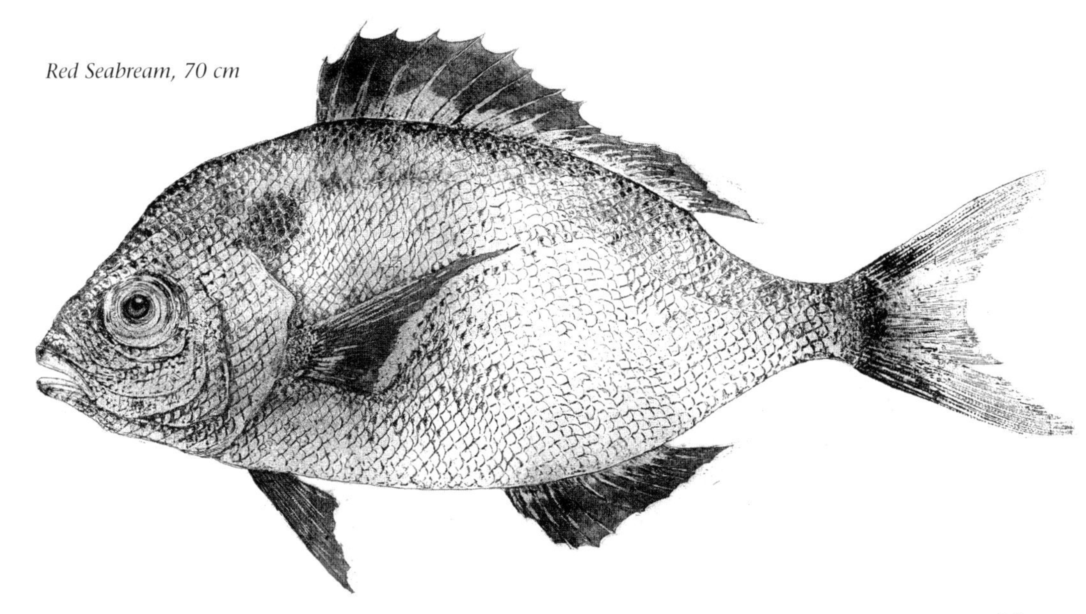
Red Seabream, 70 cm

you'll lose it. I remember well the first night I went fishing it, that at first I was losing them for quite a while – as I had too tight a grip on the line and I was hauling them too strongly, but experience taught me the trick eventually, that is to haul them in gently. They don't stay long in any one place as they always come and go with the turn of the tide. Fishermen often throw out broken rotten crabs to entice them to the place. But if spurdog or tope arrive the seabream must be left there as they can no longer be fished. They're nice fish fresh or salted. A lot are dried for the winter and there's no dish as nice or as sweet as them when they're salted, dried and preserved properly.

An Ballach [46] **The Wrasse** **Family *Labridae***

The wrasse are very abundant on this western coastline. Indeed, there's hardly any other tribe of fishes as plentiful as them. It's easy enough to recognise a wrasse from any other fish, that is by their shape and colour. There's a big soft thick lip covering the bright dense set of teeth. Aren't they the nice teeth? Isn't it often said to someone with a fine set of teeth *"is cosúil le fiacla ballach iad "* (they're like the teeth of wrasse)? There's no colour in the rainbow that isn't to be seen in its perfectly arranged coat of scales, as arranged and even as the slates on the roof of a house, as if one had started back at the tail and overlapped them out to the lips. By running your hand back on it you would not know it had any scales, it would be that slippery. But you couldn't rub your hand forward from the tail because the scales would stand on their edges against you. It will be understood that nature requires that – like the bird moving through the air – so the fish can be ploughing the seas without hindrance.

There are lots of kinds of wrasse; the *ballach breac, ballach Muire, ballach cuaiche, ballach fuarleice, ballach meilsceánaigh* and *the bochar.* The wrasse spawn in summer and they make nests in the clefts of the rocks from anything they come by. But they usually use red seaweed, oarweed and sea belt outside, and *cáilthíneach* and sea moss inside. The eggs of wrasse are often seen attached to *cáilthíneach* when it's thrown ashore. It's said that the age of the wrasse can be determined on the scales, that is, according to the small rings on the scale, and also that the old wrasse are toothless. The wrasse that are between small and big, that is half-grown wrasse, are called *bromóga*. It's a very greedy and hungry fish and it often dies as a result of its appetite. It feeds on mussels, winkles, lugworms, and on green crabs and red crabs, but it's necessary to remove the shells from them for bait. Fishing wrasse is nice work and many of them are caught off rocks with fishing rods and hand lines. Most people fish for them from boats, out on the deep and weed-covered bottom (but not too deep, about five fathoms). But they're not found everywhere.

There might only be the length of the boat between a place that's full of them and a place where there would be nothing. That was often proved before. Take for example a boat with two men in it on the wrasse fishing ground, one man sitting on the aft platform and the other man sitting on the fore beam; the man on the aft platform hauling as hard as he can from the weedy bottom, and the man up forward not getting any bite as if his line were cast into the middle of a peat bog. But if the turn of the anchor rope were taken off the fore *mullard* and a few fathoms of slack given to the rope there would be a different story. The two mens' shoulders would then be shaken with a message from the bottom and the gunwale of the boat would resound and there would be the blood of wrasse as well. The wrasse, therefore, probably have dwelling places as does every kind of fish on the sea bottom, just as every tribe on the surface of the earth. On wild rough shores with mussels they move up with the tide eating mussels and other small worms, and when it begins to ebb they move down again. But they don't all go to the bare rocks, as some always stay in the weed-covered bottom. They're different to the others. The wrasse on the bare rocks are fatter and darker in colour, almost like the mussel-covered rock. People like very much to fish on the bare rock. There's a snood on the hand line and nine or ten fathoms are thrown out on the rock. When the wrasse then takes the bait it draws the line until it runs out of the fisherman's hand and he'll then take it aboard without delay.

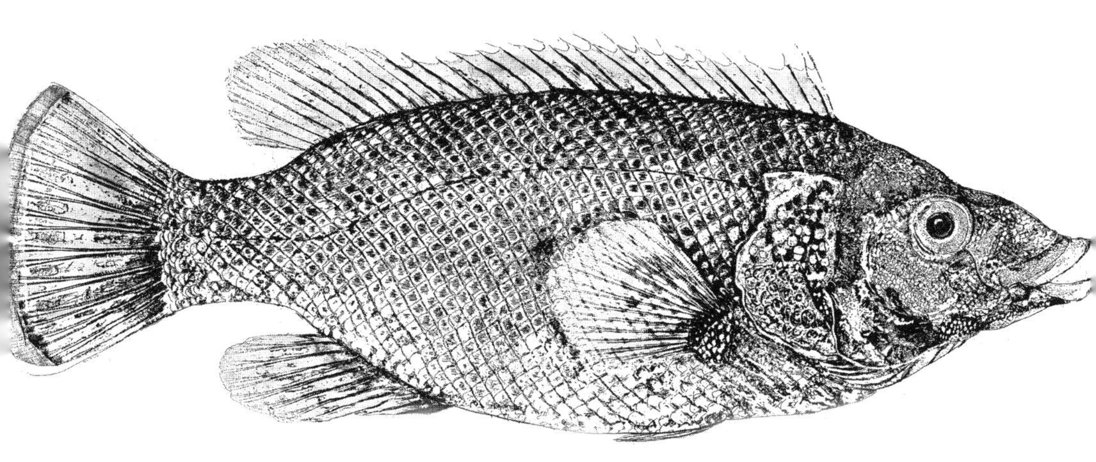

Ballan Wrasse, 40 cm

[46] There are nine different names of wrasse given by the author – *ballach breac, ballach buí, ballach Muire, ballach cuaiche, ballach fuarleice, ballach meillsceánaigh, ballach stopóige, bochar* and *bod gorm*. Four species are common on the west coast – ballan wrasse, cuckoo wrasse, corkwing and goldsinny. The rainbow wrasse and rock cook have also been recorded off *Maínis*. Wrasse are characterised by a variation in appearance and colour according to the time of year and to courtship, and the males and females are often differently marked. There are a number of hermaphroditic species that start life as females and then, as they age, change their sex to become males. While this is a familiar condition in invertebrates it is less common in vertebrates such as fish. An indication of the species described above can be gleaned from the descriptions, current and recorded use of names and the author's notes published elsewhere:

ballach breac	ballan wrasse	*Labrus bergylta*
ballach buí	goldsinny	*Ctenolabrus rupestris*
ballach Muire	cuckoo wrasse	*Labrus mixtus*
ballach cuaiche	cuckoo wrasse	*Labrus mixtus*
bod gorm	probably the male cuckoo wrasse	
ballach fuarleice	rock cook	*Centrolabrus exoletus*
bochar	corkwing wrasse	*Crenilabrus melops*
ballach meillsceánaigh	literally eel-grass wrasse	species not identified

Here's a description of some other types of wrasse: the *ballach buí* lives mostly in the weed-covered bottom and they're almost the same colour as the tops of the sea rods, that is the dark yellow seaweed that grows in the same place that they live. The *ballach Muire* is not very widespread. They live on deep weed-covered bottoms. The *ballaigh fuarleice* and the *ballaigh stopóige* are not the same colour. The *ballaigh fuarleice* are dark, almost black. They're the same colour as the slab or the rock on which they live, as for example, the *ballach fuarleice* when it goes into the weed as the tide ebbs. They're fatter also than the wrasse that don't move out of the weed, because they eat the mussels that grow on the flat rocks. The wrasse that lives in the eel grass and is called the *ballach meilsceánaigh* has big wide scales, dark green in colour, the colour of the eel grass in which it lives. It's not as nice to eat as the *ballach fuarleice*. The *ballach breac* lives in the weed-covered bottom, although the odd one sometimes goes on to the flat rock. Indeed it has a nice colour. It has all the colours of the rainbow after being taken from the sea. Some of them are very big. The *leathracha* described above are level weed-covered bottoms without hills or valleys. There are sea rods and red seaweeds growing on them. The same red seaweeds are also called *leathracha*, i.e. the name of the place in which they grow. [47] Some of the *leathracha* are very wide and quite long as well, like a big field, perhaps four or five square miles. *Leathrach Mhór Sceirde* is that big. The *leathrach* has no crest. Where crests are found is not a *leathrach* but a breaker. Those crests break early when there's any swell in the sea, but the *leathracha* don't break unless the sea is in a mad rage altogether. There's another type *Crenilabrus rupestris*, and it's called a *bochar* around here.[48] It's not very big and it lives in the weed-covered bottom.

An Bod Gorm — The Male Cuckoo Wrasse — *Labrus mixtus*

There are few fish as widespread as wrasse. In summer and autumn the places near the shore are full of them. Many are caught on hand lines and in nets during the season to be eaten fresh or to be salted and dried for the winter. They are lazy slow-moving fish in their own kingdom and spend a lot of their time asleep in their dykes. I often saw them on moonlit nights when we were foraging, lying back on their sides, dozing between the stones in the pools in such a way that we could catch them without any hurry. It's said that there's hardly any fish in the sea that doesn't take a nap at night but the eel. It's said that even the mackerel, albeit the fastest fish, takes a nap while hurrying.

The male cuckoo wrasse takes the prize for laziness and for sleep. Unless the weather is very fine, it can't be seen at all, but the female wrasse keeping it fed and comfortable. They're plentiful in certain places such as *Maidhm na mBod Gorm* and other such places. They have to feed themselves in such patches as the other wrasse aren't so plentiful to look after them. It's said that when the male cuckoo wrasse get older the strong young ones chase them away from the other weed-covered bottoms. Then they have to join forces and stand their ground in strong numerous bands, and that's probably why they're more plentiful in some areas than in others.

They're no good to eat. It's a strong firm fish about seven or eight inches long and almost the same width. It has a blue colour spotted with yellow and dark green, a small head and a big belly, a big dorsal fin and a small fin beside the tail. They're not at all bad as pot bait, once they're well rotted as the lobster isn't at all squeamish.

Male cuckoo wrasse aren't caught much by hand, as they don't like to catch any bait when they're swimming about on their own. The day that one of them can be caught is not a good day for fishing. On days when I was fishing I often saw the wrasse lazily entwining themselves between the sea rods, sometimes swimming to their tops and nosing about on the fronds as if they were trying to stand on their heads. On a dead calm day like that the male cuckoo wrasse would usually take your bait. If it does so, wind in your hand line, haul it up, raise your sails and make for home, unless you want to waste the day. There's many a day that a fisherman catches nothing; nevertheless hope always beats strongly in his heart and he hopes to God that if he doesn't succeed one day he will the next. It's a risky business; it's said "*má mheathann tú téirigh ag iascach*" (if all else fails go fishing)

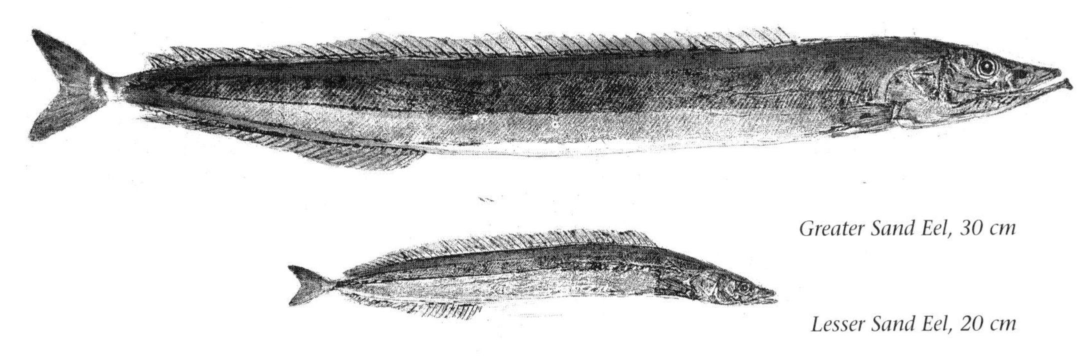

Greater Sand Eel, 30 cm

Lesser Sand Eel, 20 cm

An Scadán Gainimh — The Sand Eel — *Ammodytes sp. Hyperoplus sp.*

They come in from the sea at the end of spring and again in the autumn in plentiful shoals. There are few times in the year when some of them aren't to be found on the beaches; that means that some of them stay near the strand all the time. There is more than one type to be found. The shoals that come in the spring have fish about a foot long and very fat, in their prime, the females full of roe. The autumn shoals have smaller fish about six inches long and there are tiny ones that are little more than two inches long. Many of them come in during summer before other fish. Those big ones that come in during spring usually go to hard sandy beaches near low tide mark and the autumn fish usually prefer soft sand. Many are fished with shovels during moonlit nights, and even when the night is dark they can be seen because of the brilliance of the luminescence on them. When a shovelful of sand is turned over they start prancing about for a short while and then stay still and go into the sand if they get a chance. Their backs are sandy coloured and their bellies paler than that, the colour of the sea from the bottom – that is if you were on the bottom looking up. All fish that swim near the surface are like that.

[47] *Leathrach* is a name for the brown oarweed *Laminaria digitata,* also referred to as *coirleach* and *copóg* elsewhere in this book.

[48] *Crenilabrus melops*

They need some defensive way to confuse their enemies, as no sooner are they at the bottom than at the surface again, the herring, the mackerel, the pollack and lots of others that stay near the surface of the sea. Nature didn't forget to colour them on both sides in an appropriate way. To look into the deep water at the back of a mackerel or a herring, it's not easy to notice them, but if it turns its belly upwards it can be seen easily. On the other hand it's not easy to notice them from the sea bottom. Notice the plaice that is spotted with many colours like the sand where it lives. If it weren't for their natural defensive shades they could never protect themselves from spurdog or from other vandals that are constantly sidling about in the sea.

Sea birds such as gulls, gannets and shags that fly about looking for their chance are happy when the spurdog do the damage as they get the remains of the plunder in small pieces and those fish that are injured in the hunt come to the surface. That's when the white gulls and the shags have a feast. Isn't it strange that people who go fishing for the sand eels that are hidden in the strand know that they're in certain patches? The gulls give the game away as they walk back and forth on the beach on top of the fish getting their feed from time to time. There are few places where fish are found that the gulls don't give the game away, whether out on the strange deep, on the rocky shore or on the beach. The sand eels are a fine tasty dish when properly prepared, and therefore men, women and children don't let the opportunity slip without churning up the strand at night to collect a load of them; if it were for nothing else it's a great pastime for them and the boys and girls have great fun during the fishing season, especially when the weather is favourable, that is fine and dry and bright. Many are fished on *Trá na hAille* on the east side of *Maínis*.

Iascán an Gha Nimhe — The Greater Weever — *Trachinus draco*

This lives in shallow bays. One can often see it buried in the sand in such a way that only its eyes protrude. They're about eight inches long, a big head with two shining eyes, small dorsal fins and the fin with the sting in it at its centre; it can kill small fish with that sting. It does a lot of damage to sand eels, to shrimps, to *malraigh Cháit*, to gunnel and to many more. It can destroy fish twice its own size with a prick of the sting. It's not hunger that makes it kill some of the time, but a love of combat; that's the nature of this fellow. One day while catching sand eels on the *Ard-Trá* I saw it striking seven or eight sand eels one after the other. It was burrowing through the sand like a pig. Any one it met it knocked out. It wouldn't bring its mouth near them; which proves that it's killing is a wicked trick, like the rat killing the mouse. It's a very prickly fish to handle, and if you're not careful, you'll give it away because if it stings your hand it will give you a fright and make you shout. It's very like a bee sting except that it runs up your arm as if it were an electric current. I remember well the first day ever that one of them drove me mad with a sting. I had a blister for two days afterwards. There are some others, like a jellyfish, that can hurt a person badly, but none as vicious as this. It's no good for eating and it's not even used for bait. Indeed, no one likes to have anything to do with it. You never saw anything as amazing as the way it settles itself under the sand, with nothing visible but its eyes. They aren't around at all in winter because they retreat out onto the deep as do a lot of others. The female spawns near the shore amongst the rocks and the seaweed. During that time the male is busy with his sting chasing away any creatures that come near.

An Ronnach — The Mackerel — *Scomber scombrus*

This fish is found very plentifully on this coast in summer and in autumn. Many are caught in nets and a lot are caught even with hand lines. Indeed, it's a nice fish when it's fresh from the sea. It has a nice colour, dark green and green on its back and white on its belly. They spawn near the coast in summer, between fourteen and fifty miles from the land. It's said that they can't be caught on hand lines at the beginning of summer. But towards the end of summer and in autumn many are caught on lines. A small piece of a raw potato is a good bait, and a bit of themselves is also suitable. They're mostly fished from *púcáin* and *gleoteoga* and the boat needs to have a little speed and even still it comes from the prow of the boat when you haul it in. That's no wonder – isn't it often said that there's no fish in the sea as fast as it. There are often big shoals of them on this west coast and they come in near the shore in the autumn. Sometimes the tide ebbs away from them and they're left high and dry like heaps of seaweed on the high tide line. Lots of them came ashore a few years ago on the way to *Iorras Mór*, and they were a great boon to the local people. They're a nice fish fresh and many are also salted for the winter.

An Mac Siobháin — The Goby — Family *Gobiidae*

In the lee of the islands, away from the roughness and agitation of the waves, in a place which has a dense mat of knotted wrack and of bladder wrack covering the shore, that's where the gobies live, in the clefts and in the pools under the stones and they can attach themselves to the sides of rocks with small gripping fins on their bellies. Some off them are very small fish for there are many types, but generally they are less than four or five inches and there's no colour in the rainbow they haven't got. The most common type has a dark brown colour with patches of red and yellow, a big head and big shiny eyes on top of their heads so it can look either way at the same time, two dorsal fins with sharp spines in one of them, and there's no doubt but it's irritable and mischievous if one sets about him.
It needs to let off often as many of its neighbours are bad natured and they would prefer a good fight to anything, especially the blenny and the sea-scorpion. The three tribes mix with each other and they have many a fight and bungling when the tide rises above them. I don't know why, but it seems as if it's over food and the field of battle. The shrimps have a bad time from them as they normally feed on them. I would often come across one of their nests under a stone when I would cut seaweed, the eggs neatly placed in a limpet shell with its opening underneath and a small burrow through the sand in under it lined with some kind of lime, the goby on guard under the slope of the stone and the female bent in a coil around the nest. If an enemy comes by there's no doubt but that it will escape quickly rather than stand up and fight. In spring the seaweed harvesters catch a lot of them, as they make a very tasty meal when other fish are scarce. You need to be careful when catching them as they have sharp teeth. They also do their best to save themselves. They often hide in the clefts and under the weeds. When the weed is cut from a part of the shore they migrate elsewhere where the rock isn't bare. They aren't bad long-line or pot bait. Often on low spring tides on moonlit nights the cats go foraging, though they have no lines or hooks but only their claws. They catch a good lot of fish on the shore of every kind, blennies, gobies, scorpions and others.

An tIascán Nimhe **The Dragonet** *Callionymus lyra*

This is a fish that's not very widespread on this coast. Nonetheless, bait gatherers and winkle pickers often find them in summer under stones at the bottom of the shore. It's a nasty fish to handle, as its spines are quite sharp when it's in the water. It's almost like the seascorpion except that it's so coloured. There's no colour in the rainbow that isn't often to be found in it, and it's said that when it changes the colour of its coat that it's not a sign of good weather but of bad weather. It's coloured yellow and blue and red usually and they're usually mixed together. But whatever about its beautiful colours it's no good for the table and therefore old shore fishermen have no interest in it.

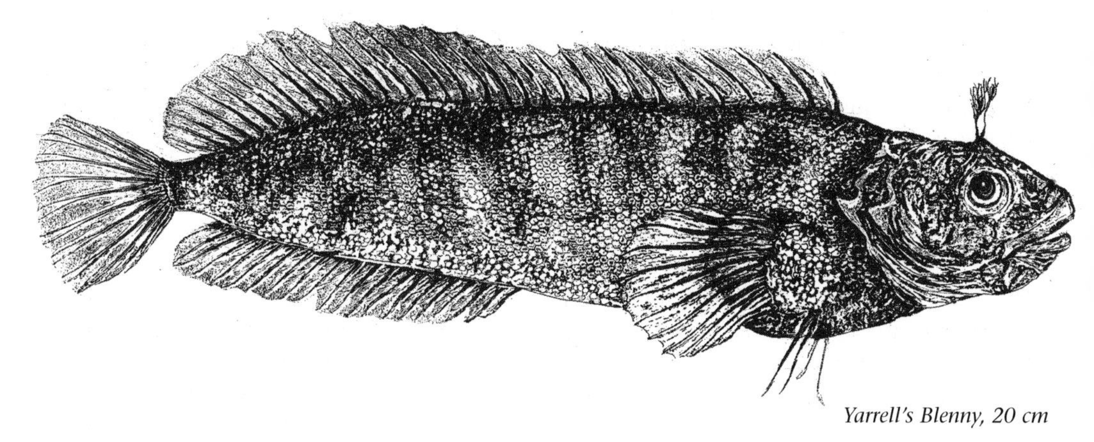

Yarrell's Blenny, 20 cm

An Ceannruán **The Blenny** Family *Blenniidae*

There are many types of blenny and they're to be seen very commonly in the pools and about the shore. It's a very tricky and clever fish. I would often fish them when I was going to school. Sometimes it would turn its cheek underneath and it would close one eye, looking at my bait with the other eye, pretending it had no interest in it. But if a *glasán* or a *malrach Cháit* or any other fish like that came near the bait, as they often do, there would be a riot. The blenny would get angry and annoyed and instead of having one eye closed as before, it would look sharply with both eyes, expand them and have a mad look in them. It would catch the small fish by the nape of the neck and I can tell you that it was in a hurry to get away when it was free of the small sharp teeth of its enemy and it would have a job to do just that. And when the blenny started to eat the bait itself it would taste it and pick at it and there was little chance of it catching the hook. Indeed, it's a good fisherman that would catch one, and indeed, if he caught one it would be a bad brat and wouldn't be satisfied until it drew blood. They often fight among themselves and it's they who snap at each other and trounce one another. And what's more, one of them keeps its head out of a cleft looking keenly at the infighting and from time to time ventures as far as the battlefield. And when it does the fighting stops for a short while, but as soon as it returns to its hide (a cleft in the rock) they start all over again. It's a fish that's not much good for eating, and they're very abundant. It has a head like a cat's and it has some of the traits of a cat as well with its bad manners. They're found in pools on low tide, on exposed shores as well as in quiet places, and when it's high tide they go up to the high tide mark and return again when it ebbs. They like a craggy shore because, when the tide ebbs, some of them stay in the cracks between boulders and they murmur to themselves just as crabs do.

An tSearróg **The Gunnel** *Pholis gunnellus*

The gunnels are not a very plentiful fish on the shores of *Maínis*. The spring and summer are the best times for them. The fishermen catch them for pollack and cod bait, and there are few bait comparable to them when skinned as they have a colourful brilliance that would entice the most clever fish in the sea. There are several types. They are almost identical. The *malrach Cháit, péist an dá shúil déag* and the *searróg* belong to the same race; there's little difference between them that's worth mentioning except that the *malrach Cháit* is bigger. It's not easy to distinguish them on the basis of shape and colour. The gunnel is long and narrow like the young eel, very slippery and full of slime. It's yellowish brown in colour with a line of black spots with white rings around them under the dorsal fin, about ten or eleven of them equidistant from one another. That's why it's called "*péist an dá shúil déag*" (the twelve eyed worm).
When I cut seaweed for fertiliser in the spring I would often notice the female in a cockle shell in a cleft huddled in a ring around the spawn, like a bird brooding over her eggs, and the other one stretched around in a ring about the shell, watching in case anything approached the nest. It's no lie to suggest that it looks after its spouse well. I wonder does it take any time off to eat its meal. I never saw one bigger than seven inches long. I don't think they grow any bigger than that. It's very hard to see them, as they are the same colour as the place in which they live. You would need a knife to lay on their backs in order to catch them as they are as slippery as a young eel. It's a nice fish and makes a fisherman happy if he catches a few of them for a day's fishing.

An Breac Giúirlinne [49] **The Barrel-Fish** *Hyperoglyphus perciformis*

The barrel-fish are strange unfamiliar fish and a lot of people are afraid of them. It is thought that the fairies have something to do with them as they're only seen in strange unnatural circumstances – on wrack, in boxes or on barrels that are covered with foot-long goose barnacles. They carry the goose barnacles between their lips like bonhams suckling a sow. The ones I saw around *Maínis* were no bigger than seven or eight inches long. Indeed most weren't even four inches and they're coloured much like the shells of the goose barnacles that are attached to them. A dark blue on top and a yellowish colour on the belly, a slimy skin with few scales, oval but somewhat flattened near the tail, fairly big eyes and soft drooping lips. It seems as if they're a strange timid race as they leave the wrack as soon as they reach land, that is if they're on the outside. But they're often trapped in a barrel or a box.
One day a large box was brought ashore on *Maínis*. Seán Antaine (God rest him) spent from early morning to the pall of night towing it shorewards after his *púcán*. It was a very

big box, about eight foot square and firmly closed each side by one and a half inch planks so that there was no way in or out for anything but water. It had a heavy growth of goose barnacles as is usual for wrack that is tossed about on the crest of the waves. When it was alongside the pier someone heard clattering and slopping of water inside. It was turned around to see if there was any hole or door on it. There was nothing but the seams between the planks that anything other than the blade of a knife would fit through. It wasn't long before a man with an axe was attacking it fearfully.
"Stay away from me", he said to the group of people crowding around him. "If it's the devil himself in it we'll have to see him without delay". While prising out the end of a plank what jumped out but a mass of barrel-fish. Some of the people on the edge of the pier got a fright and since it was night at the time and the fish were swimming at the surface, the light glistening around them from the luminescence was a beautiful sight. But one thing we all wondered about was the way they were able to enter and as they were inside there was never any way out. It was no wonder if people thought they were the fairies in the form of fish. A portent of things to come, perhaps. Others thought that since the place was very safe it was a suitable means for the female fish to put a lot of eggs in the seams between the planks. In such a place other fish couldn't get them as they're much sought after. There's no doubt but some fish are very clever during spawning. A lot of them make great efforts to save their own from enemies.

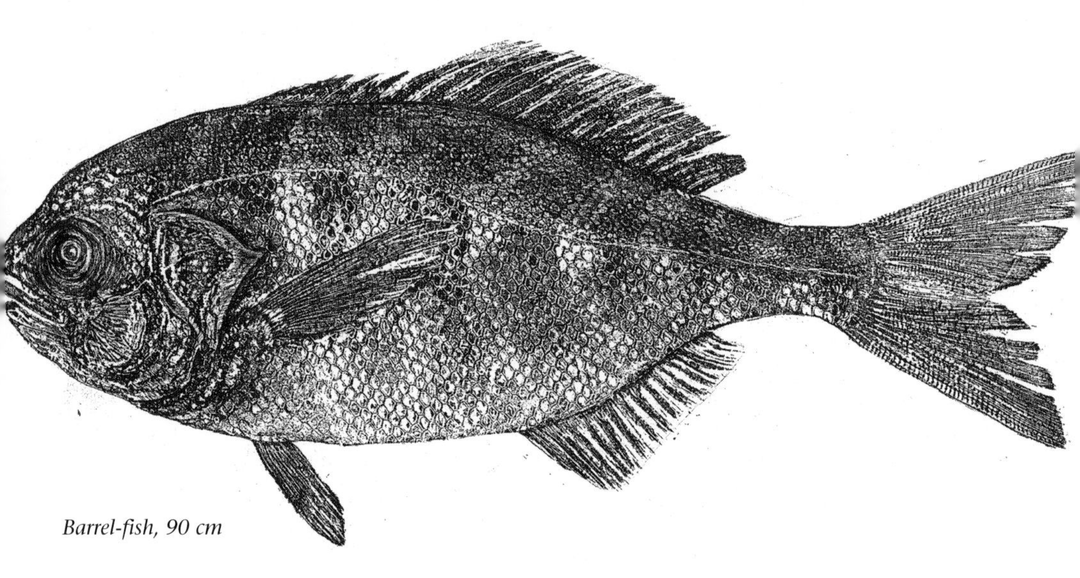

Barrel-fish, 90 cm

Another time some years ago I saw a barrel coming ashore at *Crompán an Chúir* near *Tobar Cholm Cille* (Colmcille's Well) on *Maínis*. It had a heavy growth of goose barnacles and the bung was missing, but it wasn't empty as there was a shoal of barrel-fish occupying it. They couldn't come out, as the hole was too narrow; they were swashing about. The barrel was upturned to see if they would escape from their captivity. Someone put two fingers in the hole but withdrew them quickly because one bit him and hurt his fingers. He was so angry that he caught a big stone. "Come out" he said, pushing in the head of the vessel.

He gave it another few blows until he made smithereens of it in the water. A wave came that scattered the cants and the head about the shore. The hoops rattled as they fell between the boulders. Those fish that weren't hurt went into clefts and others went out to sea. Nobody wanted anything to do with them. They doubted whether they were real and thought they had something to do with sorcery. I never heard of anyone seeing them on wrack, nor were they caught on line or in a net. I don't know if they're any good to eat; I don't think they'll be tried in *Maínis* anyway.

I remember well a fine day in autumn I was cutting seaweed on the south side of *Oileán Lachan*. However I looked out on the surface of the sea, I saw what looked like a beam coming inshore, and a flock of gulls on it, sometimes rising off it and flying amongst each other in the air, alighting on it again and pecking at each other over the barnacles. I thought it might drift eastwards outside the headland, and since the boat was on the other side of the island, I would be too late if I brought it around. There was nothing for it but to go into the water as the beam was drifting around the headland by now. There was no time to delay and I therefore let myself out into the water, a gentle breeze from the west and a flowing tide taking the beam eastwards. When I came near it the gulls left and let out a mournful complaining noise. It seems as if they didn't want to hand over possession to me. I went outside the wrack and started nudging it inwards, and as the tide was pulling me east I was moving away from the shore. I wasn't able for the strong tide; indeed I was getting rather frightened. I climbed on top of it with a leg either side and the barnacle shells quite sharp against my bare skin. It wasn't long before I felt the barrel-fish

[49] There are two different types of fish that accompany floating objects that have been recorded in Irish waters. The first is the perch-like Stone Bass or Wreck-Fish (*Polyprion americanus*), which has been recorded occasionally and caught on rod and line off the south and south-west coasts. The above description more likely resembles a second type – the Barrel-Fish *Hyperoglyphus perciformis*. The young stages of this species are typically pelagic and accompany floating objects such as wreckage and boats and are rare vagrants in the eastern Atlantic. It has been recorded off the west coast from Kerry as far north as Achill Island. . There have been occasional records in Irsih waters of another barrel-fish *Schedophilus medusophagus;* as its species name suggests; it eats the tentacles and gonads of jellyfish.

People's fear of the barrel-fish, as expressed above, has been substantiated by another account of a shoal that came ashore on Aran in 1901(Holt & Byrne 1903). The following is an extract from a letter from a Mr. Colman Costello quoted in the article: "They came after a log of timber covered with barnacles, and they were thrown ashore at the north-west corner of the South Island, where the Congested Districts Board is after building a breakwater and clearing the shore. At the time, owing to the tide being low, it was like a horse-shoe, so that if the islanders took twenty fathoms of net and put it across the entrance they would save thousands and thousands of fish; but, instead of that, when they saw the fish, from a high ledge on one side, having the barnacles like a calf would have the teat of a cow in the mouth, they all got afraid, and said they were Sheeogues and then ran away, except one old man. At the time the log struck the shore about 400 of the fish jumped on dry land, and were hopping about on the shore, so that some of them got into the water again, while others died, and were carried away by the next tide, except two that the old man took home with him. When the old man came home, and his wife and sons saw the fish, they would not allow him to take them into the house, as they never saw the like before; they were no fish, but Sheeogues resembling fish. It was from this man that Mr. Costello got them. When the log dried it appears the fish turned away to sea and scattered about. A man named ***, with another, was fishing about half a mile from the shore in a canoe, with hand lines, a few days after, and was looking out over the side as the day was bright, and saw one of these fish swimming about very near the surface. He pulled ashore, and did not go out again for three days."

attaching themselves and tickling me, one of them stuck between my shoulder blades. That's the fellow that was tormenting me and to cap it all a school of porpoises arrived, and I may tell you they weren't pleasant thoughts that crossed my mind, especially when I felt their skin rubbing both my ankles. I got the shakes when I remembered that there could even be a shark loitering about. Didn't I see one west of the island about a week ago? What would stop it? There was neither wall nor fence before it. I never heard of any mischief in the porpoises but apart from that who knows what they might think of? If they cut the legs off me wasn't it the same as if a shark did it? They passed me out and puffed as they came to the surface. I pulled myself up and tried to go on my hunkers to be safe from them. The beam rolled around and threw me head first into the sea. I tried again and again until I finally succeeded. Practice makes perfect and now I was seated on my hunkers with no worries, the beam rocking and moving, rising and falling on the crests of the waves.

A strange noise from the barnacles due to rubbing against one another and bobbing in the water, the porpoises puffing and the arch of their backs visible above the water from time to time, as if they were twisting and doing cartwheels, the gulls with their cursed screeching above me, shags and gannets diving south of me. The wind died away and therefore I didn't drift much, my cheek resting on the palm of my hand looking down at the bottom, fishes slipping lazily amongst the sea rods, moving to and fro without haste. I was thinking about the lives of fishes when I noticed the back-current was drawing me towards the shore between the two rocky points. "God help us" I said to myself "one ought to have patience". Although I was comfortable now that the fish had eased off with their play-acting, they weren't teasing me anymore. The porpoises had headed off somewhere else, as they weren't making any progress with the barrel-fish. They were too clever, hiding between the barnacles near the skin of the beam. I was so happy that I let myself down into the water and started nudging it shorewards. The fish didn't delay when it hit the shore, they let loose their grip quickly and headed off to sea. They left me wrestling with the wrack in the mouth of the waves amongst the rocks. When I put on my clothes I went to fetch the boat. I rowed around the island whistling with joy about the fine piece of wood I had got. I tied a rope to it and towed it home behind the boat. There was no sign of it being bored, and it was twenty-five feet long and a foot square, and when cut into twelve planks you never saw anything as suitable for the loft of a barn that was twenty five feet by twelve feet inside the walls.

An Lannach — The Thick-lipped Grey Mullet — *Chelon labrosus*

The mullet are abundant fish in summer. They fill the creeks and lagoons during high tide and they puddle about in the mouth of the tide. They like brackish water and for that reason they frequent the mouths of rivers and go up into pools especially if they contain brackish water. There's a brackish lake that's called *Loch na Lannach* in *Roisín an Chalaidh* and it's full of them. The female spawns during summer near the land and they all migrate together in winter to other places on the deep.

It's a wild irascible fish to catch on a hand line. It tries its best to free itself and very often it succeeds because it twists the hand line on a sea rod or on something on the bottom so as it can prise the hook from its mouth and head off again on its way. If you fish it from the shore, when you start hauling it in it dashes back and forth until it cuts the line on the sharp stones and bids you good-bye, showing that it's a very clever fish.

Nets are often set across the mouth of a creek on a low tide and when the tide rises they're raised up on stakes so as that they're like fences and the mullet above them are trapped and can't escape except for the odd one which jumps over the net fence. When it ebbs they can be picked up from the beach here and there. You need to be careful also as there are sharp spines on its dorsal fin.

They're not too nice to eat, the fish has a very heavy taste and whatever good they are they're no good for salting nor drying.

It appears that it feeds mostly on winkles and sand eels as many are found in its stomach; indeed it's a voracious hungry fish. I often saw it nosing about and digging in the mud like a pig without a ring in it, looking for food. Some of them are up to two feet in length with lots of overlapping scales covering them. Their backs are a sort of dark colour and the belly whiter. Sharp teeth and a soft palate and a rough gullet inside, two dorsal fins, sharp needle-like spines in the pectoral ones and often when I was fishing it caused me to bleed a lot when I tried to remove it from the hook, as there's no fish as wild and irascible as it when trying to capture it. They normally move about on the tides, out with the ebbing tide and back again with the flowing tide and up to the top of high tide into the lagoons, the creeks and the mouths of the rivers.

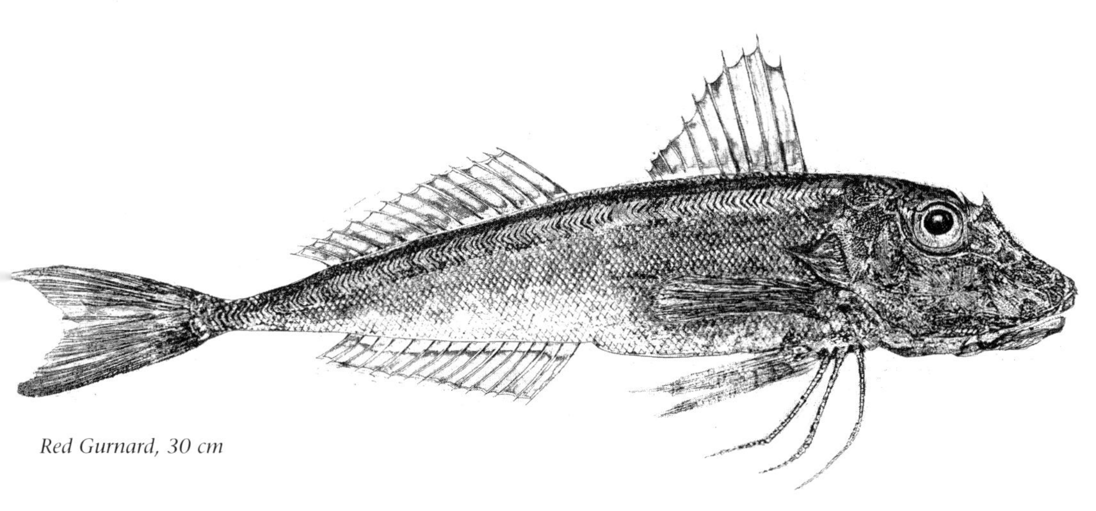

Red Gurnard, 30 cm

An Cnúdán [50] — The Gurnard — Family *Triglidae*

There are many types of gurnard. These are the ones that are common on the coasts of Connemara – *an cnúdán buí, an cnúdán dearg, an cnúdán glas, an cnúdán breac, an cnúdán soilseach,* and *an cnúdán deilgneach*. The gurnard is often described in poetry. The poet Raiftearaí mentions it in one of his songs "*Bainis an tSleachain Mhóir*". The *cnúdán glas* is a nasty fish, as it has fins that contain a lot of spines. The gurnard is a nice, mild, sweet, healthy strong fish to eat. It's said that it wasn't the fishermen who were most wanting for food during the bad times, that many fed themselves by fishing, especially by fishing gurnard. Gurnard are caught mostly by hand lines on the shores of Connemara.

An Gréasaí Cladaigh | The Seascorpion | *Myoxocephalus scorpius* *Taurulus bubalis*

This lives in clefts between rocks and under stones on rough shores. There's no doubt but it's a spiny irascible fellow. It has sharp spines on the fins like bodkins or needles and it can raise or lower them at will. If it hears an enemy coming near, it thrusts them quickly out of their sheaths and bristles with anger. It's about six or seven inches long and quite strong. It's brown with red patches, but like any others it can change colour when it wishes. They migrate to the deep in winter as nature would have it.

An Muiricín | The Armed Bullhead | *Agonus cataphractus*

The armed bullhead or pogge lives in a place where mayweed or any other weed grow together on the bottom. It's about seven or eight inches long and has a hard shell-like skin like the pipefish. Its head is like a hound's and it narrows towards the tail. It makes good use of the tail. It often twists it around a sea rod when climbing up to look for something to eat. They're no good as human food. Indeed, there aren't many to be found around the islands. They usually leave the coast at the end of autumn and migrate somewhere else.

An Leatha | The Flatfish | Order *Pleuronectiformes*

One could say that God's work is wonderful, the way the flatfish change their shape and their colour during their youth. They're like other fish originally, round, long and narrow, greyish white or white or the colour of sand or the mud where they live – that is, after being formed from the eggs and for a period of four to five weeks. After that time they gradually turn on their sides, but they stay a while on one side and at the same time the underside turns whiter and the upperside changes to the colour of the bottom, be that white, yellow, spotted, black or striped. The shape of the head changes also and the eye on the underside follows the other eye to the upper side so as both eyes are on the top. It would be no good having one eye underneath as it would have no vision with it.

I often saw hundreds of the small young flatfish on the beach east of the house. They would come in on top of the flowing tide. Some of them wouldn't be two inches long, and he who would not be in the know would swear they weren't flatfish at all but shrimps or other such fish. Another thing I noticed, there used be a wide area of stones with weed growing on them out from the head of the pier in the path of the shoals that used come into the pier. Since the weed was black and the beach white around it, there was a good view as they came through the black patch. But as soon as they changed shape and lay on their sides they didn't come that way any more but came a roundabout way. Their enemy would see them easily in the black patch but they were smart enough not to give them

[50] Six types of gurnard are mentioned by the author. Four species are common off the west coast and these are the red gurnard (*Aspitrigla cuculus – an cnúdán dearg*), the grey gurnard (*Eutrigla gurnardus – an cnudán glas*), the tub gurnard (*Trigla lucerna – an cnúdán soilseach*) and the piper (*Trigla lyra*). The streaked gurnard (*Trigloporus lastoviza -an cnúdán breac*) is also found occasionally on the coast. The author has ascribed the *cnúdán buí* to *T. lucerna in* a separate publication. The *cnúdán deilgneach* is equated with the armed gurnard (*Peristhetus cataphractum* – a species unknown in these waters) in the same publication.

that chance, as they kept to the beach that was the same colour as themselves. They're very clever fish. They often bury themselves up to the two eyes in sand so as the enemy can't notice them at all. They are caught in trawls, with long-lines and with nets on the coast of Connemara. They are a sweet and healthy fish and are in great demand on fish markets at home and abroad. The female has thousands of eggs in her ovaries and it would be no wonder if they were plentiful but very little of the fish eggs survives, as they're nice and sweet to ravenously hungry fish. There are many types of this thin flat fish to be found in the bays of Connemara. Not all of them are the same shape, the same colour nor as good to eat as one another. The types known as the turbot and the sole are supposed to be better than the flounder or the plaice or the *leatha stríocach* or the topknot. Few fish in the sea are as good as the dab for the table.

An Turbard — The Turbot — *Psetta maxima*

It's wide like the flatfish. It's often caught on longlines near the coast, but the big boats that scrape the sea bottom catch a lot of them. Most are sent to England fresh for sale on the markets and there aren't many fish on fish markets as much in demand and dearer than it. It's between one and a half and two stone in weight. It feeds on other fish, like sand eels, sprats, sole and small flatfish. Few fish in the sea have as much spawn as the female turbot. It's said that she has up to ten million eggs in the spawning season that lasts from April to June. The eighteenth century poets themselves didn't forget this tasty fish. Didn't they often write about the striped turbot? And it's no wonder, as a grander fish is hard to find on the bottom of the big sea.

Turbot, 1 m (feeds on sand eels)

An Bhóleatha **The Halibut** *Hippoglossus hippoglossus*

The halibut is not very abundant on this coast. Nevertheless, they're caught with long-lines and with trawls. They're also caught on the deep with hand lines. They're shaped like a flatfish, quite dark-coloured above and white below. The flesh is nice and tasty and it fetches a good price on the market. They're quite big and it's said some reach a length of six feet.

An Leatha Riabhach **The Dab** *Limanda limanda*

The dab is not nearly as abundant as the plaice or the *leatha dubh*. It's very like the plaice in shape – almost the shape of a plate. It's covered with small scales from the tip of the tail to the base of the gills and a border of fins encircling its sides. Dark brown mixed with yellow and white on its back, or striped, white on its belly. It doesn't grow as big as the plaice. We never caught any on the long-lines bigger than fifteen inches wide and we caught them out on the deep on fairly rough ground, where there was rough gravel and red sand with lumps of seaweed-covered rocks near enough to make us wary of following them. They have nice flesh and I think myself that it's a tastier fish than the flesh of plaice. But out into the autumn after the female has spawned they're not as good or as fat, but that's the way with nearly every fish that swims in the sea.

Lemon Sole, 45 cm

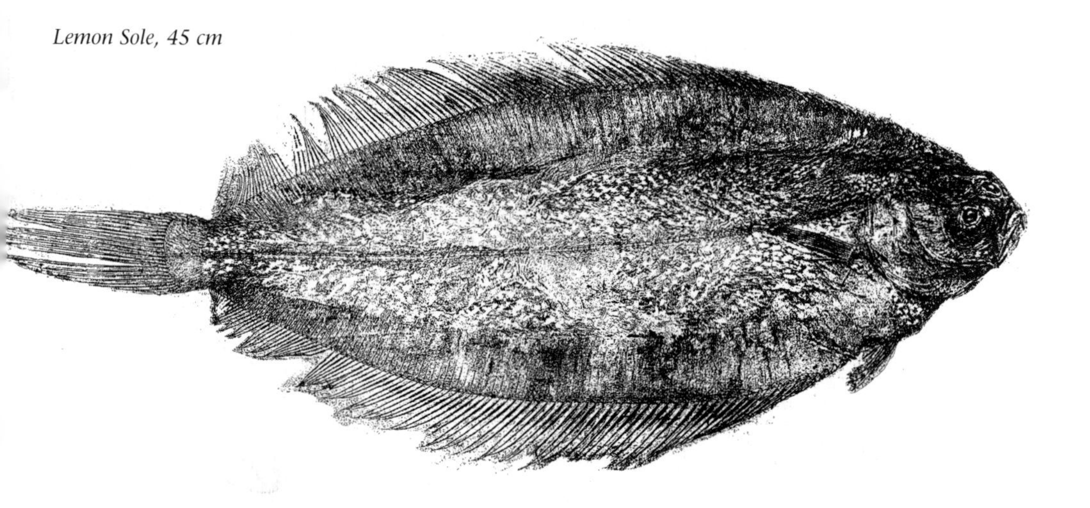

An Plás **The Plaice** *Pleuronectes platessa*

There was no flatfish as abundant on the long-lines as the plaice we would catch. It has a lovely colour and the slime of its back gives it a shine. A thin oval shape and a border of fins almost surrounding it. Its back is coloured brownish yellow and dotted with lots of red spots, its belly or more correctly its underside, white. It usually lives on white or red sand and its topside is similarly coloured to blend in. But if it hears any noise around, it buries itself in the sand, except for the mouth, the eyes and part of the top of its hard knobbly head. Some are a couple of feet in width. It's not as nice to eat as the turbot or the sole, but it's tastier and sweeter than the flounder and the *leatha leice*. It spawns in spring but it's not as nice to eat after that and neither is it as heavy nor as fat.

Plaice, 90 cm

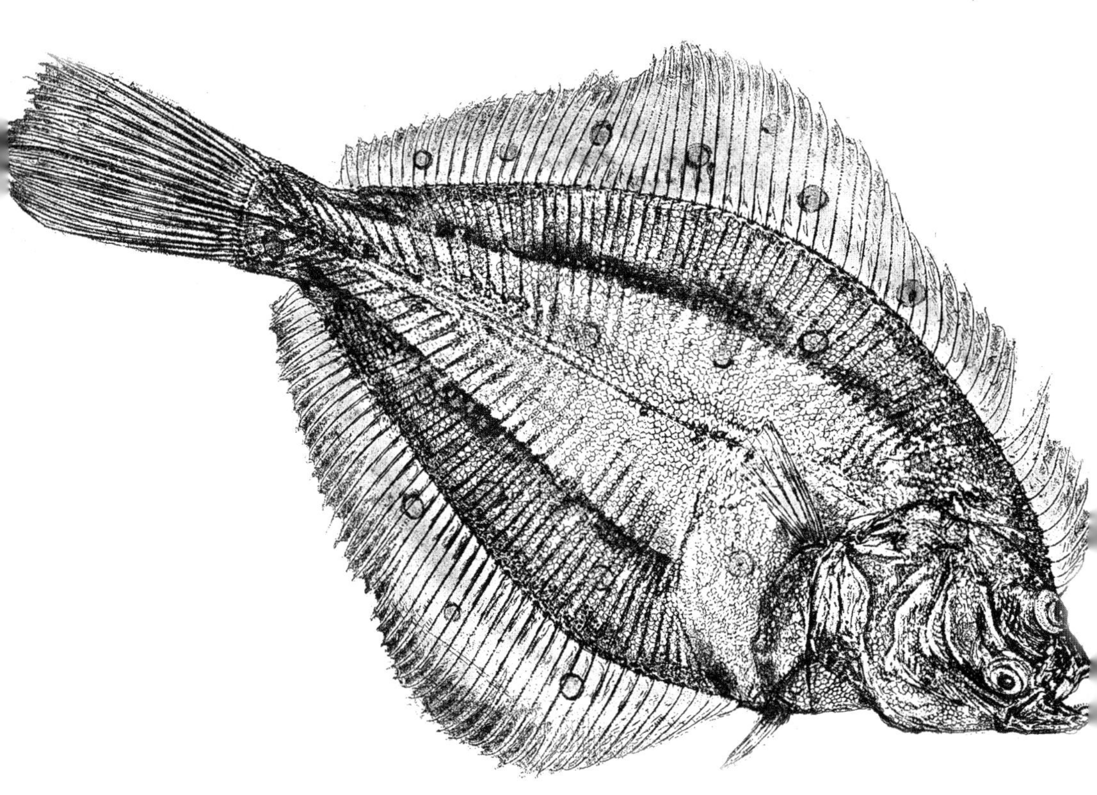

An Dúleatha — The Flounder — *Platichthys flesus*

This flatfish is white underneath and dark above. They're found commonly enough in lagoons near the mouths of rivers and in quiet shallow inlets. They normally frequent dark muddy or sandy bottoms, which would have the same colour as their backs. The flounder doesn't mind brackish water and it often goes up the mouths of rivers as far as the freshwater. They're caught with long-lines, trawls and nets in Connemara. They're not as tasty to eat as the plaice. They're the same shape, a thin oval shape and a border of fins around the edge. You can feel the scales on any flatfish by drawing your hand from its tail up along its back. They go out onto the deep in winter and the flounder occupies a dark bottom on the deep just as it does in the shallows

Common Sole, 50 cm

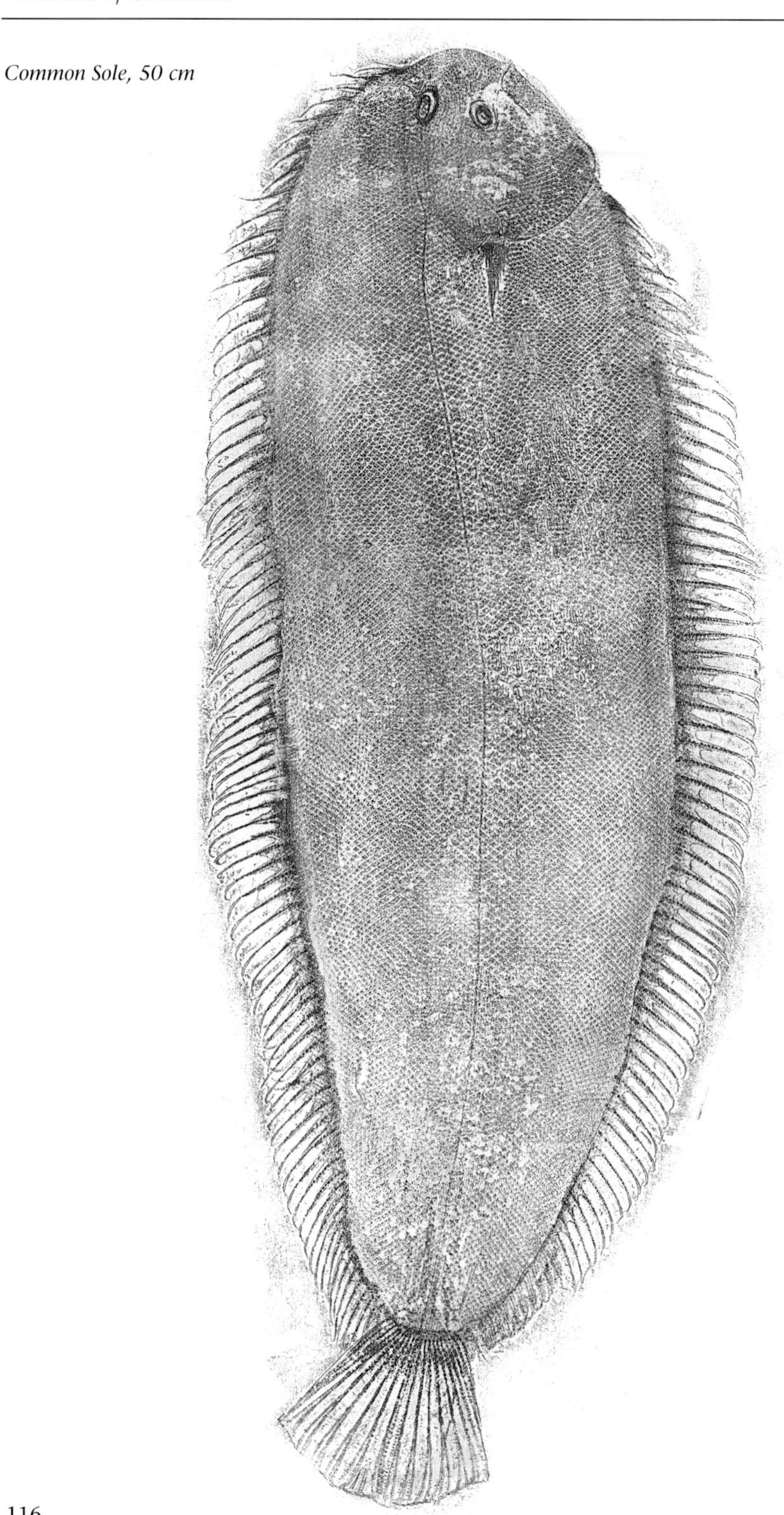

An Sól — The Common Sole — *Solea solea*

None of the flatfish tribe, apart from the turbot, is as tasty to eat as the sole; one could do with more of it. God didn't make it large. It's among the smallest of the flatfish and it's easy to recognise with its long narrow shape, like the sole of a shoe and a lacework of little fins around its edge. Brown mixed with black and yellow above and white below, but it often resembles the colour of the sea bottom where it lives. Its bones are more slender so as it can turn and bend itself in a more agile way than any other flatfish. We often caught them on long-lines near *Muic Ghainimh* and *Tonn Uí Fhloinn* – two sand banks out from *Maínis* that break during a swell. They're quite plentiful some years and other years not so. There's no bait they prefer to the lugworm and the sand eel and there are few flatfish that don't like lugworms. If the halibut is the king of flatfish in size, I think the sole family is the best for smallness and sweetness to eat, except perhaps for the striped turbot.

An Leatha Leice — The Topknot — *Zeugopterus punctatus*

This is a strange type. It lives attached to the stones near high tide. You would need a knife to remove it just as you would remove a limpet. It's round like the others, surrounded by fins, a big head and a small tail. I never saw any bigger than seven inches wide, although some may be bigger than that out on the deep. Many are caught, or removed to be more correct, when people cut seaweed for fertiliser, as they're attached to the stones under the seaweed near low tide. Grey above and pale blue below. I never saw them but attached and they increase their grip if you try to remove them, so you would have to cut the fish in order to remove it. There's no more colourful fish than them and they attached to the hard surface of the rock.

A crowd gathered on the pier in Cill Chiaráin (Kilkieran) on regatta day.

BOAT RACES IN CONNEMARA

It was a fine sunny day at the beginning of autumn, and, indeed, it was impossible to do a stroke of work. The stinging gadflies had their tongues out with the thirst, and cows with their tails curled were running and gadding about in a rage, making their way to the sea to get some respite and coolness. The granite stones were splitting in the heat, a heavy haze around the base of the sky to the west; a deaf thunder creaking and roaring now and again many miles away. The golden sun shining and beating down from the yellow-blue sky on withering lands, on big sandy beaches that were glittering and resplendent and on the sea which was as calm and even as a big glass mirror, with the reflection of the sky, the sun and the birds to be seen in it.

There were people here and there around the edge of the sea and their clothes off and pushed into a dark cleft of a rock, as it was unwise to leave any scraps of clothes on a rock or on a flag unless you wanted them to be burnt red. They were happy, gay, joyful and pleased with their carry-on; some of them puddling and paddling about as they had no swimming-stroke, some others crawling near the mouth of the tide, some others succeeding in their strokes. It had flowed a bit by now and the boats were returning from the wild rocks off the exposed shore, loaded to the gunwales with their oarweed, other boats scattering here and there out on the ocean, some of them so far out to sea that they were barely visible to the eye, like a fly out on the horizon. The crew in some of them rowing as best they could to try and approach the land while they still had the flowing tide in their favour. Other boats fishing on a cod-bank, the crew jigging with hand lines a few fathoms off the bottom and letting them down again to try and deceive the poor cod and to entice it with the fine bright bait of fresh sand eel.

"Keep at it!" now and again, a signal from the bottom that would jolt the shoulder of the man up forward. Woe is me! I who neglected to get a dark blue number six hook stuck in the upper lip of the fish with the big gob, a fish which has a cure and a healthy balm in its liver for wheezy and asthmatic people.

As the very same day was as sunny as it was, I set off swimming from *Clochar an Bháid*, as it was a heart-lifting and refreshing experience for the rest of the day to have a fine bath of salty water. When I had my clothes on after having swum as far as *Carraig na bPortán* and thrown off the tiredness and weight of the day, I headed up to *Trá na Dumhaí Bige*, and heard "scrape, scrape" coming from there in the quiet of the day. It didn't take me two shakes to approach the place where the boat was being scraped, up on two blocks such that a good sized cat would fit between the keel and the strand without touching; another block under its belly to keep it off the strand, and it keeled over from ear to tail as she would be on a very windy day on the sea with one reef in the mainsail and a deep *barróg* in the jib because of the roughness of the waves and it proudly carrying its sail.[51]

[51] The *barróg* refers to the method of reefing a jib – tying the leech and luff of the upper part of the sail together.

"God prosper ye", said I to the two who were swimming in sweat, stretched on their backs in under her cheeks, scraping weed, small limpets and anything else. The smooth skin of red deal was crinkled in spots.
"And the same to you, son" said the two of them together "isn't it a grand day?"
"Don't be talking, man," said I, "a black man wouldn't stand it".
"It doesn't matter except that we'll be burnt and roasted this evening, and what matter but the state we'll be in from the steam and the smoke from that old tar. There won't be a strip of skin on our faces nor our hands that won't be burnt"
"Ye'll be in a right mess if the steam off the tar gets in your face" said I, "ye're in for a terrible punishment. Ye're thinking about tomorrow, fair dues to ye and good luck to ye, ye're right, not like the other featherweights. Indeed, it's easy to recognise the right calibre. It's said, and it's true, that 'everything takes after its kind' ".
"Folly, folly entirely", said Seán "but well done brother, folly itself is unavoidable; its been always there and will be forever".
"What kind of talk is that?" said I, "it's not folly at all. As long as a person has his health, he shouldn't complain"
"Now you're talking", said Cóilín Mhichíl, leaving down the scraper and wiping the sweat from his face with his sleeve and pulling up his trousers and fastening his waistcord around him tightly. "What do you think of our chances"?
"You've a good chance, I'd say", said I.
"I'm afraid that if this calm persists that tomorrow's race is as far away from us as our grandfather's wedding feast" said the voice from the aft floor.

"Have courage, Seán, stir yourself and don't give in like that. The man with courage never lost it", said I, "and another thing, I don't think the day will be that quiet tomorrow. I think this is a pet of a day. That sky out there is being blown in by a south-west wind and at the break of day today there was a grumbling at *Carraig an Mhadra Uisce* caused by the high spring tide and there was a base of a big rainbow in the sea, west over *Carraig an Mhíle*.
"Bad luck to them but we're eaten by them", said Cóilín. "I think there's a change in the weather because when I was taking this out of the pier this morning, there was a big grey seal in on *Ard-Trá* and I never before saw one so far in as far as I can remember. And it's a long time since I saw Brandon as clear as I saw it at daybreak today. There's some change coming with this terrible heat; heat before rain I suppose"
"Upon my word, "said I "I don't want to take the words out of your mouth, but that old cat of ours was madly looking for a south-westerly this morning."

"Maybe it's milk it was looking for", said Cóilín, "no more than a big red cat that came around here today and started to eat the butter out of the dish. If I hadn't heard it, it would have burst" "It's a pity it didn't choke," said Seán, "as the long-line hook choked your own cat two weeks ago. There wasn't much chance of the scoundrel choking; there are plenty of ways to choke a cat besides using butter".
"We'll soon have the flowing tide in on top of us now, "said Coilin, "as a spring tide comes in fast. We're in the second day of its strength today, three days coming, three days in full strength, and three days going. I don't know if it's a big spring tide or an ordinary spring tide."

"I think the last spring tide was a big one; therefore this one is an average one. Good day to ye" said I, and went off home. They put the boat out on the water when it floated and indeed you never saw such a smooth hull. You could shave yourself in it. Everything was put in its place in the twilight. Blocks stropped. New throat halyards and peak halyards and a new tack and sheet. Soft sails lubricated with red tar and lard. The ballast fixed nicely from the baling hole up to the floor under the mast beam, and three or four bags of small stones each side of the ballast, so as they would be easily handled and possible to place up forward when the boat would be running before the wind, as the boat is better weighted down forward when running. But to make a long story short, everything was in its place by nightfall, and I can tell you that the two slept well that night, as they were very tired from the day's work.

With the dawning of the following day the two were dressed and, indeed, the morning wasn't the best either. Misty rain, and there was a strong west south-westerly wind, but at about eight o'clock it cleared up. The sun was visible by now over *Leitir Móir*. To put seven words in one, it wasn't long before its bellying sails were raised. They had a crew of four and a good crowd of people going to see the show. They hauled up on the anchor and the helmsman turned the boat to the right. The sails were sheeted in and it wasn't long before she was drawing the wind down by the flat rock of *Garraí Gainimh*. He was quite far off the wind and *Maidhm Sheáin Thomáis* put them about on the first tack. The flapping of the sails as the boat came about frightened a flock of oystercatchers that were picking food on a flat rock of dulse. There were two gulls standing on a bare rock and they didn't move; I suppose the oystercatchers remembered the big day of the swimming races the birds had a long time ago when the oystercatcher loaned the skill of swimming to the gull until Monday and the gull never repaid him. "The oystercatcher's swimming loan" is what it's called.[52]

They had a hard beat and they didn't know whether they'd be better off going out or in. They came about again off *Trá Mhóir*, and, as they did the wind shifted slightly to south south-west after a shower. There were a lot of boats heading west also, some of them to go racing and others to see the show. "It seems to me" said Cóilín, "that you're not keeping close enough to the wind; unless the wind is heading us slightly". "I think" said an old man who was sitting on the aft thwart, "that he's losing nothing. Isn't that the luff of the sail flapping? Mind that the wind isn't drawing out, and it is too; it backed out after that light shower"

"Isn't that all the better?" said the helmsman. "It's a pity it doesn't go directly south and we'd have a good breeze going west." As the boat was heading out on the deep, the wind was freshening and because there was an ebbing tidal current against the wind, it made things worse.

There were white crests on top of the waves, breaking mercilessly on the shoulders of the boat and spraying spumy seawater as far back as halfway up the mast. Indeed there wasn't a stitch on anybody that didn't look as if it hadn't been dragged after the boat. Some of them may have been muttering under their breadth "It's a pity that I didn't stay at home! Wouldn't I have found something to do?"

[52] According to this tale, the oystercatcher loaned its webbed feet to the gull and the gull never returned them. The presence or absence of webbed feet would have added significance for the shore dwellers as birds with webbed feet could be eaten by Christians during and between fasts.

There was another man from the mountains who was a passenger and who was going to watch the horse races. He happened by the village to buy fish and what did he do but join in with the company. Didn't he have friends in *Cloch na Rón* where the races would be held. Wouldn't he have a red-letter day amongst them? Yes, and a relation of his from *Léim* had a horse running on *Trá an Ghoirtín*. Wasn't that a good excuse for him, and if there was any fair play to be had, wouldn't it win if you were to believe the chat at home? The sail was barely raised that morning when the mountain man had started talking about horses, and if he got away with it, good luck to him. "If it weren't for respect for the stranger", said Cóilín, "he wouldn't get away with it".
But, on the other hand, didn't Cóilín get his own back. He (the passenger) was lying in a coil of rope in the forward hold and he bent double with sea sickness. He was shaking with the cold, and didn't care if the bay emptied on top of him.
"Hadn't I better come about shortly?" said the man aft, turning his head around and looking over his shoulder. I'm making a lot of leeway for a while now" "Go about" said Cóilín, "you'll sail above the island if the wind stays in this quarter". And he was right. He was well above it, as he had to ease off his sheets, and if it wasn't ploughing the sea, don't believe me. A white froth from its two cheeks and the stream of water from the top of the rudder foaming as if boiling and the sea like white milk with the amount being displaced by her sides. But, to make a long story short, it didn't take them long to sail by the mouths of the bays before they dropped their sails in *Cloch na Rón*.
When they dropped sail and moored the boat, they headed up to a public house to quench their thirst. Their faces were as white as chalk with sea salt and there was some also in their gullets. But before long, their gullets were scoured and as for the mountain man he was throwing it back like a river. He didn't look like a sick man now, and he showing off.
"That's it" said Cóilín, "he who's ashore is a good boatman" Your man didn't like to mention the sickness at all, in front of the company, and there wasn't a word out of him as if he had his tongue cut off. But if Cóilín hadn't said anything, I can tell you there would be a different story.
"There's no time for delay", said Seán, " throw them back and let's be out of here. It's better to be early than too late."
"Have another drink", said the bearded man from the mountain as they were going out the door. "Not now" said Cóilín, "thanks, there's a long life ahead. You know that lot don't delay when the time comes".
"You're right" said a middle-aged man, lowering his pint and licking the outside of his mouth with his tongue.

The crew headed smartly for the boat and the other group followed them down lazily. There wasn't a word out of them coming up in the morning, but they were shaking with the cold, but now if there wasn't talk and chatter, let us leave it like that.
But it's hard to beat the old saying "Most talking is done by drinkers". There was a crowd of old boatmen stretched on their flanks on the shingle at the top of the shore. That's where there was sailing! There was no good sailing boat that was on the coast in the last fifty years that wasn't mentioned so that you could imagine the boat sailing before you in your mind's eye. The group that was with Cóilín came into their company listening to the conversation and they stuck their noses in, and if there was sailing on the sea there was

sailing also on land. Even school children gathered about eventually and their mouths wide open listening attentively.
The boat with the race committee aboard was out on anchor, and it was covered in flags as a distinguishing feature from the other boats. The nobbies were the first boats to race and they luffed up, each one in turn, beside the committee boat. When they had paid their crown piece, each owner got a small flag, and no two flags of the same colour, to tie at the top of the spar, so as the committee and other people could identify them with binoculars.

The officer of the day gave them the course just as he would be reading it out of a book. Everyone in the boats listened carefully. He told them to go on anchor in one line, according to the draw of the tickets they drew that morning; their sails to be raised and ready, throated, peaked and tacked. One hearing the shot, anchor ropes to be cast into the sea and to tack out under *Cruach na Caoile*, to go right about *Sceirde Mór*, to come back with the wind following, to leave *Cruach na Caoile* to starboard, to go about the boat that was at anchor in the mouth of *Trá an Ghoirtín* by leaving her to starboard and to come back here again and "the first boat to luff up" said he "under this boat's quarter, but to abide by the rules, will have first prize; but, on the other hand, for any boat that breaks them, that will be a different story. Remember that now! Does everyone understand the conditions now? Anyone who doesn't let him speak, and let there be no excuse later."
"We understand, we understand you well", said they in one voice.
"Be ready now them." Bang! Smoke and the smell of powder! Ropes being thrown to sea, as it was no time to go hauling them. To get the boats moving, the sails to be eased out; that's when there was a commotion, a din and an uproar, everyone in his own place, and they tacking down the bay making towards the open sea. It was a lovely sight to watch, some of them sailing close to the wind below, some of them in irons beside each other and some of them luffing each other. They ploughed the seas with great strength, a bright surge of a wave in front of their stem that was spraying up on their bows. Large waves followed each other endlessly out from its cheeks with great speed. A white wave behind boiling and foaming and creating a whirlpool. The boats' ribs straining and moaning, mixed with the sad plaintive music of the sharp wind through the hard manila halyards. The masts creaking and murmuring in the beams, bending under the heavy load of the wind. The spar of the main sail bending like a fishing rod. That's when you need your sea legs, it was heeled over so much. Yes, and the boat would need to be well fitted above, between halyards, cloth and spars.

The hookers were then let off on the same gun as the nobbies, and they weren't long making way, and if ever a boat carried sail they did. The *gleoiteoga* were then let off; the *púcáin* were the last class of sailing boat. There was a big fleet of *púcáin* from every corner of Connemara, and they weren't the worst either, but the first class. The course was read out to them, and they were arranged in one line just like the others. The shot was fired and if there wasn't competition, then so be it. There wasn't such frenzied activity and commotion and bustle anywhere in the world. Yes, noise and shouting and disorder, and by Jove, if there was a rib left at the end of the day it was a wonder.[53]

[53] Folklore has it that every time someone cursed, one of the devil's ribs would be broken,

It happened that Cóilín was downwind and on the outer edge of the line of boats and wasn't that the luck of the draw? When the boats' sails filled out they were taking the wind out of each other's sails depending on their relative positions in the wind, and Cóilín was well smothered, and even if he was he wasn't too downhearted yet. At the start, the other boats sailed out above him, except for two boats. He sailed out below them until he had them off his starboard quarter. The boats above him on a port tack were hampering him a lot. He was in a flat calm. Nevertheless, when he moved towards the land he had a back-current down the bay. The other boats came about very soon but he went with the back-current, until he was afraid he'd take the limpet off the rock. The other boats by this time were out under the influence of a flowing tidal current; Seán came west about and didn't leave anything behind either. There was plenty of wind and he started to make way to windward.

"Keep moving", said the man who was sitting on the moveable thwart, "and don't keep her so close to the wind. It seems to me she's not making much headway. I'm afraid that spit will put us about and I don't want to lose any way to windward for the moment"

"It will put you about anyway", said Cóilín, "as there's a river of a flowing tide up there. You'd better not be too greedy for the moment"

"All right" said the helmsman and laid off the wind ever so slightly, and even if he did he didn't lose anything by it. He gave the boat a bit of scope and she made her way easier through the sea. She was the first boat to come about from the land this time, as the big *púcán* from *Ros Muc* was in irons as she came about, and the boat from *Caiseal* was under way and the helmsman had the tiller down and was changing his half-hitch from the port *mullard* to the starboard *mullard*. There were two other boats beside her, and the rest a good bit downwind. There were good puffs of wind by now, and it beginning to ebb, wind over tide, a lumpy sea across the mouth of the bay so that there were splashes coming in to the forward hold on the lee side, and as for a choppy sea, it was there in abundance. The boats were sailing close to each other and it was a lovely sight to watch them from the land, and if there weren't old people watching them keenly and arguing amongst themselves, then so be it. They were nearly at each other's throats with excitement for the sailing; they were in earnest too.

The *báid iomartha* and currachs were racing by now and wasn't there great enjoyment to be got from them in spite of the bad day. The rowers in their shirts were bending red deal and ash. Sometimes, the boats would get tangled in each other and that's when there was noise and commotion, oars and tholepins breaking and boats crashing into one another. They would free each other again and would start rowing, pulling the oars long and fast. A *bád iomartha* from *Iorras Mór* got the flag, and she needed all the speed she had, and a currach from *Inis Ní*, and nothing was left idle in her.

During this time the *púcáin* were ploughing the sea heading out towards the *Sceirdí*, a hard beat and a soft swell in the sea out on the deep abyss. They had one reef tied by now, and the man with the baling bucket was certainly busy. He had a pain in his back by now keeping out water, because as in the old stories, when he baled a gallon, two gallons came aboard. Indeed, there were 'white flowers on the fisherman's garden' (white horses) that day if ever there were.

"I think we'll have to tie another reef" said Cóilín, "and we'll have to put a *barróg* in the jib. Mind you isn't that boat below us hove-to?"

"It is indeed," said the baler, "she's tying a reef. No open boat can stand it any longer. Isn't it a right gale now, and I'm afraid it will get worse with the end of the ebbing tide. The sea is already very choppy".
"As we're in front and ahead of the other boats, I think we should hang on for a while; I'll be spilling wind now and then, and we'll shortly be laying off"
"Upon my word, the *Sceirdí* are still a long way off. They didn't look far away from us the night before last, when we were standing at the gable of the house that time. Didn't they look like two stranded sailing ships? Isn't it many the look they have when a change in weather is on the way? Not only that, but no sooner do they look this way than the other, but I think myself that they're under a spell".
"I wonder should I be getting a bit of speed up to go about" said Seán, turning his head around and looking at the wild rocks that were a good bit away upwind.
"You may as well dip the mainsail, there's a river out here with an ebb tide, and it will be bringing us out".

The other boats were a good bit off by now; some of them within a distance of a cast net away, some others further.
"Is it in nature's power that we'd get the better of them?" said Micil Thomáis, the tack man, who was seated on the forward thwart at the bowsprit beam.
"It is", said Cóilín looking at the man aft at the same time, and saying "don't lose any way!" "You don't need to say it, but we'll be hard pressed to make it".
"Don't worry," said Cóilín "you'll lay her." He was right, and when he came abeam of them he had to lay off and ease off his sails.
"Put out your bags of stones forward and get ready for goosewinging"
No sooner said than done. They were running now before the sea with their mainsheet full out and the other boats were coming around the *Sceirdí* and starting to goosewing. It was a dangerous place to be in them, as the wind was dead astern. You wouldn't know what side the sail should be set. The helmsman would need to be careful now, because if she gybed they were finished. She was down to the bends forward with the speed and the sea was one big white wave around them. But it didn't take long until she was coming alongside *Cruach na Caoile* and the other boats following her. When she reached the boat that was anchored at the mouth of *Trá an Ghoirtín*, you couldn't trust a gybe; he had to luff her up, and to drop sail. The other boats did likewise. If there weren't lots of people on *Trá an Ghoirtín* then I tell a lie. There were hundreds and as for horses there was a display of them. There were foot races there, and all types of athletics and bravado. Even the thimble-rigger was there with his smart tricks and his voice above everyone else's. It was he who was well able to make himself understood with his cajoling and flattering words.
"Put your money up front", he'd say, "if ye don't take a chance, ye can't win. Ye came here barefoot but ye'll be going home in a car, " and so forth. A middle-aged man going about and an old man asking him what he was saying.
"He's a thief," said the man, "he has my silver half-crown in his pocket, that it may not bring him good luck nor profit. That the devil may choke you there, and haven't you the voice".
"Amen", "said the old man, "but don't be swearing". Cóilín's and Seán's hearts were gladdened by now and Micil Thomáis was singing a song up on the forward platform and looking up at the top of the mast. Wouldn't he be up there tying the flag within another

half hour? What did that ten pounds matter to Seán and Cóilín? They couldn't care less but to see the famous flag raised. By now he was luffing up keenly and hopefully at the flagboat's quarter. Bang! The drop that was in the soles of their feet went to the top of their heads and weren't their friends ashore happy. The pier inside was one big hubbub of shouting and talking when they threw out the head of their mooring rope. "I knew this morning" said the bearded man "that ye'd be lucky and me with ye".
Micil didn't wait to look around but went up to the top of the mast in five or six bounds and attached the flag there. When the sails were folded, and the boat tied, they headed up the pier to wet their whistles. There wasn't a stitch of their clothes on their skin that wasn't wet through, and no wonder with the day that was in it. The other boats by now were luffing up one by one at the flagboat. The *Ros Muc* boat second, the *Caiseal* boat third, a boat from *Cloch na Rón* fourth and a boat from *Béal an Daingin* fifth.
There were a few other boats from *Iorras Mór*, and as an old man from *Inis Leacain* said, hadn't they sailed the same sea as the first boat? But what good was that when they hadn't got the speed – only one boat could get the first prize.
Seán and Cóilín and their crew were warming themselves in by a big fire in a kitchen in a public house at the top of the pier. There was another big crowd inside as well, and they drinking pints, some of them a bit merry. The sailing, showing off and singing started. *Cóilín* was warming the soles of his feet by the fire and he struck up a verse of a song.

I saw a time when the clans of Maínis
Bore off the palm this side of Limerick
For the beauty of their fine sailing boats
When sheeted in to come about
Did they travel not a quarter mile
With strength and vigour of their sails
And there was nowhere to be found
Their equal but the sturgeon fish.

"I'm going astray in it", said he and he started scratching the top of his head. It's beyond my power to think of another word of it. Don't let anyone who's supposed to be with us be asleep in the morning, as we won't wait for morning; We'll set sail with the daybreak".
The band of night-light had not yet disappeared from the sky, you would think that the sun was at its highest in the sky, as they made their way to the boat harbour. Noise and bustle, commotion and shouting, warps being let off, anchors weighed, folded sails being unfurled and raised on masts. Pulleys sounding. But to make a long story short, it wasn't long before Cóilín was out on the bay.
"Ye may as well put out the oars, and keep rowing a little". They looked at each other. "Laziness", said Seán, is the worst ailment. Ye should be ashamed of yourselves trying to dodge work like that, as we'll never make it down against the flowing tide. There isn't a puff of wind. The tholepins are up forward in the hold".
Cóilín and Micil went looking for them lethargically. When Cóilin went looking for the tholepins he hit his head off the beam under the fore platform, and I tell you that he hurt himself. He was dizzy, and he wasn't the only one, but everyone in the boat was, as a result of the night's carousing and revelling. It's true that "a drunken night makes a sad morning" but nevertheless there wasn't sadness without joy mixed with it. There was

gladness in Cóilín's and in Seán's hearts, and no wonder as they were bringing home the flag. They started rowing stiffly and lazily, a stroke in the forward hold and another on the aft thwart. There wasn't a puff of wind, and the sails were midships. They were in a flat calm.
"'Tis a pity a freshening wind doesn't come" said Cóilín, "but maybe it will come with the sunrise". It was true for him, because when the big golden sun started to rise up in the east, a little northerly breeze came. It was slightly better than rowing, but it was strengthening little by little "as the cat ate the mixture", until the wind kept the sail well out, and there's no need to say that the rowers were glad when they hauled in their oars. It was one tack down by the shore, on a beam reach. A look now and again from Seán under the clew of the mainsail, when he was going east through *Bealach na Srathra*, and telling Micil to stand on the forward platform holding on with his hand to the luff of the staysail for support. To keep a sharp look out, that there was a submerged rock somewhere ahead. Indeed, Micil's sight wasn't good at the time, and if it wasn't, don't blame him as he didn't sleep a wink that night.

It was nearly dinnertime when they had the boat tied up and the sails folded, and weren't the crowd at home full of joy. There's no need to mention the shaking of hands and the heaping of praise that the boatmen got and they got only what they deserved that windy day on top of the waves.
"Ye're the best of men," said one of the old people surrounding them, "to bring home the flag".
"You've said it," said Micil, "but aren't we just as bad if we don't win the day in *Leitir Meallain* a fortnight form next Monday. It's exactly as you say".
"Have some courage," said the old man, "the man with courage never lost it"

When the crew had drunk a couple of bottles of the juice of the barley in each others' company, and had engaged in a bit of bravado, arguing, and conversation, the day was losing its light and the black clouds of night were spreading, and as they did, the crew also scattered, effusively grateful, in an honest and friendly way. Everyone went home to this own cabin, where they stretched themselves out on the soft bird plumage. There's no need to say they needed it and they slept soundly till morning.

REPENTANCE

My family rose up in the morning
And made their way down to the boat
They rowed back west to the rock
Each rowing with his own stroke
They were but half way there
When Páid he looked astern dead
He saw the signs of foul weather
And the sea churned up from the head

Rise up there with you Mylie
Take down the foresail good and hard
Don't wait to tuck or to fold it
Till you go for the throat halyard
Rise up Mylie without sorrow
And bail water as fast as you can
Till I turn her head in towards the shore
As Páidín's a good helmsman

There came like an angel from Heaven
And stood on the top of the mast
Tell us all your misdoings
'Cos you're in great danger at last
Do you stay away Sundays from Mass?
Do you say the rosary at all?
Do you go any night drinking
With the woman of the big shawl?

I don't stay from Mass any Sunday
And I say my prayers as there's call
And I don't go any night drinking
With the woman of the big shawl
But I sometimes go to Sail's household
And the odd time to Peadar Mór's
Sometimes to Ward's down in Galway
When I come ashore at the Poll Mór

Don't go into Sail's household
And don't go to Peadar Mór's
You won't go to Ward's down in Galway
If you come ashore at the Poll Mór
But when Páidín came home on the Friday
The old woman was laid out on a board
And his wife and the children lamenting
To the women the drinks he did dole

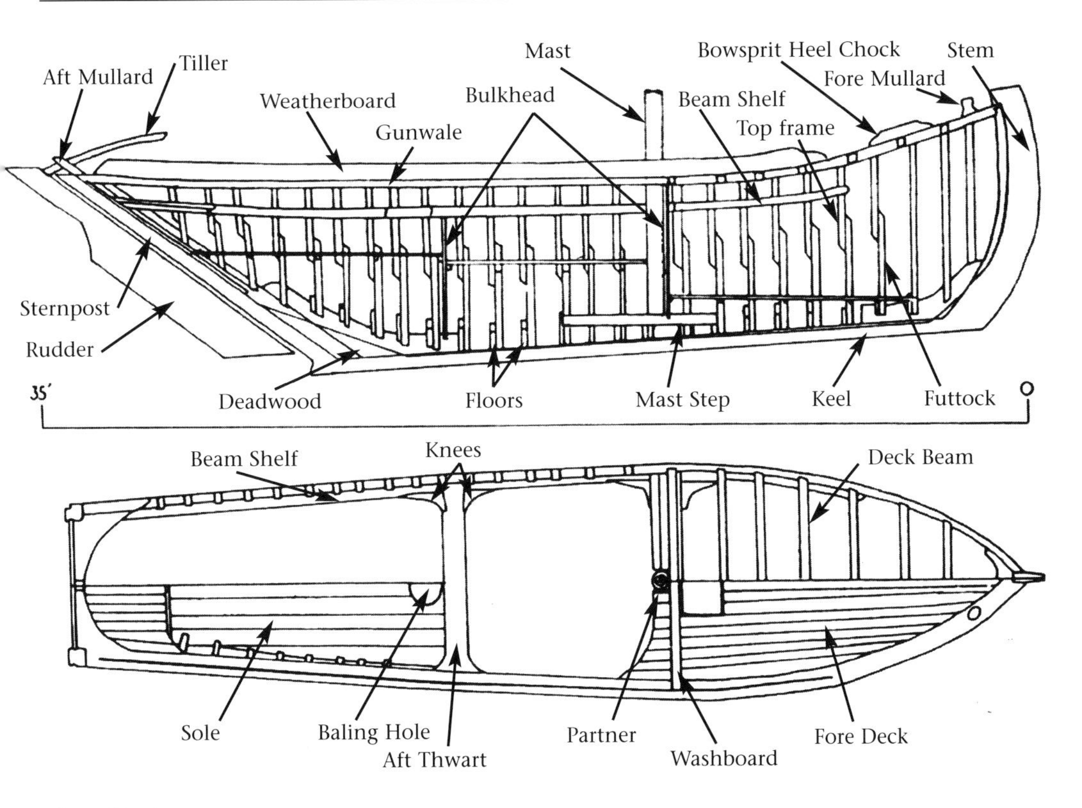

Plan of Hooker

MATERIAL FOR THE PÚCÁN

Old Páidín and Máirtín called into the wright's house in the pall of night. The lit lamp was hung on the wall and the boatwright seated comfortably on a chair warming himself by a fine hard black turf fire, whose flames were flickering glowingly, trying to reach the arch of the chimney hole, a chalk pipe between his teeth and he raising smoke above him. Wasn't he due rest and comfort after the day's work?

He took the pipe out of his mouth and he gave a warm welcoming invitation to the pair.

"Pull in to the fire. Isn't the night a bit sharp?"

"There's a cold twist in it," said the two in one voice and they sitting on two chairs.

"Didn't some wrack come ashore this morning?" said the wright. "Yes," said Páidín, "and fine planks too, fresh and clean, as if they were after coming out of a ship."

"Isn't it a shame the wind changed to the north?" said the wright. "They'll be driven to Kerry if the wind stays in this quarter," said Máirtin," but did you ever hear that it's an ill wind that blows nobody good? The people of Brandon and the Blaskets will be gathering them soon, and who'd blame them?"

"It's hard to beat a good turf fire," said Páidín, rekindling his pipe.

Right: Colm Ó Cathasaigh repairing a boat in Maínis. He belonged to a family renowned for building hookers in Geárd na gCathasach on the eastern side of Maínis.

Left: An early stage in the construction of a boat in a field – the keel has been laid and sternpost and stem attached.

"The poor have little other comfort as the proverb says – the beginning and end of one's life is to draw closer to the fire."
"It's a good sod of turf," said he, settling one foot on top of the other.
"You can't beat the turf that's next to the stone," said the wright, "even though it gives a bit of trouble."
"I'm not cutting across you there," said Páidín, "I heard you were repairing the hooker for Cóilín Beag."
"You heard the truth," said the wright.
"Any chance of you finishing?" said Páidín
"I finished this evening and indeed it was about time. Indeed, there wasn't that much work to do, a few pieces under the *ioscaidí* at the ends of the planks, as the skin was fairly rotten there.[54] A false keel and a *maide teallaigh* and some caulking because she was leaking at some of the seams on her shoulder."[55]
"The reason I'm so inquisitive," said Páidín, "I was hoping to get you to make a new boat for me, and I'd like to talk to you in time about the subject. That's the reason for my journey tonight."
"Good luck to you," said the wright, yawning and stretching himself.

[54] The *ioscaidí* represent the area under the aft platform.

[55] The *maidí teallaigh* are floor timbers under the foredeck on which a non-combustible surface is laid so that a fire can be lit on it.

"When can you attend to me?" said Páidín.
"Anytime you're ready for me," said the wright pointing his pipe towards Máirtín.
"I wouldn't like to let the opportunity pass", said Páidín.
"It's said that he who does is often worse off," said the wright.
"A lot of nonsense is spoken" said Máirtín, throwing a thick spittle into the fire. "I'd like to know from you how much wood, iron and the rest I'll need."
"When I get the details from you," said the wright, "I'll make an estimate."
"The likes of Mícheál Phádraig's is what I have in mind – eighteen feet in the keel, six and a half feet in the mast beam and about three feet and four inches in depth and twenty five feet above."
"You're not far off," said the wright, " because it was me who built Mícheál's boat."
"Indeed, that's the truth, but not a muscle in my heart remembered it," said Páidín.
"There's no harm done," said the wright.
"You've those details already," said Páidín.
"Do you like her to have a big draught?" said the wright
"I don't", said Páidín, "I'm not telling you your business; I like her to have a slight rake and a neat freeboard. A nice side and line counts a lot, a smooth form and shape, graceful like a seagull, able to carry a good load for her size, put together strongly and well for sailing. You know the rest."
"Strict rules," said Máirtín, "but she's not very good for a load, although she's diligent and enduring and there are few days, no matter how bad, that she can't cope with. She's a bit feeble for bringing seaweed in from the wild rocks. When I was returning from the sea last

The boat builder Joe Bháitéir Seoighe constructing a bád iomartha on Inis Bearachain.

summer with a load of seaweed, weren't her ribs twisting and groaning, proof that I had one foot often close to the grave."

"I'd say there are few boats in these harbours as old as her," said the wright.

"There aren't, nor anything near it," said Páidín. "Wasn't she on the gurnard banks at *Carraig Iolra* during the bad times?"

"It's time for her to rest from now on," said the wright, as he started to oil a saw.

"The tool has to be kept in condition," said Máirtín. "If you don't mind, I'll give you a hand." "More power to you." said the wright.

"There's sense in that; you'll find a rag in the corner of the tool box."

"The wood and the rest would cost a fair amount of money," said Páidín, as he scratched the back of his head and put his cap out of place.

"It will cost you nine or ten pounds at least," said the wright and he doing his best to sharpen his cooper's knife with a file. "I'd say that you'd nearly know yourself how much is needed."

"Did you ever hear that two peoples' opinion is better than one's? Apart from that, I'm not as knowledgeable about those matters. It's said that one person is ignorant in another person's home," said Páidín who was sharpening a pencil.

"Alright," said the wright, "we'll be starting therefore, in God's name. Are you ready?"
"Fire ahead," said Páidín, sliding out on a piece of paper that was in front of him.
"A piece of beech for a keel, eighteen foot clear by nine inches, by three inches, straight and smooth with few knots; a piece of oak for stem and false stem, seven feet in length by eighteen inches wide, four inches thick – it doesn't matter if it's a bit bent because of the curved bow of the boat. It will be easy enough to pull the saw through it. Have you that much noted?
"Indeed, I have," said Páidín, stretching himself.
"Keep going then," said the wright.
The material for a sternpost and rudder post, eight feet by eight inches by three inches; it will be easy enough to make two equal lengths of it. The floors now, I'll make twenty, about two and a half feet in length, four inches by two inches, I'll get that much from a slab fourteen feet by eighteen inches by two inches."
"You'll have plenty to spare," said Máirtín, interrupting him.
"Wait a while now till I see," said the wright, "I'll get four out of its width, and five out of its length, isn't that twenty? And the piece left over will be needed for *líosaí* and the beds for the sweeps." [56]
"You're right," said Máirtín.
"The frames now," said Páidín.
"About forty," said Páidín.
"Right, one at each end of the floors," said the wright. Each one will be about three feet by four inches by two inches. We'll get enough from three slabs of oak, fourteen feet by eighteen inches by two inches. There will be sixteen from the slab. The surplus will be needed for *crannáin* and transom frames; there will be some left over."[57]
"There should be," said Páidín. "There'll be seven or eight feet to spare after the frames if I'm right."
"You're not far off," said the wright. "We're coming to the tops of the frames now. Do you think larch is all right for them?"
"I know it is," said Páidín.
"Put down two slabs, the same length, width and thickness of larch."
"Two slabs won't be needed," said Páidín.
"I know," said the wright, "but, son, there will be breasthooks, aprons, cleats, knees, dowels, and other pieces needed. They say that a surplus is better than a deficiency."
"I understand you now," said Páidín.
"We have the backbone, front, back and the ribs," said the wright.
"The skin now, I've pine beams for it."
"Watch that they're not faulty or bored by shipworm," said the wright.
"It's not likely," said Páidín.
"I sounded them. I knocked on their ends with a small stone, and Cóilín had his ear to the other end until he got a message through them. He tapped lightly again with the nail of his thumb, the sound came to me as sweet and musical as you ever heard. That means they're healthy. Isn't that so?"
"You can't beat that," said the wright.

[56] The *líosaí* are pieces of wood attached to the sweeps to protect wearing against the thole pins.

[57] The *crannáin* are V-shaped frames laid on the deadwood.

"It's amazing how sound and noise moves through the wood and it strong and vigorous after the passage, but it's said that there's a certain spark in everything. How long are those beams?"
"Thirty feet by fourteen inches square, they're the ones Cóilín and I got, the big day of the south-west wind a long time ago."
"You put yourselves at risk with them too," said Máirtín.
"And there was a great number of them came in that year," said Páidín.
"Wasn't that ship wrecked on the *Sceirdí*, and it was said at the time that the jack-o-lanterns led them astray."
"Indeed they could do it," said the wright.
"A lot of planks will come from even one of them, about seven inches they'll be in width, by about three quarters of an inch thick. The lowest plank will be eighteen feet, and there'll be a couple of inches of it lying into the rebate, from there up the planks will be getting longer because of the round belly of the boat. There won't be much to spare from thirty feet up from the waterline and it's usually white deal that's used in the upper planks."
Páidín spoke and said that he had plenty of white deal, but that he thought that it wasn't flexible enough, that it wouldn't be easy to bend from the shoulder.
"Don't worry," said the wright. "I'll steam most of the upper planks. I'll guarantee that they'll be rebated there with no bother. There'll be material for aft platforms, ceilings, stringers, locker seat and gunwale as well as the skin in that beam, I think."
"I thought there might be," said Páidín.
"The weather boards," said the wright. Haven't you got planks? Cut one on them; eighteen feet long by seven inches, by an inch and a half."
"Alright" said Páidín.
"We'll need supporting frames for the platforms, and a locker seat," said the wright.
"I've a piece of red deal for that," said Páidín.
"I've material for a mast step of hard wood and another block of black oak from the shore. You never saw anything as smooth nor as heavy as it; I thought it would be good material for pulleys and blocks."
"You thought right," said the wright, "because it's as hard-wearing as you ever saw. Have you material for a mast and a bowsprit?"
"I can say that I have a fine piece for a mast. A ship's sail spar that I found ashore on one of the islands last winter. The best of red deal, twenty eight feet long and nearly three feet around, a grain so straight that it would cleave from top to bottom."
"Twenty five feet will be needed by seven or eight inches square," said the wright.
"I have a spar of Newfoundland wood, twenty five feet long and strong enough for a bowsprit," said Páidín. "Fifteen feet is what's needed, isn't that so?"
"The surplus is yours. Indeed, you got a lot of the wrack that came ashore recently," said the wright.
"As I'm telling you, my son, it wasn't unknown to myself, as it's many a knocking over and a heavy fall I got on uneven shores, trying to make a way between high cliffs on dark nights that you wouldn't see your hand stretched in front of you, the screech of a spumy sea from the white breakers, nearly taking my breath away, on hands and knees and climbing most of the time. Often, when I was walking in foam, I would fall in to a water hole, as I didn't know where to place my foot. It's quite abominable work."

"I understand you well," said the wright, "indeed, I haven't walked much since that time long ago when the paraffin barrels came. I got fifteen of them one morning."
"You made a fine penny," said Máirtín.
"I didn't, and not a brass farthing, because the peelers took them," said the wright.
"Wasn't that the bad state of affairs, but that was the way at the time," said Páidín.
"Didn't they play the same trick on us all. They took away the barrels of cod oil too. They had help too."
"Bad scran to it as a wrack," said the wright, "woe to him who ever put himself in danger with it. Weren't good men often lost because of it?"
The tool was oiled by now. The toolbox was divided into sections so that each piece could be put in its own place, planes, chisels, wedges together. Bradawls, gimlets, augers and caulking irons in their own places. Hammers, mallets, axes, adzes, a big saw and little saws in another corner and so on.
"We weren't long with them," said Máirtín
"Thanks," said the wright, "it was always foolish to be averse to help."
"There's hard cold weather on the way," said Páidín, "and the cat putting its backside to the fire"
"Put a few sods on it," said the wright, "or it will soon go out."
"I've two stumps of bog deal for knees," said Páidín, as he put down the fire, "one of them eight feet by eight inches square and the other six feet by a square foot."
"We'll get eight slabs out of them, two inches clean. We'll have plenty for knees," said the wright.
"The rest will be good for a fire because it's full up with sap," said Máirtín. "It's said this country was full of woods in the old days, and doesn't it show all the signs of it with all the tree stumps in the bogs and the swamps."
"There were lions and other wild beasts in those woods," said Páidín.
"There were no lions nor pigs in them," said Máirtín.
"Isn't it in other countries they are?" said the wright.
"Maybe you're right," said the other. "I only have what I heard."
"Have you material for beams?" said the wright.
"I have a twenty six foot plank. An aft beam, a fore beam a mast beam and a stepping beam will come out of that."
"Nine inches by three inches?" said the wright.
"Right," said Páidín.
Máirtín by now was crouched, looking in under the coffer. It was a mouse he heard gnawing wood. "Isn't it a wonder they wouldn't be afraid of the cat?" said he.
"Indeed," said the wright, "if he made a nest in that one's ear, he wouldn't move, he's so lazy. He's old now, but he wasn't so good even at his best."
"There's little of the material we didn't talk about, apart from iron, oakum and nails", said Páidín as he rekindled his pipe.
"You'll get two stone of grey nails, an inch-and-a-half and a stone of two inch for the skin; a half stone of black inch-and-a-half nails; three twelve foot bars half inch square iron, two stone of oakum and two stone of putty. We'll have the leftovers. I'm sure you have material for a rudder, spar and sweeps," said the wright.
"You can say that," said Páidín

Pulley blocks for a sailing hooker.

"It seems to me," said the wright, hanging the kettle, "that we don't need much more. Nothing is done in a flash. Have you anything else on your mind, Páid?"
"I don't think so but I'll have to get gudgeons and pintles for the rudder, a mast iron, a crance for the bowsprit, rings for the top of the mast, top and front of the spar, a sheave to put in the mast for the main halyard and blocks with brass pins in them for the jib and peak halyards. I'm sure that the black oak is good enough for blocks."
"Leave the details to the smith," said the wright. "He's the boy who won't be long making hooks, and rings and everything else like that you'll need." Máirtín stood up as he was supposed to be getting ready to go sailing.
"Don't be afraid to stay for a bit", said the wright, "ye won't go anywhere until you have a sup of tea."
They stayed, as they would be as well off trying to empty the bay as to refuse. The tea was soon ready. They sat in to the table. Blue lightning shone on the window.
"There's a change in the weather," said Páidín. "The wrack will be driven out."
"Don't you think that it was from the ship that the people of the west end of the village saw that the planks came?" said the wright.
"What else," said Páidín, "didn't Colm Thomáis and his crew see her clearly below them in the sea, the white sails raised to the tops of the masts, the sail spars swinging

back and forth with the movement of the waves, and planks coming to the surface from time to time".

"I don't know if she was far out," said the wright.

"Twenty three or twenty four miles out, a while out from *Sceirde,*" said Páidín, but she wasn't on the bottom but floating below the surface. It looks as if there was something heavier than wood in her, if not she wouldn't be as deep in the water."

"Maybe" said Máirtín, "there were guns and bullets below the wood. A trick like that is often done to confuse the enemy."

"I think," said Páidín, turning away form the table, that it's time for us to be heading home."

"Indeed, there's a part of the night spent," said Máirtín, cutting a bite out of a piece of tobacco with his penknife and passing it over to the wright.

"I won't, thanks," said the wright taking out his pipe "I don't chew."

They bade goodbye and a blessing to the wright and headed off.

"It's a wonder he's not lonely in that cabin," said Páidín.

"For whom?" said Máirtín.

"Don't you think I'll need up to four score yards of canvas for sails?"

"There'll be plenty there," said the other.

"Indeed, it's going to cost me, between everything."

"There's no doubt," said Máirtín.

"I have to speak to Cóilín so as he'll be ready to make the sail. I have to get hemp bolt-ropes and thread. I think I'll get good enough baft for sixpence a yard."[58]

"I wouldn't give a halfpenny more for it. I'll have to leave you now. This is the head of the boreen," said Máirtín.

"Good night to you."

"And the same to you," said the other and each one went towards his own cabin.

[58] Baft is a type of coarse cotton used as sail cloth

Harvesting seaweed on an exposed shore. If the tide were ebbing men would often walk into the sea to gather loose weed.

KELP MAKING

I'm someone who spent the beginning of my life living on an island in the west of Connemara, listening to the perpetual lonely murmuring of the sea arriving continuously in big waves from the strange abyss in the west, breaking fiercely and bluntly against shore and beach. It doesn't matter whether it's a smooth level beach or a rough mussel shore. With the amount of swell and tossing of the sea from day to day and from year to year, there are storm beaches of big stones that are as round as eggs on top of the shore. But even if the sea is like that, it's from her that most of the people of Connemara make their living and not by fishing alone but by making kelp. This is hard bothersome work, and it's going on for a long time. It's from seaweed that kelp is made. There are many types of seaweed and there are special names for each type of them as follows; mayweed, oarweed, sea thong, bladder wrack, knotted wrack, sea oak, furbelows, sea belt, toothed wrack, channelled wrack and so on. There will be a description of each of these later on. The oarweed and the mayweed, that is red seaweed, are the best for making good kelp.[59] The other types are also made into kelp, but they make only bad kelp, or second grade kelp as they call it. When bad weather comes, which removes the seaweed on the deep bottoms and on the flat rocks, it's thrown in on the shore and on the beaches, and the kelp makers put it and the sea rods up to dry. It's spread on the rocks and it's dried. When it and the sea rods are dry, saved and the salt dries on them, they're made into big cocks and covered with ferns, briars and sods. This is called winter seaweed and it's left like that until summer comes.

The seaweed is harvested with a *croisín*, and two or three men go out in each boat to harvest the oarweed. Working with the *croisín* is hard, bothersome work, because it's difficult, even very difficult, to remove the oarweed from the rock. The *croisín* is about sixteen feet in length and there's a piece of wood across one end of it about eight inches long that's called the knife. The boat anchors above the oarweed rock, the *croisín* is thrust down to the bottom of the sea and twisted, and as the man in the boat is twisting the *croisín*, the oarweed is turning about the knife on the bottom and when the knife is full with oarweed it has to be hauled. There's about a stone weight of oarweed on each *croisín*. It's easy enough to harvest oarweed in the quiet sheltered bays, that is, areas that are sheltered and protected from the big sea by islands or by a series of rocks. The oarweed which grows there is not as strong nor as fat as the type that grows out on the face of the open shores or on the wild rocks where there are strong currents of the open sea and where the waves are forever fiercely and angrily frothing, coming in from the open abyss with lightning speed under their white caps, swallowing each other as they reach the shallows, and competing to wreak vengeance on the bold black cliffs, spraying the spumy sea into the skies, and sending a big mass of foam flying like a gull looking for fish on a stormy day – the noise of those waves like thunder of a thousand miles away.

[59] There are three main classes of algae or seaweeds, based on their colour – green, brown and red. The oarweed and mayweed are classed as brown algae.

Right: Burning weed in a kelp kiln on the Aran Islands.

Left: Seaweed harvester in Connemara and a stack of sea rods.

At the end of summer and the beginning of autumn the coast of Connemara is alight. There are hundreds of kilns to be seen. Aren't they a lovely sight, their smoke rising slowly skywards in the quiet of the evening, submitting to every breath of wind, however slight, to signal to everyone from what quarter of the sky the wind is blowing. The smell from the same smoke is a healthy fragrance. The burning is hard work. The kelp makers say there's no bother with the seaweed until the burning starts. A stone wall is made beside the cock, ten feet long, three feet wide and a foot high. There are two lines of stones and it's heaped with wrack between them. The seaweed, which is put in the bottom of the kiln, is then well teased apart. Fires are lit in every part of that bed within a couple of feet of each other; then a mat of sea rods above the glow. A mat of seaweed above that, and from then until midday there are two men keeping it topped up with seaweed with all their heart and soul. At about twelve o'clock mid-day, it's let burn down and cleaned. Whatever kelp is in it is then well and truly mixed, with kelp rakes and loys; it's then topped up again until evening. It's heavy work to mix a kelp kiln. There are five or six men, feeling as if their skins are fire, mixing and agitating until they are tired and exhausted.

The following morning, it's a hard slab like a rock, about a ton weight. It's then broken into twelve pieces so as it can be brought easily to the boats. In the area I'm talking about, *Caiseal* and *Cill Chiaráin* are the two places for the kelp market. [60] A lot of it is sold every year in those places. During the burning season the market takes place every fortnight. There are hundreds of kelp makers there on the day of the market, and piles of kelp next to each other from the top to the bottom of the pier, small piles and big piles, according to the capabilities of the teams of workers.

The sampling man goes around with a hammer and bucket, taking a small bit off each slab. The kelp makers know him as well as a bad halfpenny. When the sample is taken he brings it into the assayer's office, and the name of the person who owns the pile is on a ticket in the bucket. The man inside has a glass as a means of assaying, and according to

what the glass shows he will pay its value to the kelp maker. Kelp was very valuable at the time of the Great War – twelve pounds a ton. Before that it was only four pounds. Before this it was weighed on the pier and sent by ship to Scotland. It was processed in Glasgow. It had many uses; iodine is extracted from the first grade, that great and valuable stuff that's talked about far and wide as a medicine. Soap can't be made without it, and it's said that some of it is used for making glass.

[60] Kelp making, which was well established by 1720, lasted for over two hundred years on the Irish coast. In the eighteenth century Irish kelp makers went to Scotland to teach the craft. The kelp was used at that time for the extraction of salts that were used in the manufacture of soap and glass. European wars resulted in increased prices for the kelp. During the French Revolution kelp was fetching more than £20 a ton in Britain. In the early nineteenth century the importance of kelp as a source of salts diminished. The newly discovered extraction of iodine and potash, however, ensured a continuing demand for it. E. Bullock & Co. opened a factory for iodine extraction in Galway and John Ward & Co. opened another in Ramelton, Co. Donegal. E. Stanford, an English man who later pioneered the extraction of alginates from seaweed, opened a factory near Spanish Point, Co. Clare in 1874. By the end of the nineteenth century other sources of iodine outside of Europe resulted in the closure of many of the factories in Ireland and Britain.

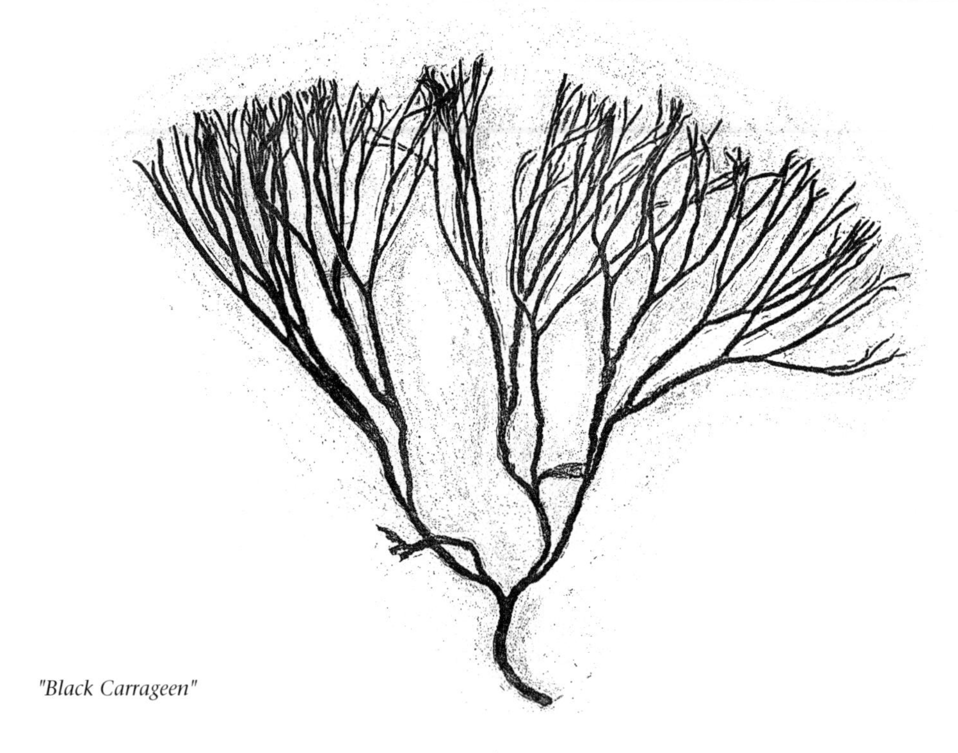

"Black Carrageen"

Carrageen

SEAWEED

An tEireaball Cait The "Cat's Tail"

The *eireaball cait* ("cat's tail") grows on the deep and, indeed, the name suits it well, it resembles a cat's tail so much, a hard slender rod with grey black fur growing densely on it. Some of them are fairly big also. Some of it gets thrown ashore in winter mixed with seaweed. The seaweed harvesters have to separate it from the other types and let it go to waste. It's no good as manure or as anything else. There's a type that comes in from the sea that's called *gruaig na caillí mara* ("the hair of the sea witch"). It has large broad fronds but is almost similar to the *eireaball* except for a different structure. They both grow on the deep in a fairly sheltered place between the arches near small sandy holes on the weed-covered bottom.

An Scothach The Mayweed *Laminaria hyperborea*

At the end of April the kelp makers are ready to go to work on the mayweed. Their potatoes and corn are planted in a hurry for the season. You'd see them in the evening looking out to sea hoping to see the sea swelling and breaking over a reef or shallow bottom. That's a good sign, as it's the white breakers and the swell of the sea that are the harvesters that will take the mayweed from the weed-covered rocks. Isn't there help and a livelihood for the poor close at hand under the crests of the waves during that time? The mayweed is the best of seaweed. It's said there isn't much difference between it and the oarweed as regards adding strength and vigour and weight to the kelp. The best iodine is extracted from itself and the sea rods and oarweed all burned together. That's the way it's normally done, especially in Connemara, although other types are burned mixed through these without taking much from the kelp.

The mayweed grows on the deep. It begins to grow at the beginning of spring and it's ripe for falling around Mayday, or its time is past as they say on the coast. The tuft of mayweed grows on top of the sea rod tufts. They're much the same in shape, shaped almost like your hand – the palm the heart of the clump and the fingers the fronds – except that they're a foot or more in length and in width. The heart of the mayweed clump begins to grow on top of the other one, and at that point the fronds of the lower clump gather densely together from the top to give the mayweed clump a chance to spread and grow. As time passes it doesn't neglect to get a grip from leaf to leaf on the sea rod tuft until it has plenty of fronds to support it underneath. Time passes until the mayweed clump is mature, the heart which is attached to the top of the other one begins to narrow gradually, from five or six inches at the start to a couple of inches at the end. If bad weather and a swell come, which often happens, thousands of millions of clumps fall off the top of the sea rods. But, suppose the sea was quiet and the weather fine during this time for a few weeks, wouldn't you think the mayweed would stay as a laughing stock on top of the rocks? There's little danger of that. Nature rarely fails, and it's said that God never closes a door but that he opens another one. He didn't fail here as ever, as the little winkles that are called the *sceanairí* (cutters) go about their business willingly and it doesn't take long for those abundant hungry hordes to bore the necks between the two parts of the weed and they don't leave much go to waste that isn't eaten. Anyway, they like them a lot and maybe they grow impatient when the weed gets longer and they have to do the work. And for that matter, even if the swell breaks it off, they eat it, and they attack the heart first, it's the sweetest part for them. It's said that unity is strength and that's right as regards the boring and eating of this mayweed. Even if there's a plentiful throng of them helping one another they can't be accused of dodging work nor of laziness, as they are the harvesters of the mayweed, or at least help it along if the swell fails. The kelp makers aren't very grateful to them because of the damage they do in boring and eating it, but even Homer sometimes nods.

The fresh clumps of mayweed are beautiful when they come ashore from the sea, especially when the rays of the sun glisten and shine on them, they would remind you of gold, and it's a golden harvest too for the poor kelp makers who need it, to help them make some money for themselves and their families. They distribute the amount of seaweed that comes ashore among themselves and spread it on the ground, using ass or horse, and if the shore is not suitable for them there's nothing for it but for themselves to haul up by creel on their backs. They cast lots for it when it's divided up. Often there's an odd sea rod through it; the *ceanna slat* grow on them and the mayweed is the flower of those *ceanna slat*. It's necessary to start with the clumps near the sea: the work is easier to carry out as the surf threw them ashore. The last ones to be cast up are the first to be gathered and the first covering to be left until last. When the day's work starts, it's spread out, it's cocked every evening to protect it from the dew or in case of rain, and it's spread again early the following day, and the same again for a few days or until such time as it's dried and seasoned enough, when big cocks are made of it and some sort of caps are put on them to keep them safe until the burning season at the end of summer. A lot of it is taken from the deep sheltered holes in the lee of the small islands with iron hooks that have thirty-foot long shafts of red deal. I often got up at cockcrow to go gathering it; you would think that it was the middle of the day by the seashore with the noise and bustle of people, grapnels being hauled, people heading off in twos and threes in every direction. We would sail out with the moon at the end of night with a westerly wind under full sail and other boats ahead of us and behind us until we reached the harvesting ground on the deep hole of *Oileán Lachan*. It's a wonder the harvesters don't hurt themselves with the long shafts of the hooks, as the place is very narrow, two men in each boat, every one of forty with a hook and they twisting them above each others' heads every now and then. On taking the seaweed up from the bottom they must stretch those poles across three or four boats. Nevertheless, they don't make contact with each other, they're well used to the work. But if there were an inexperienced group in that small area of sea, I guarantee that some of them would have sore heads; when they wouldn't have much experience they wouldn't be able to look around and bring up mayweed at the same time. The long narrow poles would remind you of straight bare trees, if they weren't being lowered and raised and intertwined in each other during the mens' work on the playing field. As long as the season lasts a lot of work is done. Two men harvest and bring ashore three loads of a three-ton boat. Isn't that amount many the full hook-load, about two stone weight in each hook-load, from the bottom, on average? That would mean that each person of the two would put up to four hundred hook-loads into the boat. At the beginning of the season there's a lot of it growing high on the sea bottom and it's not so hard to load it. I often heard from the old people that they themselves saw the time when a two man crew used take five loads ashore for six days a week, perhaps without anything to eat throughout the day but a few cold boiled potatoes and a drop of buttermilk that they'd bring with them in the morning. "That's when there were strong healthy men" they would say, "unlike the emaciated people around today. Tea and white bread and too much care and feebleness are the cause of that wasting".

In the mayweed season a lot of fish shoals come in from the deep sea to the west. They follow each other – the big follow the small. Some of them don't stop or stay still until they reach the mayweed area. There are a lot of pollack, coalfish, pilchard, sand eels, gunnel, pipefish, whelks, prawns and lots of other types, not to mention winkles and *sceanairí* and others, all of them in one big assortment rushing along with the hunger, some of them eating the weed and others eating and swallowing each other according to their capability, their strength and their cunning. Spurdog often get the smell of the blood and the strife and when they arrive on the spot it's a right battle, as they do damage to pollack and coalfish. A lot of the other smaller tribes hide in the mayweed and under the cheeks of the boats if they're there, until there's an end to the battle – which proves that the fish have a great liking for the mayweed. Indeed, they and the *sceanairí* do a lot of damage to much of it during the season.

If the sea is troubled as it comes ashore on an ebbing tide, you will normally see women, men and children out to their armpits in the mouth of the waves gathering it and bringing it ashore on the strand in a creel. If it were allowed to dry the sand would ruin a lot of it, or the undertows would bury it in the soft strand. They work as hard as they can for a couple of weeks; anything that's left after that time is too rotten to handle. Two or three people can get the material for three or four tons of kelp out of it, if the weather is suitable. A hundredweight of kelp is extracted form twenty hundredweight of the wet mayweed. It doesn't wither in the wind or sun like other types. When it's dried and seasoned about three times its weight has been lost by those two agents. That's a return of about one hundredweight of kelp from five hundredweight of the dried weed.

The shores and deep holes are normally full of mayweed by Mayday, but it's not normal to lay a hand on it as the people believe that the fairies are busy that day moving abode from one place to another. For that reason they have a day off. There's a little tale told in the folklore about a man in the townland who didn't believe those kinds of things. He headed off to sea one Mayday morning to bring a load of seaweed ashore, but if he did, let him be, because with the first hook he put down to the bottom on *Poll Domhain Oileáin Lachan* a gust of wind lifted him overboard after the hook, even though the morning was so quiet that it wouldn't budge a hair on your head. His partner had to throw him the end of a rope as soon as he could, and he was on his last gasp when he came aboard, and to top it all, he spent the following week sick in bed. From that day that old Cóilín was swept overboard like a wisp of hay very little was harvested on Mayday. The people understood better that old habits shouldn't be broken, that perhaps the fairies had something to do with that episode. Anyway little mayweed was harvested there on Mayday since then.

The mayweed doesn't last long in clumps without rotting. Within a couple of days it's quite sick, especially if there's much of it piled up and no salt drying on it. It heats up and produces grubs. Then large flocks of gull and terns gather to have a feast on those small white maggots. That company doesn't always agree about the food. Now and then they have bouts of fighting, so that all that's visible around them is a shower of feathers, sand and weed all mixed together. The amount of mayweed on the deep stays fresh for a couple of weeks due to its being moved about by the pull of the sea. Isn't that a great advantage for the poor kelp makers?

The landlord had never any rent or power over the deep holes, although he tried once to keep them for himself. I often heard the old people talk about the dispute that arose between themselves and the landlord that time. It appears there was a war on at the time and the price of everything was high compared to the period before then. As a result of that, the landlord thought he would have a hand in the profit and raise the rent. He started cajoling and flattering the people saying there was very valuable material being extracted from the seaweed, that the mayweed pools should be protected before another group of people came into the townland to take it, and so on. The tenants saw the bait and didn't yield to him. That made him mad, and he took some of them to court for taking the mayweed. He made out that if it were left alone it would come ashore on his land with the swell and the gales. He wasn't right there; it normally doesn't move off the deep in any bad weather. He didn't get any satisfaction form the court as the judge wasn't able to make any sense of the case, though the landlord and his assistants pursued every avenue they could. It was necessary to re-awaken books that hadn't been used for ages and to brush the spiders' cobwebs, mildew and dust form them. But it was no good as there was no information about the law of the mayweed in them. The judge, therefore, could make no judgement. He closed the case by ordering that a message be sent to the government to instruct the Admiralty that an article be included on the law pertaining to mayweed in the law of the sea. The judge thought that was the right thing to do. No one heard any more about the affair, but plenty of mayweed has been taken from those holes since; I think it's about sixty years or more since that time. No one was ever stopped since and no government or landlord interfered with the harvesting of the seaweed.

As most sowing is done before the mayweed season not much of it is used as potato fertilizer but it's put on turnips and mangels now and again. It's good fertilizer but nevertheless it pays more to make kelp out of it and that's exactly what's done.

Indeed, it's hardly worth my while to recount in any more detail what happens during the mayweed season as it's nearly the same story every day – dividing it out, putting it up on the land and drying it, taking it in the boats, bringing it ashore, spreading it and cocking it. The last day of the season comes when all that's to be found are rotten slimy cut fragments full of white maggots that are of no use or value. It would need to be worth the trouble of taking it and bringing it ashore – the remains from the harvesters, the *sceanairí* and the fish.

I well remember a day at the end of May. Indeed, none of the boats were even loaded to the gunwales but were coming in with a light load from the sea. When the sun was going down in the sea to the west and the *Beanna Beola* to the north were changing strange wonderful colours due to the last rays of the sun shining on them during that time, the dry mayweed was being cocked, as the dew was beginning to fall heavily on the shore. The shag and the cormorant were heading out to the lonely rocks for the night, the seal, who was fending for himself since the previous morning in the bay, was now wandering back past the point to reach his own dark cave, shoals of sand eels hiding themselves under the sand before the tide ebbed, people returning to their houses after having cocked the mayweed, and what they had harvested that day spread out, hoping that tomorrow would be fine. Weren't they thinking already of harvesting oarweed with the *croisini?* The lamps were being lit, as the daylight was fading and the dark colours of night were spreading, everything going to rest. Isn't it as well for me to follow suit and to end this, to say goodbye to the mayweed until another time, and to start describing another type, to get to know it better.

An Fheamainn Gheimhridh [61] The "Winter Weed" *Laminaraia hyperborea*

This is called winter seaweed because a lot of it comes ashore at that time of year and people spread it as winter manure on their land. It's a good help, and therefore the shore people are very happy whey they see the big red clumps glistening on shore or beach. It's good fertilizer and there are a lot of other types mixed through it as the harvesters of the sea gather all before them.

The sea rods are often attached to the clumps coming ashore, and maybe even have big stones attached to the holdfasts, proving that the swell of the sea has a lot of power. People often have to break the sea rods from the tufts as the rods are not used for fertiliser but are put aside for kelp. When there's a swell in the sea the people have to go into the water because if the weed were exposed on an ebbing tide the undertows would bury it in the soft sand and it would be useless. You would often see men and women on frosty mornings in the middle of winter up to their necks in the sea on the beaches, others helping by bringing out empty creels and bringing full creels ashore on the dry strand. The sea would often also break in one big confusion on top of them taking their legs from under them and throwing them ashore like sea rods. That didn't bother them in the slightest, hadn't they plenty of experience of the antics of the sea? They would be out again immediately in the breakers. Those of them who were knowledgeable enough about the tricks of the sea could stay on their feet and let the wave break over them, by standing with their shoulders rigid against the waves. You can do that. I can tell you that the water would be quite cold when you first walked into it. Nevertheless, after a while you would feel nice and warm from the work, filling the creels or taking them ashore and breaking the sea rods from the tufts if they had any, and often they did.

It's good kelp material and if the weather is good some of it is dried on the stone walls and made into stacks until the burning season the following summer. It's said that it doesn't lose anything with age either but it's so squashed and pressed together in the old stacks after the year that you would nearly need a pincers to separate it on the day of burning. It's hard work to tease and pull apart a stack, but it's done gradually in time. This type is called *ceanna slat*, and on big low tides in spring, as they are exposed on very low tides only, a lot of them are cut for fertiliser, especially in a year when there isn't any winter manure made. The people have to cut them, often with bent sickles, and take them aboard their boats with iron hooks. It's hard work too, but those who live from the sea have nothing easy; they never had and probably never will have.

[61] *Feamainn gheimhridh* represents the fronds ("leaves") of *L. hyperborea* that are thrown ashore in winter.

An tSlat Mhara [62] The "Sea Rod" *Laminaria hyperborea*

The sea rods grow out on the big deep and some of them are up to twelve foot in length, especially those that are in the valleys sheltered from the pull and agitation of the sea. You must understand that there are dips and heights, hills and valleys on the sea bottom just as there are on top of the land. The sea rods are like forests and they are constantly being moved and swayed here and there with the movement of the sea; just as trees are by puffs of wind. If you were out on the sea on a fine day you would see the fish wandering about and weaving slowly between the rods and there's no colour in the rainbow that wouldn't be seen mottled and mixed all over the place. It's a beautiful and wonderful sight that would make the finest artist green with envy.

In winter the swell removes a lot of the sea rods and even though they don't float, a lot of them are washed up on the shores and beaches. When there are big clumps of them at the top of the shore, they're in one big jumble, twisted and intertwined amongst each other with the result that it's difficult to remove one of them. The power and working of the sea is beyond description.

There's no kelp material as good as them, and therefore, many are put on walls to dry them in winter, and when they're dry and seasoned they're as hard and sinewy as a piece of rope; the mesh in lobster pots is often made from them. They're not strong enough for the ribs. It's said that pots made from hazel are better than those made from willow. Maybe the lobster is fond of them because they came from their own kingdom. They're great for kindling a kiln in the morning and for keeping it red for the day when the weather is bad. They light easily because of the amount of sap. They're the best feather in the cap of the kelp burner at any rate.

Children often make balls from the holdfasts, and hurleys from the rods so as to play hurling. Knife handles are also made from them; when the rod is fresh and iron is thrust into it and when it's dried it will have a great grip on the blade. They're often thrown on the beach beneath the boats' keels when they're being launched or taken ashore; aren't they good and hard and slippery for them to run on? It makes the work easier for the launchers also.

They're a valuable type for kelp; the people share them just like anything else. They dry quickly on the stone walls due to the wind coming through the gaps. The tufts are often left on them and they're put on the east side of the wall, the sheltered side. The rain has no effect on them there and they're made into stacks when they're bone dry of salt water. The poet himself did not forget them in the song:

Wasn't Maínis the fine townland, reported this man Maitias
With the best of land in plenty, as fertiliser it comes ashore
Ye may talk of the wood of Garman or the woods of Ballinahinch now
But what comes ashore as sea rods 'neath my house is worth far more

There's no doubt but he had a lot of truth in that, because the amount of kelp extracted from them over a period is quite a lot. It's said that you can get up to a hundredweight of kelp from two tons of them fresh from the sea. Then, when there are thousands of tons

[62] The sea rod is the stipe or stalk of *L. hyperborea*.

coming ashore every year, it's many a ton of kelp can be made from them. I've no idea what price kelp is now, and therefore I'm stopping now and leaving the rest until another time. It's said that it's best to leave a part of every story untold.

An Fheamainn Mhín [63] The "Smooth Weed" *Laminaria hyperborea*

When the mayweed falls this type grows on top of the rod. It's almost like the mayweed but it's not as heavy or as bulky. At the time of the longest day it's mature and with the pull and swell of the sea it falls and is washed up on beach and shore. The kelp makers haul up the amount that comes ashore with a creel to the drying ground in order to dry it and they harvest a lot of it with big hooks in the deep holes. They take it ashore in boats and when it's dried and saved they make big cocks of it until the burning season comes. It's then put in the kilns mixed with other types. It withers a lot in the wind and sun and it doesn't produce as much iodine as the mayweed or the oarweed and you can't get as much kelp from it either.

As the sowing is finished by the time it comes ashore it's not used as fertiliser. Nevertheless, it's often put on turnips and on other such produce and even if it is, it's not bad. The people often go into the water to gather it up, one person up to his armpits filling a creel with it, another person bringing it in on the dry strand and unloading it so as to give the man out in the water an empty creel each time. It's necessary to do that, especially if there's a swell, as the undertow buries the smooth weed in the sand when it's thrown ashore on the beach. Sandy weed is no good for kelp or for anything else. As well as that it's heavy to put up on the land.

An Choirleach nó Duilleacha The Oarweed *Laminaria digitata*

Out into the middle of May, when the mayweed is dry and saved, and the big cocks put aside, the people begin to think of the *croisín* and the cutting of oarweed, as the season is close at hand; wouldn't it be a good thing to get another couple of tons out of it with the fine weather?

The oarweed grows in long thin slippery very smooth leaves that reach four or five feet in a year's growth. It's coloured dark brown with no root or indentation from the holdfast on the rock up to the top. There's a narrow round stem between the holdfast and the leaves that's as sinewy as a piece of rope. Most of them are exposed on a low spring tide, and indeed, it's a lovely sight during that time. There's not much difference between it and the mayweed for kelp; they're better mixed together. The kelp that's extracted from them is spotted with every colour of the rainbow. On low spring tides in summer and in autumn during fine weather and on quiet seas you would see a lot of boats beside the small islands and the lonesome rocks, densely packed by the shores, the crews doing their best with sickles and knives stripping the rocks and making heaps of it here and there until the tide turns. Then they load that which is nearby into the boat by hand, and that which is not convenient to load into the creels they work with ropes. One person stays in the boat and the other man hitches the end of the rope under the bundle of seaweed. The

[63] The term *feamainn mhín* is used to denote the young fronds of *L. hyperborea* as they appear at the beginning of summer.

man in the boat hauls in a line of seaweed and settles it in the hold of the boat, he coils the rope and casts it back to the man who is gathering it, and so on until the last lot comes aboard and the boat is loaded. They sail off home then, quite tired, with the flowing tide, as the low tide lasts only a short while. They work hard enough, I tell you.

It's worked with *croisíní* on a neap tide. There's no work as hard as working the *croisíní*, especially on the exposed shores of Connemara, and there's nowhere, no matter how exposed, that it doesn't grow and the darker and heavier it is the better as regards juice and strength and weight in the kelp. You can't beat oarweed from *Sceirde*. But, indeed, you need fine weather and a quiet sea to get the best from these remote lonely rocks, as there's a swell in the sea there, even on the most beautiful day, and *Leic Mhór Charraig na Meacan* is nearly as bad except that it's not as far from home.

When a three-ton boat is loaded by two men with their *croisíní* they have earned their keep. They often have to get into the water during that time. Nevertheless, they take it on board bit by bit until they've the boat loaded down to the gunwales. As a lot of water comes in with the weed, it's necessary to bale the boat with the bucket now and then. I often counted the number of *croisín*-fulls of oarweed that would fill the forward hold when I was harvesting, and with good oarweed of two years' growth forty fills would do the trick. That would be one sixth of the load; that would mean two hundred and forty would fill the boat. The oarweed was vigorous and heavy, plenty of sounding and growling to be heard as it separated from the rock, heaps of mussels attached to the bottom of the holdfast, and the feet covered in little limpets, the long dark brown sturdy leaves shiny and smooth, greying with growth at their tips, and long white worms twisting on them, the heavy healthy smell of the sea from it, giving an extra appetite to the harvester, something which is not often necessary, as the kelp harvester is always hungry, and often has not much to relieve the hunger.

Though strange to relate, it's far easier to haul it during a flowing tide than during an ebbing tide. The knobbly holdfasts haven't as strong a grip on the granite, I don't know why. When there's a flat face on an oarweed rock it's not so difficult to tear the weed away. It removes itself once the *croisín* is given a tug after a small twist, so that the leaves are twisted on one another like a thick cable. Then, when there's a batch of it aboard, it's jammed under the gunwale and when the boat rises with the tide there are many of the holdfasts supporting each other on the rock until they start growling and sounding. In that way the boat has a lot of power when it rises and you could lift a hundredweight in one batch with that attempt. You can do that on rough exposed shores only, where there is a couple of years' growth and where there's no slime on it, because it's too slimy in the lee of the islands and it would slip out of a grip before you could tie it to be lifted off the bottom with the power of the rising boat. The area is normally not more than five or seven feet deep on a low neap tide. It's easier to lift it when the *croisín* is kept out a little, that is to say, it's not thrust straight below you. You have much more power to tear those holdfasts off the rock if you have the *croisín* at a slight slant. I was often harvesting in places where I wouldn't take in a pound weight at a time, of red slender-stemmed oarweed, where there were murlins growing through it. That's the hard one! You would be as well off to drag the broad-footed devil by his tail. You would need a thousand *croisín*-fulls to load her up.

About an hour-and-a-half before low tide the boats arrive on the harvesting ground above the oarweed and after an hour-and-a-half of the flowing tide they leave for home. When

Hookers from Connemara with cargo of seaweed tied up at Galway Harbour,

they reach the strand beside the drying area they start to unload. One person usually loads it into creels on the gunwale and two people, up to their hips in water, carry it on their backs. The boat is as high up as the tide will allow and as it flows it floats up nearer the drying ground. When the last bundle is on the ground it's spread out. It's cocked every evening to protect it from the dew and spread again in the morning, it's turned over at midday and so on for two or three days until the salt is dry on it. It's then left in stumps for a week until it's dry enough to put into the big stack. It's left like that until it's time to burn it, that is unless it's sold dry to some company and that's often done. At a couple of shillings a dry hundredweight it would pay its harvester better than making kelp from it and to get eight pounds a ton, not to mention the trouble of burning it.

The shore has been divided for a long time among the people, as far down as the bottom of a low spring tide, and their share of the shore is in relation to their land holding. There's a boundary between each tithe so that everyone knows where his own portion is. Wouldn't you think that they couldn't but stray across the boundary, as they would be near it when harvesting? Kelp makers are decent likable people and if they trespass slightly now and then there's very little argument between them. Maybe if there's a cranky cross person you would hear some complaining and barking from him sometimes, but it's not worth two pins.

There was rent and tax on the oarweed as well as on the land. Indeed, there wasn't much of the price of the kelp left when the rent was taken out of it; it was easy to count. The kelp makers were working for the landlord. The rent money – about four hundred pounds a year – wouldn't last him long. He was getting between sixty and eighty pounds from the kelp makers. Those in the know who had dealings with them said that four hundred pounds wouldn't last an hour for some of them going about their business in the big cities of England, between horses and drink, reveling, sport and fun. It was worthless to them; wasn't that a good one! They thought little of the amount of sweat lost by the poor creatures who earned it for them. They were feeding and fattening themselves and having a good life on the backs of the poor, like insects sucking the blood and the marrow out of an old sheep, bringing themselves to a state of bursting with fatness.

At the beginning of this century the people of *Maínis* had to go to court against Colonel Houlihan (Ó hUallacháin) of Tuam, the bad landlord who was their master.[64] He was trying to impose a heavy rent on them because "the borders of gold" as he himself said, belonged to that part of his land. The oarweed was that golden lace. A few good Irish speakers from amongst the kelp makers went to Dublin to the court. But to make a long story short, the tenants got the upper hand that time, although it was a wonder they did. It was thanks to Father Mícheál Mac Aoidh and his other friends who took sides with the seaweed gatherers and fought faithfully and diligently against tyranny and bad laws. Some of them have passed away, God rest their souls.

A lot of oarweed is harvested in spring as fertiliser. It's better than mayweed for promoting growth and flowering. It needs to be exposed a bit to the weather on the ridge until it's discoloured by rain or dew. It turns white after being heated and dried by the sun followed by rain. It's better if it's dry when spreading. Indeed, not a lot is harvested especially as fertiliser as the people don't have a lot of it. It's left for kelp. The problem is its scarcity, unless there were a fine summer and a quiet sea so that you could get out onto the breakers and the exposed rocks. The amount that's near home doesn't last long, as the people don't have a lot of shore.

[64] The landlord in question was Colonel John Philip Nolan of Ballinderry near Tuam, a Member of Parliament. It is reputed that he bought the land in Maínis from money earned from his invention of a range finder for the 303 Lee Enfield rifle and the sale of the rights to its manufacture to the army of Russia (Liam Ó Mainnín, pers. comm.).

There was a dispute between the tenants and the landlord about the oarweed harvest. The landlord took them to court. He thought it would be plain sailing and no wonder. On the day of the hearing one of the harvesters had a *croisín* to show the judge how they used them to harvest. Mícheál Shéamais took off his clothes down to his trousers and his shirt. "Keep out of my way" said he to the crowd around him, although all he had beneath him was the bare dry floor. He was twisting and pulling, now and again wiping his forehead with his sleeve, as if he was drying the sweat from himself, just as he would do out at sea. Someone threw his *báinín* under the knife of the *croisín,* thinking that better than doing nothing. It didn't take long to put a twist in it, to lift it high, the judge looking on all the time; but the end of the story was a judgment of a couple of pounds each boat, about a quarter of what was demanded. It wasn't too bad for the poor people as they earned a fair bit from the seaweed and the other man got his share. They would have had a hard time of it if it weren't for their good friends in *Cumann na Talún* who were on their sides and against the other man. *Cumann na Talún* did a lot of good at the time, but that's another story for which we have no space here.

An Chopóg [65] — The Oarweed — *Laminaria digitata*

The *copóg* and *coirleach* are very much alike, except that the leaves of the *copóg* are wider and not as long and folded in at the top. It normally grows in a quiet area, especially if there's a strong current. It's exposed on a very low spring tide. A lot of it is cut with knives and sickles at the time, to put ashore in creels or to load into boats. On neap tides *croisíní* are used. It's not as difficult to harvest as the *coirleach,* as the holdfast hasn't such a strong grip on the rock, as there are a lot of encrusting weeds on the rocks. Where they're found many attach themselves to the edges of the holdfast that makes it impossible to remove them. The *copóg* is as good as *coirleach* for kelp and if it dries without being exposed to rain, you can get a hundredweight of kelp from twenty hundredweight of *copóga* from the sea. Many are thrown ashore in winter when the weather is bad. They're found amongst the others and they're put ashore as they're not bad as winter manure, but it's necessary to place stones or some weight on them as they are light and the wind could easily blow them away. They wither a lot in wind and sun, a lot more than the *coirleach.* They fade from brown to white in the rain or the dew. When it's added to knotted wrack or bladder wrack in spring for manure you need to expose it and let it fade before the sods are turned. As with the *coirleach,* that's the best way for crop growth. They are of great benefit to the planter at the time of harvest in a favourable year. During the kelp-burning they are the mainstay of the kelp maker, as they are excellent on top of sea rods and in a bed under the fire in the early morning to get the kiln going, and if the kelp maker gets a rainy day there's no danger of the kiln being put out if there are some of them in the cock. They're good kindling and along with sea rods good friends of the kelp maker. As they grow in sheltered places they can be harvested in bad weather when it's not possible to get near the *coirleach* and the kelp maker therefore keeps them for the rainy day. You would see harvesting going on in the shelter of coves and creeks during stormy weather and high sea swells. It's hard to tell them their business, they whose ancestors before them were in the same business, keeping watch over the shores and the antics of the sea in the west of Ireland.

[65] The *copóg* is a form of *L. digitata* that is shorter and wider and of a lighter yellow-brown colour than the *coirleach* and grows in sheltered situations.

An Rufa — The Sea Belt — *Laminaria saccharina*

The sea-belt grows in sheltered coves or in any place sheltered from the lashing of the waves and the strong puffs of wind. It looks very like the frills of a woman's dress of long ago. That may be also the origin of the name. It has brown and yellow leaves, five or six feet long and about six inches wide, full of folds and fairly indented on the edges with short narrow stems. They grow back to back on the rocks with the result that some of the holdfasts grow on top of one another. You'd find the odd one growing amongst the oarweed and when the harvesters are lifting the oarweed they don't leave them behind. They wither a lot in wind and sun and lose about one fifth of their weight. They're not much good for kelp. Nevertheless, they're dried in autumn, when there isn't much oarweed to be found. Indeed, there are few types the kelp maker doesn't use – anything that adds weight to the kelp. A lot is washed ashore in winter amongst other types. There's no distinction made but all types are spread in the field as fertilizer. It's necessary to put a weight of soil or stones on them before the wind scatters them in the air. They don't float but are pulled about by the tide, like the mayweed or oarweed.

An Chlaimhe — The Furbelows — *Saccorhiza polyschides*

The furbelows grows between the sea rods and the oarweed though it often goes amongst the oarweed. It's more abundant some years than others. Big strong vigorous branching tufts up to five feet in height from the rock, with a holdfast as big as a football and it and the rest of the plant hollow inside. Some are up to half a hundredweight, though they have no goodness or sap in them. They're harvested for kelp. It's hard to dry them because of their volume, but nevertheless, when they're spread on shores the wind and sun dry them with time. Another thing, they're not affected by wet weather and therefore the kelp makers bring ashore a lot of them during bad weather.

Many are often thrown ashore in winter when there's a swell in the sea. Those that are not too big are left mixed with other types and put out as winter manure on the fields. Indeed, it would have to be worth the trouble, as they're not good material for getting flowers or other plants to sprout. It's said that the smallest thing can cause great trouble and so it is with the furbelows that was the cause of a boat sinking.

A *bád iomartha* from *Leitir Mealláin* was returning from *Carraig na Meacan* with a load of furbelows and oarweed. There were two men rowing and a woman on the aft beam baling. At that time the women were as adept in boats as the men, well able to cut seaweed and everything else. Anyway, there was a furbelows holdfast hanging off the heaped load in the water at the boat's side. The woman thought she'd haul it aboard but failed and one of the men came to her aid and when the two tried to haul it, the pile of seaweed above the gunwale slipped, and the boat capsized and the crew and the seaweed were thrown overboard. My grandfather and his brother Páidín were coming from *Árainn* in a *púcán* with a load of potatoes, and however the man who was out forward in the boat looked underneath the sail he saw the boat going down. They made their way there as fast as they could; they barely arrived in time as the woman was going down, but with the blessing of God my grandfather managed to grab her by the hand. They hauled aboard the two men, who were bad enough, but the woman was at her last gasp. They made no delay but started to massage her until they saved her from death's door. They put some of their own dry woollen clothes next to her skin, and to make a long story short, she improved greatly within a short while. They attached the end of a rope to the boat which was floating below the surface and since there was a full set of sails of a favourable wind it didn't take them long to tow her to *Trá Fhada Mhaínse*. The furbelows and oarweed were missing. When the boat was baled and those who were snatched from the sea had their hunger relieved they bade farewell to the people of the village and headed east towards *Leitir Meallain.*

A lot of oarweed and furbelows is still harvested on *Carraig na Meacan* as much as it was eighty years ago. People still put themselves in danger and are drowned but I have no intention, especially now, of describing any more of those episodes, and as a result I intend to lower my sails and spend some time thinking of the antics of the sea and the accursed furbelows that nearly sent those people to another life. As they are now gone to their eternal reward, God rest their souls.

An Rúálach **The Sea Laces** *Chorda filum*

This is like the sea thong except that it grows very long and that it's full of water. It's most abundant in sheltered bays and it normally grows on small stones or on empty shells. The cords often intertwine due to eddy currents and form what look like cables that would be twenty fathoms in length, stretching up from the sea bottom. It's no good as fertiliser or kelp. It often comes ashore mixed with other seaweeds and indeed it's also a tangled mess. Nevertheless, it must be separated from the rest and thrown aside. It's not a good place to go swimming amongst it and if some of it were to get caught in your spindle-shanks you would be in great danger. Therefore, one stays away from where it grows. Boatmen also often find it troublesome as it gets caught between the heel of the keel and the lower tip of the rudder, that is unless the boat were clean, and if things get caught in that cleft it's God's justice as it's indifference is the cause of it. [66]

There are people who are lazy and who let things pass and put them on the long finger, but if a sea lace or a lobster pot rope keeps them on anchor for a while and they in a hurry, as seafarers usually are, that's when they're sorry they hadn't bridged that cursed cleft before then. I will guarantee that when they get the chance that they will solve the problem by attaching a small piece of leather to the heel of the keel with a few nails so that it's back as far as the pointed tip of the rudder. Then the gap would be well closed.

An tSraoilleach **The Murlins** *Alaria esculenta*

The murlins grows on wild exposed shores through the oarweed in certain places. It is difficult to harvest with a *croisín* as it has a strong grip on the rock. Not only that, but it's not easy to raise the oarweed itself which is found in the same place, and therefore the kelp makers avoid it. But during low tides when the exposed oarweed is cut the murlins is left through it even though it's not much use for kelp, and it withers a lot in the wind and sun as it contains a lot of water. It's not much good as fertilizer either, but nevertheless when it's in the pile with others it's let go. The holdfasts themselves are the

[66] Being clean means the presence of a heel or small extension of the aft end of the keel which passes behind the lower tip of the rudder so as a rope cannot rise between the rudder and the stern post

THE BOLD HORSEMAN

1.

It was late last night that I spied the bold horseman,
Advancing, and not yielding to the downpour,
Dressed in his suit of armour, flanked by his sword,
And from there down each detail was in order.

2.

It is no lie or jest to tell, that surprise upon me fell,
If I can now but half my tale relate,
But be sure and take good care, you simple soul, beware,
For you don't hold the lease on Muínis.

3.

As far as I am told, he's a son of Grand Signor,
Who was driven off his course and thwarted,
Coming to make sport to the lighthouse at *Iorras Mór*,
And I'm certain he held gold in plenty.

4.

Were Fionn to live this long, and an election to put on,
Many's the man, with laughter, would roar,
And the horse on which he rode when he turned up at my door,
Would banish from the glens the hornless doe.

5.

Wasn't he the placid horse, the finest in all of Ireland,
Who would, for speed, the March wind out-run,
For he surpassed them all at racecourses big and small,
From England all the way to *Barr na Cruaiche*.

6.

His saddle came from Spain, his bridle German-made,
A pair of horseshoes, in grey steel, from the King of France,
And I'd be surely bound that his match could not be found,
As a horseman, this boy was so advanced.

7.

We must now undertake, a solid court to make,
With one acre of land underneath it,
And a set of mighty guns, resting up along the front,
To overcome the enemy's great power.

8.

'Tis my pity the tribe of Gael, the noblest of mankind,
So bravely they line up to front the faction,
For if we fail to take the lead, and facing danger, not succeed,
I fear Ireland will get no satisfaction.

best parts of it. It's almost like oarweed except that the leaves are very flimsy, veined and slightly indented on the edge and the holdfasts are more flattened on the rock. It normally grows among the stalked oarweed and it would be as easy to drag the devil by the tail as remove it.
One night a long time ago that some of the young lads of the village wanted to play a trick on Micheál Mharcais, the local poet, they got a big quiet dog and dressed it up in murlins and oarweed so that it was covered in weed from the end of his tail to the tip of his nose. It was unrecognisable. They dressed a boy as well, and they put a belt of oarweed on him, lots of murlins around his neck and his waist and trailing down to his heels. They put him astride the dog, a strand of murlins as a halter in his hand, and a stirrup of the same material that he made taut with his feet. In this disguise the two sailed pass the poet's door. When he heard the commotion, he got up and stood between the two door jambs and looked at the spectacle for a while. A shower of rain fell and the lovely bright moon came out, and the oarweed, furbelows (as there was furbelows under the child's belt and he had a sea rod on his shoulder) and the murlins on the dog glistened resplendently from the light of the moon and stars, and to top it all, there was a multi-coloured bright luminescence dancing and throbbing on the coats of seaweed fresh from the sea. That didn't upset the poet; there wasn't a chance of that. He went in, sat down, put a palm under his cheek, looked into the fire and started to compose the song *An Marcach Tréan* (The Bold Horseman) about the boy and the dog. Micheál composed many songs in his lifetime. *Loch na Nidhe,* which he wrote about the queen of the fairy dwelling is a fine song. It's a long time since I learned *An Marcach Tréan* off by heart.

An Ríseach — The Sea Thong — *Himanthalia elongata*

This is like yellow twine. A lot of it grows on the shores of Connemara. In summer and autumn a lot of it is harvested for kelp. It's full of sap, slime and dye. It's doesn't rot as quickly as oarweed in bad weather, and therefore, when the weather isn't the best, a lot of it is taken ashore in boats, in from the islands. It can't be harvested with *croisíní,* as it's too slippery; it would slip off the blade of the *croisín.* If there's a big low tide it's cut with knives and sickles, or the boat can be let through it and it can be hauled aboard by hand because it floats. When the wind is onshore it's often harvested on a low tide and it floats up to the high tide mark with wind and current. That's called a wind ebb tide.
There's nothing wrong with it as fertiliser if it's exposed to the weather for a week. It's a very heavy type, it's twice as heavy as oarweed. Nevertheless, it floats lightly on the surface of the water and the oarweed and mayweed do not. It's harvested yearly, as the swell would remove it if it were too long. It's necessary to burn it mixed through other types because it's damp and heavy and full of sap. It adds a lot of weight to kelp but it's not recommended as good kelp material, unlike sea rods or oarweed. Amongst the sea thong is a good place for wrasse; there are little worms where it grows that the wrasse like a lot. I often set a net in such a place and even if I did I never had any cause for complaint.
It was wet weather at the beginning of autumn and therefore we were harvesting sea thong this particular day on *Leic na Cora.* We were harvesting some here and there and moving from rock to rock as usual. We filled her to the gunwales with the sea thong. We had to cut furbelows for the top of the load, as it can't be made from sea thong because

it's so slippy. At any rate, we loaded her down to the gunwales, but to make a long story short, when we were halfway home the wind strengthened and as we were loaded deep, the odd splash came in. We turned the head of the boat into the wind, and as we did, the sea thong slipped to one side with the result that she put her beam under the water and filled. The seaweed went overboard and my brother and I were in the water. Another boat that was coming in from the sea picked us up and we attached the end of a rope to the boat that was floating submerged and towed it ashore.

I remember well a fine day in autumn that myself and another man were burning seaweed. After dinner time there was about a ton of sea thong next to the kiln. A boy came around and said that the kelp man was in the village, and however I glanced back I thought I saw him.

"Look at him back there" said I.

"Indeed and that's him" said Pádraig with a frightened look. "Upon my soul" said he, "hurry up and put that pile of sea thong out of the way".

"I'll put oarweed on top of it", said I.

"What are you saying?" said he, "how do you know that fellow won't turn it up; we'd be in a right mess then"

"What about throwing it on the sheltered side of the kiln in the smoke?" said I.

"O, don't do that whatever you do" said he.

"Why not?" said I.

"Never mind the why not, but the same thing that happened the other man will happen to you. Throw it down by the cliff on the shore. It's no time for talk."

There was a heavy mat of seaweed on the kiln and as there was it gave us both time to do the business. I nearly hurt a man who was at the bottom of the cliff when I threw the first lot down; it nearly fell on top of him. Discretion was the better part of valour as far as he was concerned. When he started with a cursed look on him, he spoke angrily but we didn't wait to hear much of his complaining. But to shorten the story, when the coast was clear, "Hi, Pádraig" said I, "whatever happened to that other man?"

"O yes", said he, "the kelp man was passing by and he thought the smoke of the kiln would be a good hiding place. And wasn't it, but for the wind changing and the kelp man standing there, the sea thong in front of his two eyes when the smoke cleared, and to make matters worse, a small bag of stones".

"Wasn't it a sad state of affairs?" said I, "or did he get a reduction in the price for the kelp?"

"A reduction?" said Pádraig, "he didn't get a penny for it, but had it coloured with limewater so he couldn't sell it anywhere else".

"Wasn't it a bad law?" said I.

"There's no doubt", said he, "but there was a hard life in those times", as he lit his pipe with a piece of sea rod.

"Look at him coming this way" said I. Who was it but the very same man that we were calling the kelp man.

"Indeed" said Pádraig "he's a travelling man", and didn't Pádraig curse him. I had to take my creel and bring back the sea thong, and when we had it burned with the oarweed, it was time to let the kiln out and clean it and to put away the amount that was melted as the last of the sea thong was burned.

Tying a climín (seaweed raft) near Ros a'Mhíl (Rosaveal).

An Fheamainn Bhuí **The Knotted Wrack** *Ascophyllum nodosum*

The knotted wrack is the pick of the bunch for fertiliser. There's no shrub growing out of the ground that it cannot make grow. It's hard to beat it and the bladder wrack when they're mixed together. It's said that they're best like that. The knotted wrack grows near the half tide level, mixed with other types or on its own. It's quite full of sap and it doesn't wither too much with wind and sun. That means that there's little water in it. During an ebb tide, on a fine spring day, it's a lovely sight glistening under the sun's rays. It would remind you of melted gold, the branching slippery tufts swaying to and fro as the tide ebbs away from it. A lot of it is harvested in spring and loaded into boats and two men need to work hard with two good sharp knives to load a three-ton boat to the gunwales during that time. Indeed, it's hard work and I often had a backache from bending to shave the rocks. The flowing tide waits for no one and it's necessary therefore to make haste and load the boat in time. The team normally cut as fast as they can until low tide and they have a good part of the shore bared by then, the seaweed in heaps here and there around the boat. They load the nearby clumps with pikes and the rest with creels. When the boat is afloat and full up they sail home and unload when it's high tide.

Often when the wind is favourable, they don't bother with a boat, but cut it and leave it scattered all over the shore under the care of the flowing tide and the favourable wind, and indeed those two elements don't neglect their duties and leave it carefully up at the

Towing a climín (seaweed raft) near Ros a'Mhíl (Rosaveal).

top of the high water mark without even a tuft missing. It's often also made into a *climín* (seaweed raft), that is to say oars are laid out on the shore, a round heap of seaweed is made on top of them, and it's tied with ropes, and when it floats it's rafted with a long pole to its destination; normally the journey isn't long. It's left at the top of the high tide until the owner gets a chance to draw it up to the field. If it's left in a heap for a week it heats up, it decays and maggots appear. Therefore, it's necessary to be put in order soon after harvesting it. It's said that it can add weight to kelp, although it's not recommended for the testing glass, but kelp buyers don't often resort to the testing glass.

An Chaisíneach **The Channelled Wrack** *Pelvetia canaliculata*

This is the type of seaweed furthest up on the shore, and because of that it doesn't grow very fast. It seems that it needs the heat of the sun for a good while, because during a neap tide it's often without a drop of saltwater near it for a whole week and what's more it doesn't affect it; the small leaves about three or four inches in length are fairly shrivelled due to the exposure but they regain their shape and vigour as soon as they get the taste of saltwater again. It's that sparse that it's hardly worth the trouble of harvesting it. It's good kelp material, that is to add weight to it as it's full of sap but it's said that it's not much good in the sample. You would often see cows and calves and asses down on the shore eating it off the rocks. It seems that they like the small brown branches because they lick their lips after a meal of channelled wrack. It turns green with the rain and a lot of slime appears on it. In the old days it was favoured as a food for pigs; when it's boiled and mashed with potatoes they would have a great liking for it. There's no doubt that it's very healthy and fills the stomach. During the summer it's a pastime for children to harvest it

Channelled Wrack, 15 cm

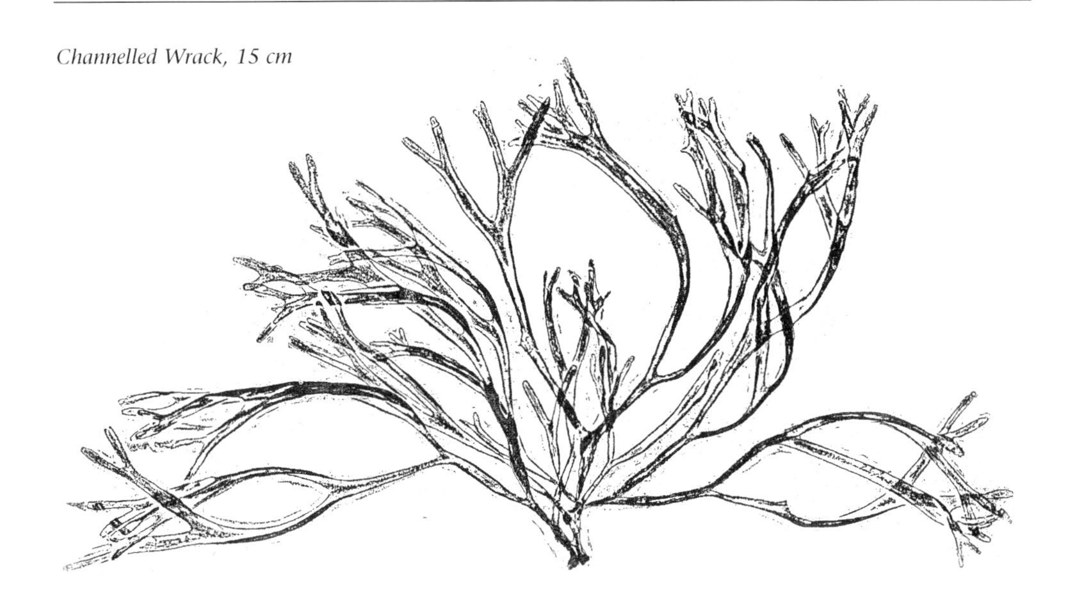

and dry it and burn it in small kilns, imitating the kelp makers and learning their craft. It often causes arguments also. Where there is a crowd of them together they steal it from each other when they get the chance. He who is weak is often left behind. That scrap doesn't last for long as they're friends again the following day. It's said that a quarrel between friends doesn't last.

An Mhíoránach The Toothed Wrack *Fucus serratus*

The toothed wrack is not bad as fertiliser when a year old, but there's no good left in it if older than that – getting older, getting worse. The brown serrated fronds grow near the low tide level, in quiet areas. It withers a lot when exposed and it doesn't rot easily in bad weather.

A lot of it is thrown ashore in bad weather. It's left mixed with the other types and put out on the land as fertiliser. If the fronds are long or big in volume the fertiliser itself is no good. It has no bladders, and therefore it doesn't float, but floats under water like the furbelows or the mayweed. It's a hard non-succulent type like the sea oak. If you were to spread it in spring under the potato sets on the ridges you will see yourself that the stems that grow are short and the day the potatoes are harvested in the autumn it will be in its own form as it was the previous spring, especially if it had two years' growth. It's not much good for kelp, but nevertheless it is harvested during wet rough weather as it's very resistant to rain. Kelp makers prefer to work with it than to be harvesting any other type that rots easily. As well as that it adds some weight to the kelp but it's not much good for the sample.

In the old days when boats were carrying seaweed to County Clare some of the year-old toothed wrack was mixed with the bladder wrack and the knotted wrack and even if it were the buyers had no objection. It's said that it's not bad for certain soils, that is to have

Toothed Wrack, 60 cm

it mixed with other types. It's not the same seaweed that is suitable for loamy soil and for sandy soil, for heath or for gravelly soil. Oarweed is better for gravelly soil than for loamy soil, and toothed wrack is better for loamy soil than for sandy soil. As the loamy soil requires less fertiliser the poor seaweed is most suitable for it.

An Barrchonla The Bladder Wrack *Fucus vesiculosus*

There's not much difference between the bladder wrack and the knotted wrack as fertiliser. Neither of them can be beaten for potatoes or vegetables, nor for meadows if it came to that. The bladder wrack is best at a year's growth when the brown-leaved branches reach about a foot in length. Nevertheless, it's often let go two years as it's longer and stronger and the harvesters can therefore load a boat more easily. It grows between low tide and high tide in quiet areas near the knotted wrack; these two are often harvested mixed together. It's said that's by far the best way for sandy land. That much of it that grows near the edge of the sandy shore is no good because of the number of small limpets on it. It floats on top of the water like knotted wrack, as there are many bladders on the fronds. It's harvested from boats in spring as fertiliser for potatoes and other crops. It's also harvested "by wind". It's cut from the rocks on low tide and left scattered on the shore under the care of tide and wind that deposit it on the top of the high water mark with the change of tide.

It's not much good for kelp and therefore kelp makers don't get much from it. The knotted wrack is much better than it for putting in a kiln. The bladder wrack is a soft yellow succulent seaweed which can produce a good fertile crop if the year is good, or as the old people say " March dry and windy, April soft and wet, May showery and bright and autumn pleasant and sunny." Those are their portents and they're usually correct. On the east side of *Maínis* there's a couple of miles of smooth level beach spreading out northwards and southwards and it dries out for a half mile to the east in the bay on a big low spring tide. Often in winter you would see men quarrying stones from the cliffs on the face of the land and when the tide is low they make sure to carry these stones out on their backs or with a barrow on to the hard bare beach. Other times when the day is right and the tide is suitable they load them into their boats and when they reach the right place they throw them into the sea. Then again on the low tide you would see them arranging the stones one after the other as if they were making a road. Yes, indeed, they are arranging the stones in such a way that seaweed will grow on them in time. [67] If you happened about in a few weeks you would see tiny little brown leaves growing on the surface of the granite. That's the bladder wrack beginning to grow. It's not usual for knotted wrack to grow on movable stones; it needs the stone to be more fixed and reliable. Within a year the series of stones have a dense coat of bladder wrack. There's about a hundredweight on every two square yards. The man who planted the stones can see the result of his work. He can cut a boat-load in the place which was bare a year previously.

In the old days the landlord and his followers would bark at poor people, trying to raise the rent because of that kind of work, just as they would if any improvement were made to the house or to the land. Though the landlord spent most of his time living it up in London and in other fancy places, he didn't have to go to any soothsayer to find out what his tenants were doing on the lonely remote islands in Connemara.

An Chos Chrua [68] — The "Hard Stem" — *Fucus vesiculosus*

This seaweed grows in that place where there is a continuous rushing and beating of breakers against the bold wild cliffs, and therefore, don't blame it for not looking very tidy. Indeed, it has only a rough black stem without branch or otherwise, standing as straight as a willow rod on the hard surface of the granite. It's not surprising that it only grows about five or six inches, as when winter's strong violent waves break against the shore they don't leave a bit of it on its stems that it doesn't tear off without pity or compassion. It and the *cosa dubha* look the same except that the *cosa dubha* have little branches and they grow in less exposed places. This doesn't mean that it isn't bad enough, as wild waves of the big sea continuously splash in that place where they're found, but the patches of rock where the *cosa crua* grow win the battle. Not even the dulse itself can grow on it because of how wild and beaten the crests of the boulders are.

They're very scarce. Although it's said that they're a great material for kelp, that is to add weight to it, and it's not troublesome – it's not worth it, and the same goes for fertiliser. These people who mess around with seaweed like to see something as a result of their

[67] The cultivation of seaweed is the oldest form of aquaculture in Ireland.and seaweed farms were well established by the middle of the eighteenth century. According to Wilkins (1989) seaweed farming was concentrated on that part of the coast from County Down around the north of the country and down the west coast as far as Clew Bay. He states, "Apart from isolated references to County Kerry, there is no record of seaweed farms on the other coasts of Ireland".

[68] *An chos chrua* refers to bladder wrack that grows in a stunted condition without air bladders on exposed shores

Spreading seaweed on potato ridges, An Cheathrú Rua (Carraroe).

work. As for wasting time with an unproductive stupid type of which a person wouldn't harvest three creels in a day – well that's another story – the man who would be seen on the crest of a rock cutting it with his knife would be the object of laughter as he would need a sharp knife as it's as hard as oak.

An Chos Dhubh[69] The "Black Stem" *Fucus vesiculosus*

This type grows on rough exposed shores. The area is not quite as bad as the place where the *cosa crua* grow. They're also very alike, except that the *cosa dubha* have fronds and they're softer to the touch. They're very good kelp material because they add good weight to the kelp except that they're not good enough for the sample. They're not much good as fertiliser; in any case they're not found widely. Some years they grow well and in others they grow poorly. But the same is true for every kind and since the seaweed that grows above low water needs wind and the heat of the sun, it's understandable that its growth and vigour would depend on a favourable year.

An Chasfheamainn The Spiral Wrack *Fucus spiralis*

The spiral wrack grows just below the channel wrack. It's barely covered by a full neap tide. The fronds are brown and curled and about six or seven inches in length. Kelp can be made from it but it's not much good, although it's put out as fertiliser in times of want. It's not much good for rapid growth. It's too hard without much sap.
The old people say that it would be boiled in the old days to give to pigs, " and even if it was, " they say, "they would love it when potatoes were mashed and mixed through it". Kelp makers often harvest it to make caps for the cocks; it's a good roof for protecting the cock from the rain. It doesn't get any allowance for keeping the cock dry as every bit of it is burned in the kiln if possible. It combines the good and the bad together. Indeed, the spiral wrack is not abundant enough on the shore that it would do any harm to kelp in any case. There's little of it compared to the other types.

An Fheamainn Bhoilgíneach[70] The Spiral Wrack *Fucus spiralis*

These small yellow brown branches are fairly scarce, the odd bundle of them here and there between the knotted wrack and the spiral wrack. It's not difficult to recognise it as it has a lot of small bladders and a type of jelly like honey inside them. Therefore, it's not easy to dry it. It would make bad kelp in any case, but it's not bad as fertiliser. Its scarcity on the shore is its main fault – " as scarce as *feamainn bhoilgíneach* ". It's said that it's good for pains in the bones. There's no doubt that applying a streak of it, as hot as can be tolerated, between two cloths to the skin where the pain is intense, lessens the pain. The old people have great faith in it, at least those of them who have the misfortune to be crippled with rheumatism.

[69] *An chos dhubh* refers to bladder wrack that grows in a stunted condition without air bladders on exposed shores

[70] *Feamainn bhoilgíneach* denotes the ripe spiral wrack with its rounded reproductive bodies on the tips of its fronds. The same name is commonly ascribed to bladder wrack (*F. vesiculosus*) in other parts of Connemara.

An Fheamainn Ghruánach **Wrack with tube worms** *Fucus* with *Spirorbis*

Wrack with tubeworms is no good for kelp or for fertiliser. Nevertheless, it's often cut when it grows among other types; it's easier to do this than to separate it. It's a hard seaweed without much sap and its fronds spotted with white because of the number of tubeworms attached to them. It normally grows near the sandy shore, on the sides of the stones. It's like the bladder wrack except that the bladders are smaller, and, what's more, it doesn't float as the bladders are pierced by the tubeworms. It's not right for kelp because of the tubeworms and if they managed to be in the sample it would be bad news for the kelp maker. It's not good as fertiliser as it doesn't dissolve well and therefore would have no effect on the crops when they're harvested in autumn and the poor farmer would not have the fruit of his labours.

Na Crúba Préacháin **The Sea Oak** *Halidrys siliquosa*

The sea oak is a hard non-succulent type. It's no good as fertiliser or as kelp. Therefore, it doesn't cause much trouble on the shore. A lot of them can be seen growing in pools beside high tide, big brown fingerlike fronds like a bird's foot, the branches all mixed up in a mess. They're very abundant in pools that have sand on them, in the lee of the islands. The swell removes a lot of them in winter and they're thrown ashore in bad weather. Those who spread fertiliser have to pick them out of the rest of the seaweed, work that they don't like at all. Sometimes kelp makers repair their oarweed and mayweed cocks with them. They're used also for animal bedding in winter because the island people have no heather or sedge – which shows there's hardly anything that can't be put to some use. There are many flowers and plants on the sea bottom that the people still know little about, but with time a different story will emerge. It's said that all knowledge is gradually gained. That may be the case with seaweeds and plants below the wave crests.

An Leaba Phortáin **The Black Carrageen** *Furcellaria sp.*

The black carrageen grows in pools near the low tide. The little dark brown branches are very like carrageen except that they are harder and rougher. Ignorant people often harvested them as carrageen. It's no good as fertiliser nor as kelp, and because of that it doesn't attract much interest. Crabs often collect it to put into their clefts, and I can tell you that they make themselves nice comfortable nests. Usually there is a pair hauling it together and making small bits of it with their claws, so that it's suitable for their purpose. However lazy they are any other time, they work hard during summer continuously providing some food for eating and hauling bundles of seaweed into the trenches between the rocks, especially that one which is called the black carrageen.

An Carraigín **The Carrageen** *Chondrus crispus*
Mastocarpus stellatus

I think there's a lot of people all over Ireland who have never yet heard of carrageen – not only have never seen it with their eyes. There are many who have seen it dried, saved, bleached in packets making its way to the markets of England and America, who haven't managed to see it growing in nice little dark branches about four inches high – as a lace around the edge of the coast on a low spring tide in the neighbourhood of the oarweed – above it – and the sea rods below it protecting from the strong ferocious violent waves of the sea. These weak and feeble branches needed that protective wall because on the west coast of Ireland, and no wonder, the currents arrive continuously with great speed from the strange abyss during low tide with a westerly or a south-westerly wind. The wind makes white claws of the currents and when they beat strongly against the shore with force and energy, then, if the sea rods weren't a shelter belt for the carrageen its days would be numbered – that's to say its ribs would be torn from the chalk covered rocks and would be swept off the shore altogether. Because of that, if it weren't for the sea rods I wouldn't be able to put this draft on paper as the carrageen wouldn't be there at all and that would be the greatest deprivation for the human race, especially those whose life's misfortune and trouble it is to be plagued and tormented by wheeze and cough, by shortness of breath and other ailments like that at home and abroad. That valuable healthy little branch which grows from the hard surface of the rock is an unction for those people.

The shoredwellers start to gather the carrageen on the low spring tide near St. Patrick's feast day. About two hours before the low tide you would see the pickers hurrying to the shore with creels, with baskets, with bags and with buckets. Not only do they pick it on the shores of the land but also go out in boats to the exposed rocks on the open sea. It is exposed within an hour and a half of low tide, but as soon as the first tuft of it is exposed, the pickers are working as if they had fire on their skin. You would see women, children and old people in one line at the edge of the sea up to their floating ribs going around small boulders and harvesting with their two hands as hard as they can and filling their baskets and creels. They're the old boys who won't be suffering and crippled from rheumatism; unlike a lot of others who don't need to wet their skin from one end of the year to the other. The carrageen tide is over about an hour and a half after the tide begins to flow. They return home then, and I can tell you that you never saw people so famished with hunger after moving and sidling about the shore for all their worth.

Good pickers who are well versed in the craft would be able to harvest six creels of carrageen that day, if the tide lasts and the shore is even, not being too bothersome altogether and having a good growth. After being harvested there's still more work to be done before it's ready for market. It's spread out on the land first. It's black-coloured then. It needs a day or two of drying and sun first, a few showers or a day's rain or a few nights' dew to bleach it. It turns red and white then. After that it's turned again to bleach the underside. When it's white enough it needs another good day to dry; it's ready to sell then. The seller needs to have it well dried. A wet creel full makes two stone weight when it's dry. Like any other people, the carrageen harvesters are cute enough also and they don't like to part with it without "baptising" it – to fool the buyer. When there's a lot of it piled up it, it becomes damp and it changes to a state where you can't handle it. It smoulders and smoke comes out of it as if from a lime-kiln.

The carrageen was quite expensive during the Great War. The picker had two shillings a stone. It seems as if the harvesting of carrageen has been going on for a long time, as there's a song made about it. Here's a verse of it:

It's long I've heard of carrageen, but don't know what it is,
If the Queen of England knew that there was such a thing,
She'd raise the taxes up as high as the 'poor rate',
And 'tis what the old woman said who was a hundred years and one,
From now on I'll have tobacco or fingers I'll have none

It's said that Irish carrageen, when dresssed properly, is excellent and no one ever ate anything as healthy. A lot of it was used in America and England. That's the basics of carrageen harvesting in Connemara but there may be some difference between the work there and in other coastal areas of Ireland.

An Cháithlíneach — *Callophyllis laciniata*

When the winter swell scours and cleans the sea bottom and flat rocks and weed-covered rocks it leaves behind the *cáithlíneach*. A lot of the small red branches are thrown ashore mixed with other types when the weather is bad. It's very like carrageen except that it's not as fat or as valuable. Kelp makers have no trouble from it because it doesn't suit them. It's good as fertiliser and because of that it doesn't get left on the shore when the time comes to put out fertiliser. Asses have a great liking for it as it's nice and tasty to eat for them and because of that they hurry from the fields to the heaps of weed to keep their teeth busy as long as the load is being heaped. It saves the driver from cursing, as there's no animal in the world as sluggish if it puts its mind to it. It has nearly the same taste as the *cáithleach*. They probably belong to the same type also.

An Cháithleach — *Dilsea carnosa*

The *cáithleach* grows on the deep between the sea rods and on the rods. It's very similar to the *creathnach* but its fronds are wider and stronger and it's not as tasty or as good to eat and therefore it doesn't cause much bother. A lot of it gets thrown ashore in winter and in spring from the swell of the sea. Winkles have a great liking for it and they make a meal of it to feed themselves. It rots quickly as it's very soft and it's not easy to dry it. It's left mixed with the other types when fertiliser is put out, as it's not bad for promoting growth.
It grows in a place that's good for wrasse. It probably provides food for them when they're hungry and it's useful also for putting in their nests during the spawning season, easy to tease apart and to make suitable. It resembles *cáithlíneach* a lot except that the *cáithlíneach* has small branches. I suppose they belong to the same type of seaweed. Neither of them is good to eat.

An Chreathnach Dhiúilicíneach nó an Duileasc — The Dulse (growing on mussels) — *Palmaria palmata*

This dulse grows in small red-brown branches on the mussels that are attached to the rocks on the wild rough shores near half tide. It's almost like the dulse that grows on the *cosa dubha* except that it's sweeter and better to eat. A lot of it is picked in summer and in autumn on the shore. The mussels are left on it although it's difficult to dry them with it because of the fish and the water in the shells. There's no doubt that the buyers like to see the shells on it, as that's a sign that it's the right type. It needs a few days' drying to be seasoned enough to keep throughout the winter. It's a nice tasty healthy food when it's boiled and properly prepared. It's not bad cold either. There are certain things missing from the human body which are found in it and which strengthen the blood and put marrow and pulp in the bone.

A boy once went from the shore to a house in the mountain to look after cows as is normally done in Connemara. He often previously brought a small bag of dulse as a present to the woman of the house. He excused himself this time and spoke thus: "I'm sorry, my good woman, that I haven't got a scrap of dulse with me today as it's a *mallmhuir* (neap tide) now".

"Well, my son" said she "if we had even a bit of the *mallmhuir* itself we'd be happy enough. The inferior stuff itself would be better than nothing."

She was under the impression that the *mallmhuir* was something to eat until he explained the story to her to some extent, but she wasn't happy with that. He had to give a precise account of neap tide, waning spring tide, spring tide and big spring tide.

During the time of the Famine when the people were dying of hunger and distress all over the place, a lot of them fed themselves on the fish of the sea and on the gleanings of shore and strand. It was good to have dulse that time and not only for the coastal dwellers but for a lot of others also who were fleeing from need and want. A lot of walkers and wanderers came to Connemara to keep themselves alive. Indeed, you can still see the remains of those times, in the guise of big heaps of shells and fish bones that are to be seen and found near the ruins of houses in *Mainis* and other places. There were happy honest, decent people once living in them until the wheels of fortune turned against them and landlords and those of the iron crowbars dispersed them far and wide as they did to a lot of others, but that's a story that doesn't belong to the dulse.

An Chreathnach Chosa Dubha [71] — The Dulse (growing among *Fucus*) — *Palmaria palmata*

This dulse grows on a type of seaweed called *cosa dubha*. It's usually found on rough exposed shores only and the small brown-red branches reach about six or seven inches. When the sea is calm during fine weather in autumn, boats full of men, women and children go out to the wild rocks to pick it. They have creels and buckets and lots of bags and the person who is very skilful at picking can pick a hundredweight that time. When they are picking it they don't let themselves go hungry, because it's nice and sweet and fresh to be turning one's eye-teeth on. They keep the teeth busy and there's no doubt that's a good way of keeping them from rotting, and on their way home if anyone is afraid of a major illness they will continue chewing it and they'll have no cause for worry. Heavy drinkers make a soup of it so as they can throw back a good amount of drink without any effects. When the salt is dried on it it's a healthy thing to chew between drinks.

There's a story still in the folklore about the dulse of *Carraig an Ghlainigh*. The rock was in the possession of the landlord's agent, and since want respects no law, some of the tenants had to go and take their share. Their hunger was a great help to him. The bailiff caught a boat crew picking dulse for themselves on the rock. They were taken to court, but there

[71] The *creathnach chosa dubha* is dulse that grows among stipes of *Fucus* on exposed shores.

seems to have been some point in the law that there would have to be grass growing on this rock, because the bailiff went to sea the night before the court sitting and he didn't return until he fixed a green scraw on the top of the bare rock. He gave it a couple of blows with his shoe and looked at it under the moonlight and said: "I'm good at getting my own back for the taking of the dulse. They'll pay dearly for it."
The time passed and the day of the court arrived. The bailiff swore there was grass growing on the rock; the dulse pickers were sentenced and had to pay a heavy fine. But as far as they were concerned it was "the law to the devil" and "to hell with the court".
A group going fishing the following day early saw the scraw and a flock of gulls carrying it diligently from the top of the rock until they threw it down the cliff into the sea. It appears they didn't like any interference in their own kingdom.
Much dulse and sloke has been picked on it, and life has changed a lot since then. It's still fixed there, about a mile south east of *Maínis,* near *Inis Muscraí,* and not a blade of grass has yet grown on it although it's almost eighty years since the green scraw was planted on it by moonlight.

An Turscar Tra — The Cast-up Seaweed

There are all kinds of everything that grows on the big deep in the cast-up seaweed, cut and ground and mixed together in a multicoloured way by the swell of the sea. In spring, during potato sowing there's a lot of it to be found on the beaches. Some of it is as fine as tobacco that you would put in a pipe. There's nothing wrong with that, as there would be no need to cut it or to tease it apart while it's being spread on the ridge with the bladder wrack or the knotted wrack. It needs to be exposed to the weather for a while before the potato sets are laid on it. It might ruin the sets if it were too fresh form the sea. It's not a good thing to cover fresh or wet seaweed with earth; the sun and wind are good for it. Those who are engaged in this sort of work know that from long experience, and therefore strive to do everything as correctly as possible.

An Caonach Mara [72] — *Polysiphonia sp*

The *caonach mara* grows in the pools and on slimy rocks on the bottom of the shore; at a certain time of the year it grows on seaweed also. It's normally coloured green and about half a foot in length.
It would remind you of grass. It's not used at all. The brown type is the most abundant as it grows on seaweed during May. The sea is full of it at the beginning of summer and fishermen don't like it at all because it gets caught in their nets when they're set, especially wrasse nets as they're stretched on the bottom. It's very difficult to pick it out of them as it's very fine and as it were stuck in the meshes. Indeed, fishermen are reluctant to set any net on the seaweed-covered bottoms until it's thrown ashore with bad weather. The beaches and shores are full of it then and it no good for anything.

[72] The name *caonach mara* is usually applied to small red seaweeds such as *Polysiphonia,* one of which (*P. lanosa*) grows parasitically on knotted wrack. The green colour alluded to by the author is confusing and he may be including sea moss (*Enteromorpha sp.*) in his description.

An Fíorshleabhcán **The "True Sloke"** ***Porphyra linearis***

The true sloke grows on flat smooth rocks on exposed shores near the high neap tide mark. It's most abundant in spring and early summer and the small delicate purple leaves are as slimy as anything you ever saw. It's very difficult to pick when it's wet as it will slip out of your fingers, but on a fine day it can be pulled in strips from the rocks because it sticks to itself with the dry weather all over the place. It makes a tasty sweet soup when it's boiled and prepared and it's healthy too, although it's not easy to save like the dulse because it's soft and juicy. Nonetheless it can be kept fresh for a good while once cooked and it looks not unlike a young green cabbage that would be well boiled.

Often during fine weather in spring the coastal dwellers go out in their boats to the small islands and the wild rocks, where the gull and shag live, and, even if they do, they bring home a quantity of it in the evening. A lot of it grows on *Carraig na Meacan*. Indeed, a lot of all kinds of *dúilfheamainn* grows on it, about half an acre of high cliffs and a storm beach of big stones that are as round as eggs on the south east side of it. There are many caves with seals on the south-west side and deep tidal pools on the north-east side where red seaweed stays. This is the easiest side to come ashore if the sea is quiet. Indeed, it's a very rough place even in summer and it's terrible altogether in winter and only on certain days can it be approached. Isn't it a lonesome place for the sailor who's buried there? He's there by himself for hundreds of years, five or six miles from land in the middle of the sea between *Árainn Mhór* and Connemara. People often say a prayer for his soul, because there's still a headstone standing above his grave. Boats usually go ashore there after winter looking for wrack, and that's what happened many years ago the day the body was discovered. It's said that it was covered with seaweed and it's thought the wild sea birds or the sea surf may have done the work. It's not known what happened the boat he was on. In any case, he has a remote lonely place where the waves are bellowing and bursting against the cliffs, the seals crying when they need to, the shags and the gulls with their own strange music, and the people who come to pick the sloke give God's blessing to the souls of the dead.

An Sleabhcán Cuircíneach **The "Tufted Sloke"** ***Porphyra umbilicalis***

This type grows lower on the shore than the true sloke, as it's not exposed until half-tide. They're not too difficult to pick because the dark green branches are that twisted that your fingers can get a good grip of them. Like the other types, it's in season in spring and summer, and during that time a lot is picked, although it's not as sweet to eat as the true sloke. Most of it is eaten fresh as it's not easy to dry and when it's boiled with onions and milk and butter it makes a fine tasty sauce for potatoes. The shags and the gulls probably find it sweet because they often fill their bellies with it when they're too lazy to go fishing. You would often see them in squadrons in the mouth of the waves watching each other with envy and suspicion, now and again pecking each other spitefully. At other times, the whole company would start beating each other with the result that there would be a shower of feathers around them.

It seems as if it likes warmth in order to grow, because it grows best facing the sun. But that's the way with a lot of other types, those ones growing on the south face of the rocks can be recognised by their quality in comparison with those on the north side

An Sleabhcán Slámach The "Soft Sloke" _Porphyra purpurea Porphyra leucosticta_

The soft sloke grows in pools on the shore near low tide. The leaves have tubeworms and sand attached and therefore they're no good for eating. It's very like the true sloke except that the leaves are bigger. Only the ducks bother with it, when they go fending for themselves on the shore. They don't mind the sand; they're quite adept at swallowing it. Once a man came down from the mountains to our village and he couldn't tell one kind from another. When he set off for the shore, he didn't stop until he reached the place the soft sloke was growing. He started picking it and putting it in his bag as fast as he could. An old woman came by and told him it was no good for eating, "but keep walking", said she "and I'll put you right". She brought him to the true sloke. He thanked her and bent down to pick and fill his bag. Indeed, he wasn't making much progress because it was so slimy that it was slipping between his fingers when he tried to tear it from the rock. But gradually and with practice he had a fine quantity of it to take home after the low tide. It's said that practice makes perfect.

An Meilsceánach The Eel Grass [73] _Zostera sp._

If it weren't for the place in which it grows you'd think it was long luxuriant grass about four or five feet in length. Some of it is exposed on a very low tide and a lot more which never dried. The winter swell removes a lot of it and the wind sends it ashore on the surface of the sea. It's no good as fertiliser or kelp, as it has no sap. Nevertheless, it's not left on the shore; not only that but the people share it among themselves just like any other type. They put it up on the spreading ground to dry. It fades from green to white with wind and sun and when it's dried and seasoned I can tell you that it's a good material for a bed and comfortable for an old cow or an old ass, and for people also if it comes to that.[74]

As the roots stay in the strand from year to year in lines above each other, the patches in which it grows are higher than the rest of the strand. Therefore, pools of water rest between the clumps of eel grass. People often go looking for flatfish on moonlit nights in autumn. You would see men and women up to their knees walking about carefully in the water in the holes between the green banks until they step on the flatfish that are buried lightly under the sand. Then the spike (of the fish spear) is placed between the feet and then carefully and quickly through the fish, it's lifted up and thrown in the creel or basket. He who knows the craft will undoubtedly have an amount of fish going home in the dead of night with a flowing tide. It's truly a healthy work to be dabbling about in the sea, and if the spearer has a good appetite don't blame him. I often used see the flatfish knocking us over because the big flatfish is a strong fish and if you didn't manage to stand on its head you would be in danger of being knocked over when it jumped out between your feet with an energetic dart.

[73] The eel grass is not an alga but is the only flowering plant which grows in the sea around our coasts.

[74] The presence of fleas was a problem for the crews of some sailing hookers that carried turf to the Aran Islands. Pillows stuffed with dried eel grass ensured that no fleas would be present in a boat. (Seán Ó Ceoinín, *Leitir Ard, Carna* on Raidio na Gaeltachta).

Wrasse, squid, rays and other fish also live there, and it's they who have a nice protected place, curling around between the blades like rabbits or mice in a cornfield. There's no one tribe of those fish which isn't the same colour as the place, so that it's very hard for the enemy to see them if they stay still, without making a sound or a clatter.

LIST OF NAMES OF INVERTEBRATES

Bairneach	Limpet	*Patella sp.*
Bairneach Iascáin	Common Limpet	*Patella vulgata.*
Bairneach Mín	Blue-Rayed Limpet	*Patina pellucida*
Bláth Mara	Daisy Anemone	*Cereus pedunculatus*
Breallach	Sand Gaper	*Mya arenaria*
Buirlín	Purse Sponge	*Grantia compressa*
Bundún Leice	Sea Anemone	Order *Actinaria*
Cíoch Charraige	Sea Anemone	Order *Actinaria*
Cluaisín	Variegated Scallop	*Chlamys varia*
	Queen Scallop	*Chlamys opercularis*
Crosán Faoileáin	Cushion Star	*Asterina sp.*
Crosán Grianta	Sun-star	*Solaster sp.*
Crosán Ladhrach	Common Starfish	*Asterina rubens*
Crosán Mín	Sun-star	*Solaster sp.*
Cuachma	Buckie or Common Whelk	*Buccinum undatum*
Cuán Mara	Sea Urchin	*Echinus sp.* and *Paracentrotus sp.*
Cudal	Common Cuttlefish	*Sepia officinalis*
Diúilicín	Mussel	*Mytilus edulis*
Faocha	Edible Winkle	*Littorina littorea*
Faocha Bhiorach	Tower Shell	*Turritella communis*
Faocha Chapaill	Dogwhelk	*Nucella lapillus*
Faocha Faoileáin	Top Shell	*Monodonta sp.*
Faocha Ghliomaigh	Hermit Crab	*Eupagurus bernhardus*
Feannadóir	Sting Winkle	*Ocenebra erinacea*
Finicín	Cowrie	*Trivia monacha*
Gabhal Mara	Crawfish	*Palinurus elephas*
Garbhán Carraige	Acorn Barnacle	*Balanus sp.* and *Chthalmus sp.*
Giúirlinn	Shipworm	*Teredo navalis*
	Goose Barnacle	*Lepas sp.*
Gliomach	Lobster	*Homarus gammarus*
Láimhíneach	Squid	*Loligo sp.*
Láir Bhán	Cuttlefish	Order *Decapoda*
Luaineachán	Swimming Crab	*Macropipus sp.*
Luch Mhara	Sea Mouse	*Aphrodite aculeata*
Lugach	Lugworm	*Arenicola marina*
Miongán		Class *Gastropoda*
Muirín	Great Scallop	*Pecten maximus*
Oisre	Oyster	*Ostrea edulis*
Portán Clismín	Masked Crab	*Corystes cassivelaunus*
Portán Faoileann	Spiny Spider Crab	*Maia squinado*
Portán Glas	Green Crab	*Carcinus maenas*
Portán Iarainn	Spider Crab	*Hyas araneus*
Portán Rua	Edible Crab	*Cancer pagurus*

Ribe Róibéis	Shrimp	*Palaemon sp.*
Ruacan	Cockle	*Cerastoderma edule*
Ruarámhach	Rag Worm	*Nereis sp.*
Scian Mhara	Razor Shell	*Ensis sp.*
Seilmide Cladaigh	Periwinkle	*Littorina sp.*
Sligín Slámach	Saddle Oyster	*Anomia ephippium*
Slobán	Sea mats and Sponges (see also seaweeds)	
Smugairle Róin	Jellyfish	Class *Scyphozoa*
Súmaire Cladaigh	Sea-cucumber	Class *Holothuroidea*
Teanga Chait	Sea Mat	Order *Cheilostomata*
Tonachán Trá	Sand-hopper	*Talitrus sp.*
		Talorchestia sp.

LIST OF NAMES OF FISHES

Ballach	Wrasse	Family *Labridae*
Ballach Breac	Ballan Wrasse	*Labrus bergylta*
Ballach Buí	Goldsinny	*Ctenolabrus rupestris*
Ballach Cuaiche	Cuckoo Wrasse	*Labrus mixtus*
Ballach Fuarleice	The Rock Cook	*Centrolabrus exoletus*
Ballach Meilsceánaigh	"Eel Grass Wrasse"	
Ballach Muire	Cuckoo Wrasse	*Labrus mixtus*
Bochar	Corkwing Wrasse	*Crenilabrus melops*
Bóleatha	Halibut	*Hippoglossus hippoglossus*
Bod Gorm	Cuckoo Wrasse (male)	*Labrus mixtus*
Bolmán	Scad or Horsemackerel	*Trachurus trachurus*
Bran	Red Seabream	*Pagellus bogaraveo*
Breac Eitill	Atlantic Flying Fish	*Cypselurus heterurus*
Breac Geal	Sea Trout	*Salmo trutta*
Breac Giúirlinne	Barrel-Fish	*Hyperoglyphus perciformis*
Cadóg	Haddock	*Melanogrammus aeglefinus*
Ceannruán	Blenny	Family *Blennidae*
Cnúdán	Gurnard	Family *Triglidae*
Cnúdán Breac	Streaked Gurnard	*Trigloporus lastoviza*
Cnúdán Buí	Tub Gurnard	*Trigla lucerna*
Cnúdán Dearg	Red Gurnard	*Aspitrigla cuculus*
Cnúdán Deilgneach	"Spiny Gurnard"	
Cnúdán Glas	Grey Gurnard	*Eutrigla gurnardus*
Cnúdán Soilseach	Tub Gurnard	*Trigla lucerna*
Colmóir	Hake	*Merluccius merluccius*
Concar	Conger Eel	*Conger conger*
Dúleatha	Flounder	*Platichthys flesus*
Eascann	Eel	*Anguilla anguilla*
	Conger Eel	*Conger conger*
Faoitín	Whiting	*Merlangius merlangus*

Fíogach	Spurdog	*Squalus acanthias*
Freangach	Spotted Dogfish	*Scyliorhinus canicula*
Glasóg	Coalfish	*Pollachius virens*
Gobóg	Tope	*Galeorhinus galeus*
Gréasaí Cladaigh	Seascorpion	*Myxocephalus scorpius* and *Taurulus bubalis*
Iascán an Gha Nimhe	Greater Weever	*Trachinus draco*
Iascán Nimhe	Dragonet	*Callionymus lyra*
Langa	Ling	*Molva molva*
Langa Carraige	Rockling and Forkbeard	*Gaidropsarus sp.* *Ciliata mustela* *Enchelyopus cimbrius* *Phycis blennoides*
Langa Gorm	Blue Ling	*Molva dypterigia*
Lannach	Thick-Lipped Grey Mullet	*Chelon labrosus*
Leatha	Flatfish	Order *Pleuronectiformes*
Leatha Leice	Topknot	*Zeugopterus punctatus*
Leatha Riabhach	Dab	*Limanda limanda*
Liamhán Gréine	Basking Shark	*Cetorhinus maximus*
Luathóg	Eel (young)	*Anguilla anguilla*
Mac Siobháin	Goby	Family *Gobiidae*
Malrach Cháit	Gunnel	*Pholis gunnellus*
Mangach	Pollack	*Pollachius pollachius*
Muiricín	Armed Bullhead	*Agonus cataphractus*
Péist an Dá Shúil Déag	Gunnel	*Pholis gunnellus*
Plás	Plaice	*Pleuronectes platessa*
Roc	Ray	*Raja sp.*
Ronnach	Mackerel	*Scomber scombrus*
Ronnach Spáinneach	Garfish	*Belone bellone*
Scadán	Herring	*Clupea harengus*
Scadán Gainimh	Sand Eel	*Ammodytes sp.,Hyperoplus sp.*
Scoirneach	Smooth Hound	*Mustelus mustelus*
Scolabord	Skate	*Raja sp.*
Searróg	Gunnel	*Pholis gunnellus*
Siorc	Shark	
Siorc Gorm	Blue Shark	*Prionace glauca*
Snáthaid Mhara	Pipefish	*Syngnathus sp.*
Sól	Common Sole	*Solea solea*
Trosc	Cod	*Gadus morhua*
Troscán Stopóige	Pouting	*Trisopterus luscus*
	Poor Cod	*Trisopterus minutus*
Turbard	Turbot	*Psetta maxima*

LIST OF NAMES OF SEAWEEDS

Barrchonla	Bladder Wrack	*Fucus vesiculosus*
Caisíneach	Channelled Wrack	*Pelvetia canaliculata*
Cáithleach		*Dilsea carnosa*
Cáithlíneach		*Callophyllis laciniata*
Caonach Mara		*Polysiphonia sp.*
Carraigín	Carrageen	*Chondrus crispus* and *Mastocarpus stellatus*
Casfheamainn	Spiral Wrack	*Fucus spiralis*
Claimhí	Furbelows	*Sacchorhiza polyschides*
Coirleach	Oarweed	*Laminaria digitata*
Copóg	Oarweed	*Laminaria digitata*
Cos Chrua	Bladder Wrack	*Fucus vesiculosus*
Cos Dhubh	Bladder Wrack	*Fucus vesiculosus*
Creathnach Chosa Dubha	Dulse	*Palmaria palmata*
Creathnach Dhiúilicíneach	Dulse	*Palmaria palmata*
Crúba Préacháin	Sea Oak	*Halidrys siliquosa*
Duileasc	Dulse	*Palmaria palmata*
Duilleacha	Oarweed	*Laminaria digitata*
Eireaball Cait	"Cat's Tail"	
Feamainn Bhoilgíneach	Spiral Wrack	*Fucus spiralis*
Feamainn Bhuí	Knotted Wrack	*Ascophyllum nodosum*
Feamainn Gheimhridh	"Winter Weed"	*Laminaria hyperborea*
Feamainn Ghruánach	Wrack with tube worms	*Fucus* with *Spirorbis*
Feamainn Mhín	"Smooth Weed"	*Laminaria hyperborea*
Fíorshleabhcán	"True Sloke"	*Porphyra linearis*
Gruaig na Caillí Mara	"Sea Witch's Hair"	
Leaba Phortáin	"Black Carrageen"	*Furcellaria sp.*
Meilsceánach	Eel Grass	*Zostera sp.*
Míoránach	Toothed Wrack	*Fucus serratus*
Ríseach	Sea Thong	*Himanthalia elongata*
Ruálach	Sea Laces	*Chorda filum*
Rufa	Sea Belt	*Laminaria saccharina*
Scothach	Mayweed	*Laminaria hyperborea*
Slat Mhara	Sea Rod	*Laminaria hyperborea*
Sleabhcán Cuircíneach	"Tufted Sloke"	*Porphyra umbilicalis*
Sleabhcán Slámach	"Soft Sloke"	*Porphyra purpurea* and *P. leucosticta*
Slobán		*Cladophora sp.* (see also invertebrates)
Sraoilleach	Murlins	*Alaria esculenta*
Turscar Trá	Cast-up Seaweed	

LIST OF PLACE NAMES*

Irish Name	Translation	English version**
Aill na nGlasóg	The Cliff of the Coalfish	
An Aircín	The Creek	
An Aird Mhóir	The Big Headland	Ardmore
Árainn		Aran
Árainn Mhór	Big *Árainn*	Inishmore
An Ard-Trá	The High Beach	
Béal an Daingin	The Mouth of the Secure Place	Bealadangan
Bealach na Srathra	Straddle Pass	
Na Beanna Beola	Beola's Peaks	The Twelve Bens
Bóithrín na Trá	The Little Road of the Beach	
An Caolsháile	The Narrow Sea Inlet	
An Caiseal	Stone Fort	Cashel
Carraig an Ghlainigh	The Rock of . . . ?	
Carraig an Mhíle	The Mile Rock	Mile Rock
An Charraig Fhada	The Long Rock	
Carraig Iolra	Eagle Rock	Eagle Rock
Carraig na bhFreangach	The Dogfish Rock	
Carraig na bPortán	The Crabs' Rock	
Carraig na hEilite	The Rock of the Doe	Seal Rock
Carraig na mBan	The Womens' Rock	
Carraig na Meacan	The Rock of the . . . ?	Carricknamackan
Ceann Léime	Leap Head	Loop Head/Slyne Head
Cill Chiaráin	Ciarán's Church	Kilkieran
Cill Rónáin	Rónán's Church	Kilronan
Cloch na Rón	The Seals' Rock	Roundstone
Clochar an Bháid	The Stony Place of the Boat	
Clochar an Mhadra Uisce	The Stony Place of the Otter	
Crompán an Chúir	The Inlet of the Foam	
Cruach na Caoile	The Stack of . . . ?	Croaghnakeela Island
Cruach na Cora	The Stack of the Narrow Crossing Place	St. MacDara's Island
Cuan na Gaillimhe	The Bay of *Gaillimh*	Galway Bay
Dúleic	Black Flagstone	Carrickadoolagh
Dún Ghudail	The Stronghold of *Gudal*	Doonguddle
Fínis	Wood Island	Finish Island
An Foiriún	Feraun	
Gaillimh		Galway
An Garraí Gainimh	The Sandy Field	
Garraí na nGéabha	The Field of the Geese	
Glaise na bhFoiriún		
Inis Leacain	Flagstone Island	Inishlackan
Inis Múscraí	Island of *Múscraí*	Inishmuskerry

Iorras Mór	Big Peninsula	Errismore
Inis Ní	The Island of *Nidhe*	Inishnee
Leathrach Mhór Sceirde	The Big Deep Flat Seaweed -Covered Rock of *Sceirde*	
Leathrach na mBran	The Deep Flat Seaweed -Covered Rock of the Sea Bream	
Leic Mhór	Big Flagstone	
Leic Mhór Charraig na Meacan	The Big Flagstone of the Rock of the . . . ?	
Leic na bhFaoileán	The Seagull Flagstone	
Leic na Cora	The Flagstone of the Narrow Crossing Place	
An Léim	The Leap	
Leitir Calaidh	Harbour Hillside	Lettercallow
Leitir Mealláin	*Mealláin's* Hillside	Lettermullan
Leitir Móir	Big Hillside	Lettermore
Loch na Lannach	The Lake of the Grey Mullet	
Maidhm an Urláir	The Breaker of the Floor	
Maidhm Mháirtín Thaidhg	Máirtín Thaidhg's Breaker	
Maidhm Mhicil Bhuí	Micil Buí's Breaker	
Maidhm na mBod Gorm	The Breaker of the Cuckoo Wrasse	
Maidhm Sheáin Thomáis	Seán Thomáis' Breaker	
Maínis	Island Plain	Mweenish Island
Muic Ghainimh	Sand Bank	
Na Mulláin Dubha	The Black Boulders	
An Mullán Domhain	The Deep Boulder	
Mullán na mBod (Gorm)	The Boulder of the Cuckoo Wrasse	
An Mhuráite Dhomhain	The Deep Fishing Ground	
Oileáin Árann	The Islands of *Árainn*	Aran Islands
Oileán Barra (Bior)	Spike Island	Birmore Island
Oileán Lachan	Duck Island	Duck Island
Poll Domhain Oileán Lachan	The Deep Hole of Duck Island	
An Poll Mór	The Deep Hole (Mooring)	
Roisín an Chalaidh	The Small Peninsula of the Harbour	Rusheenacholla
Ros Muc	Peninsula of Rounded Hills	Rosmuck
Sceirde	Remote Sea Rock	
Sceirde Mór	Big Remote Sea Rock	Skerdmore
Na Sceirdí	The Remote Sea Rocks	
Stopóg an Táilliúra	The Shallow Rocky Seabed of the Tailor	
Tobar Cholm Cille	Colmcille's Well	
Tonn Uí Fhloinn	Flynn's Wave	
Trá an Ghoirtín	The Beach of the Small Field	Gorteen Beach
Trá Dheiscirt	Southern Beach	
Trá Fhada Mhaínse	The Long Beach of Maínis	

An Trá Mhóir	The Big Beach
Trá na Dumhaí Bige	The Beach of the Small Dune
Trá na hAille	The Beach of the Cliff
An Trá Rua	The Red Beach

* These are the place names of the original text, but exclude names of places outside the area that is the subject of the book (e.g. Kildare, Blasket Islands) and places mentioned in poems and songs.

** The English version as used by Ordnance Survey of Ireland.

Index of English Names of Fishes, Invertebrates and Seaweeds

BIBLIOGRAPHY

Anon. 1978 *Ainmneacha Plandaí agus Ainmhithe,* An Gúm. Baile Átha Cliath.

Breathnach, Diarmaid agus Ní Mhurchú, Máire 1994 *Beathaisnéis a Ceathair 1882 – 1982,* An Clóchomhar, Baile Átha Cliath.

Calleia, Harry 1985 *Full Circle,* Galway Hooker Association, Annual Newsletter.

Campbell, A.C. 1989 *The Hamlyn Guide to Seashores & Shallow Seas of Britain and Europe,* Hamlyn, London.

Colgan, Nathaniel 1911 *Gaelic Plant and Animal Names and Associated Folklore,* Clare Island Survey, Proceedings of the Royal Irish Academy, Volume XXXI.

de Bhaldraithe, T. 1988 *Seosamh Daibhéid agus Cuid Dá Chairde,* FEASTA, (Deireadh Fómhair).

De Courcy Ireland, John 1981 *Ireland's Sea Fisheries: A History* The Glendale Press, Dublin.

De Valera, M. 1958 *A topographical guide to the seaweeds of Galway Bay with some brief notes on some other districts on the west coast of Ireland.* Institute for Industrial Research and Standards, Dublin.

Fahy, Edward 1985 *Child of the Tides – A Sea Trout Handbook* The Glendale Press, Dublin.

Farran, G.P. 1946 *Local Names of Irish Fishes,* Irish Naturalists' Journal, Vol. VIII.

Foster, John Wilson 1997 editor, *Nature in Ireland – A Scientific and Cultural History,* Lilliput Press, Dublin.

Guiry,M.D.& Garbary,D.J. 1991 *A geographical and taxonomic guide to European seaweeds of economic importance. In: Seaweed resources in Europe,* Eds: Guiry, M.D & Blunden,G. John Wiley & Sons, England.

Holt, E.W.L. & Byrne, L.W. 1903 *On the British and Irish species of the family Stromateidae.* Scient. Invest. Fish. Brch. Ire. 1901 5 70-76.

Mac Giollarnáth, Seán 1947 *Cladach na Farraige,* Oifig an tSoláthair, Baile Átha Cliath.

Mac an Iomaire, Séamus 1938 *Cladaigh Chonamara,* Oifig an tSoláthair, Baile Átha Cliath.

Mac an Iomaire, Séamas. 1985 *Cladaí Chonamara,* An Gúm, Baile Átha Cliath.

McNally, Kenneth 1976 *The Sun-Fish Hunt,* Blackstaff Press, Belfast.

Miller, Peter and Loates, Michael J. 1997 *Fish of Britain and Europe – Collins Pocket Guide.* HarperCollins Publishers, London.

Ó Ceallacháin, C.N. 1985 *Feamainn,* Comharchumann Chois Fharraige

Ó Madagáin, B. 1978 *Dialann Dúlra,* An Clóchomhar, Baile Átha Cliath.

Quigley, D.T.G. 1986 *A Specimen of the Barrel-Fish Hyperoglyphe perciforma (Mitchill,1818) (Lirus perciformis Regan, 1902) from Achill Island, Co. Mayo* Irish Naturalist's Journal Vol.22, No 2

Ridge, Seamus. 1969 *Conamara Man,* Prentice-Hall Inc., New Jersey.

Robinson, Tim. 1990 *Connemara, Part 1 Introduction and Gazeteer,* Folding Landscapes.

Scott, Richard J. 1983 *The Galway Hookers, Working Sailboats of Galway Bay.* Ward River Press.

Went, A.E.J. and Kennedy, M. 1976 *List of Irish Fishes, Third Edition,* National Museum of Ireland.

Whilde, Tony 1994 *The Natural History of Connemara,* IMMEL Publishing Ltd., London.

Wilkins, N. 1989 *Ponds, Passes and Parcs – Aquaculture in Victorian Ireland.* The Glendale Press,Dublin.

Tír Eolas is a small independent publishing house based in Doorus near Kinvara, Co. Galway. Since its first publication in 1985, *Kinvara, a Rambler's Guide and Map*, the company has continued to produce high quality books, guides and maps that provide information on Irish history, landscape, culture and tradition.

Tír Eolas has published seven **Guides and Maps**, covering the Burren, South Galway, Kinvara, Medieval Galway and Loch Corrib. They give detailed information on the archaeological and historical sites, the birds, animals and flowers to be seen and the natural features found in the area covered by each map. They are the ideal aid to the discovery and exploration of the Burren and South Galway.

Books from Tír Eolas

TheBurren Wall, by Gordon D'Arcy, 2006
The Burren and the Aran Islands have some of the most distinctive stone walls found in Ireland. This book celebrates and informs about the natural and social history and the aethetic qualities of the Burren Wall in photographs, illustrations and quotations.
ISBN 1-873821-16-6 PB

Alive, Alive-O, the shellfish and shellfisheries of Ireland, by Noël P. Wilkins, 2004.
Drawing on mythology, archaeology, history, oral tradition, biology, economics and a wealth of personal experience, this book tells the story of Ireland's shellfish and shellfisheries.
ISBN 1-873821-20-4 PB

The Shores of Connemara, by Séamus Mac an Iomaire, translated by Pádraic de Bhaldraithe, 2000.
A naturalist's guide to the seashore and coastal waters of Connemara, Co. Galway and an account of the life of the people who lived there in the late nineteenth and early twentieth century.
ISBN 1-873821-14-X PB

A Burren Journal, by Sarah Poyntz, 2000.
Sarah Poyntz's diaries give a striking picture of life in the unique landscape of the Burren. She describes the changing seasons, the birds and animals, the wild flowers for which the Burren is famous and the lives of the people of the village of Ballyvaughan. The illustrations by Anne Korff and Gordon D'Arcy bring her words to life.
ISBN 1-873821-13-1 PB

The Book of the Burren, edited by Jeff O'Connell and Anne Korff, 1991.
An introduction to the geology, natural history, archaeology and history of the Burren region. 2nd edition 2002.
ISBN 1-873821-15-8 PB

The Book of Aran, edited by John Waddell, Jeff O'Connell and Anne Korff, 1994.
An introduction to the natural history, archaeology, history, folklore and literary heritage of the Aran Islands.
ISBN 1-873821-03-4 PB

Kinvara, a Seaport Town on Galway Bay, written by Caoilte Breatnach and compiled by Anne Korff, 1997.
Social history and folklore seen through photographs.
ISBN1-873821-07-7 PB

Women of Ireland, by Kit and Cyril Ó Céirín, 1996.
A biographical dictionary of Irish women from earliest times to the present. It documents the rich and varied contributions women have made to the shaping of Irish history and culture.
ISBN 1-873821-06-9 PB

The Shannon Floodlands, by Stephen Heery, 1993.
A natural history of the callows, the distinctive landscape seasonally flooded by the River Shannon.
ISBN 1-873821-02-6 PB

Not a Word of a Lie, by Bridie Quinn-Conroy, 1993.
A portrait of growing up in a small community in the West of Ireland.
ISBN 1-873821-01-8 PB

For further information,
Tír Eolas
Newtownlynch, Doorus, Kinvara, Co. Galway.
Tel/Fax: 091 637452.
e-mail: info@tireolas.com
Order on-line: www.tireolas.com